Melville's
Protest
Theism

MELVILLE'S PROTEST THEISM

The Hidden
and
Silent God
in
Clarel

STAN GOLDMAN

NORTHERN

ILLINOIS

UNIVERSITY

PRESS

DeKalb

1993

© 1993 by Northern Illinois University Press
Published by the Northern Illinois University Press, DeKalb, Illinois 60115
Manufactured in the United States using acid-free paper ∞
Design by Julia Fauci

Library of Congress Cataloging-in-Publication Data
Goldman, Stan.
    Melville's protest theism : the hidden and silent God in Clarel / Stan
Goldman.
        p.   cm.
    Includes bibliographical references (p.   ) and index.
    ISBN 0-87580-174-9
    1. Melville, Herman, 1819–1891. Clarel.   2. Melville, Herman, 1819–
1891—Religion.   3. Theism in literature.   4. God in literature.   I. Title.
PS2384.C53G65   1993
811'.3—dc20   92-19791   CIP

For my only son,

DANIEL NADAV GOLDMAN,

whom I love.

CONTENTS

ACKNOWLEDGMENTS

EVERY BOOK IS A COLLABORATION, never the product of a single author, but always the work of many co-authors. I wish to thank all my co-authors who gave me ideas, words, and advice. The theologian G. Tom Milazzo first suggested the term "protest theism" to describe *Clarel* when we read Melville's cantos five years ago. The many insights I received from theological conversations with Professor Milazzo since then are reflected in the pages to follow. The Romanticist and Poe scholar G. R. Thompson read the manuscript carefully and kept me organized. His editorial skills made my dense argument accessible. Three Melvilleans helped maintain my sense of mission. William B. Dillingham first encouraged me to write on Melville's poetry and listened patiently as I wrestled with the iconoclastic ideas of Herman Melville. I am indebted to James Duban for sharing his own meticulous scholarship with me and for his unrelenting faith in my work. In an age of ideological constriction, Vincent Kenny responded graciously and enthusiastically to my manuscript despite our different interpretations. My greatest indebtedness is to the three generations of Melville scholars whose critical works have helped me in the development of this study. I thank all the editors of Northern Illinois University Press for completing the review process quickly and for treating me so well. An earlier form of Chapter 4, "The Small Voice of Silence," appeared in *Texas Studies in Literature and Language* 31 (Fall 1989), published by the University of Texas Press, and I am grateful for the publisher's permission to print the material here.

Beyond these, I acknowledge a huge debt to my parents, who began my education and still give me all the emotional and financial support that an academic son could ever want. I am grateful to my wife, Liliana, who helped me continue my education and taught me not to live as hard a life as possible. Above all, however, I owe my intellectual sanity and theological identity to Herman Melville, whose extraordinary poem *Clarel* has helped me with my own ceaseless spiritual struggles.

Trinity University
San Antonio, Texas

Melville's
Protest
Theism

Ah, exile is exile, tho' spiced be the sod,
In Shushan we languish—
Languish with the secret desire for the garden of God.

—"The Devotion of the Flowers to their Lady"
Herman Melville

Introduction

In 1856, MELVILLE JOURNEYED TO PALESTINE. Over the next twenty years he would write the most complex theological exploration of God, doubt, and faith in nineteenth-century American literature. Equating the journey and poetry, he titled the book *Clarel: A Poem and Pilgrimage in the Holy Land*. The poem's intimidating length (about twenty thousand lines) and deliberately tortuous syntax have been an effective barrier for most Americanists and even many Melvilleans. Moreover, the theological reflection represented in the poem by the characters and the narrative voices is certainly not expressed simply or clearly. Reading *Clarel* requires a tolerance for ambiguity, a commitment to oppositions, paradox, and uncertainty. These literary qualities are valued by both New Critics and Poststructuralists, but the theological reflection is dense and unsettling—difficult for many literary critics to sustain through one hundred and fifty cantos. The title of the poem, however, explains Melville's theological task. The first word of the title refers not only to the poem's main character but also to the sense of clarity (ironically) combined with the Hebrew word *el*. *El* means God in Hebrew and was also the name for the God of gods of the Canaanite pantheon. Characters are often given the epithet "Eld," a favorite Melvillean pun in *Clarel* that conflates old age with God. The idea of clarity combined with *el* suggests a semantic compound in the name "Clarel" and implies a quest for the clarity of God.[1] *Clarel* is a long, difficult narrative poem and pilgrimage in search of a clarification of God and faith or, more exactly, an understanding of the relationship between the human and the divine.

*M*ost studies of *Clarel* have failed to demonstrate the nature and strength of the faith represented in the poem. Placing *Clarel* in a biblical context, however, reveals the theological values of reverence, charity, hope, and faith rather than the self-sufficiency, endurance, despair, pessimism, and agnosticism that have usually been read from the poem. By focusing on only one half of the evidence—Clarel's suffering, doubt, and disappointed love— critics often miss in the poem the "intuitions of some things heavenly" (*Moby-Dick*, "The Fountain"). For instance, Vincent Kenny writes that "all of *Clarel* comes down to this dilemma: a wish to believe and an inability to find the way."[2] Melville does, however, offer a biblical way to God and faith that is unique—what I shall call Melvillean "protest theism": a paradoxical combination and coalescence of both protest and love based on the need that the unsatisfied heart has for God. Protest theism explains what kind of biblical protester (Protestant) Melville was and represents an attempt at finding or establishing the limits within which faith is possible and life endures and has meaning. The theological reflection represented in *Clarel* is not atheistic, nihilistic, nor agnostic, but a biblically rooted, nonsectarian, nondogmatic faith that empowers human beings to protest and to lament human fate but nevertheless to give the human heart in love to God. Although the theology offered in the poem is enhanced by and unfolded within the context of the Bible, it is not a normative biblical faith, but a distinctive theological reflection. By reading *Clarel* intertextually with the Bible, one can go beyond setting, character, plot, and symbol—what most critics have focused on—to the importance of biblical metaphors, idioms, genres, and narrative voices as the key indicators of meaning in the poem. A biblical and theological exegesis of Melville's *Clarel* reveals a theologically unique faith.

The methodology of this study has three interconnected approaches, all of them exegetical or text-centered: (1) biblical, (2) narratological, and (3) theological. My interpretation of *Clarel* is generated by the difficulties of the text, not by a prior ideology or literary hermeneutic.

The major difficulty is that *Clarel* is made up of an intertextual mosaic of conscious biblical quotations, perhaps unconscious elusive biblical allusions, deliberate reinterpretations of biblical prooftexts, extensive biblical glosses, and biblical resonances interpolated into every canto of the poem. Although the pilgrimage in Palestine is represented through other literary and historical texts (and paintings), the poem is overwhelmingly biblical. Melville's concatenation of biblical verses, allusions, images, and ideas provides much of the fascination and power of *Clarel* as well as its coherence and unity. In fact, the dialog that takes place between the Bible and *Clarel* is one of the unifying structural principles of the poem. *Clarel* is not just the plot structure of the whence and the whither of a circular pilgrimage beginning and ending in Jerusalem. *Clarel* is so deeply anchored in the Bible that one could claim that the principal organizing structure of the poem is the biblical words, images, and ideas strung together, throughout the cantos, like pearls.

I call the literary relationship between *Clarel* and the Bible a dialog because a dialog implies a certain reciprocity. When these two libraries of texts converse intertextually, new meanings are produced which neither the Bible nor *Clarel* has independently. In other words, my methodological approach is to use the Bible as an interpretive gateway into *Clarel* and to use *Clarel* to reinterpret biblical themes and passages. The intertextual relationship between the Bible and *Clarel* goes both ways. This study, however, does not primarily trace sources or specific references back to the Bible. Nathalia Wright, in her *Melville's Use of the Bible*, and Walter E. Bezanson, in his introduction and notes to the Hendricks House edition of *Clarel*, have already demonstrated the Bible's referential power for Melville.[3] The parallels I suggest between the Bible and *Clarel* stem from identifiable biblical metaphors, themes, genres, and idioms; however, these biblical words are recontextualized and reinterpreted and essentially become Melville's own. Thus I do not think that the traditional literary terms "allusions," "quotations," or "references" do justice to the two-way interpretive task of reading the Bible and *Clarel* and prefer the term "intertextuality." The Bible, especially certain parallel biblical co-texts such as Job, Psalms, Jeremiah, Lamentations, the Gospels, and Ecclesiastes, is *Clarel's* co-text. Just as the New Testament authors both identified with and separated themselves from some of the central ideas of the Hebrew Bible, Melville both continues biblical traditions and abandons them. He identifies with the Hebraic notion of a hidden God but rewrites key biblical passages such as Psalm 23 and Isaiah 52. Faced with the destruction of orthodox faith in nineteenth-century America, Melville paradoxically preserves biblical voices and texts by weaving so many passages into his poem, but he also breaches biblical traditions by rewriting, recontextualizing, and finally reinterpreting biblical texts. In other words, Melville seems to be engaged in a nineteenth-century rearguard maneuver to preserve the biblical voices and, at the same time, to help breach them by documenting his characters' doubts and rejections of biblical authority. What Matthew Arnold believed about Christianity in 1875, Melville perhaps believed about the Bible: "men cannot do without it" and "they cannot do with it as it is."[4] For good or bad, the Bible was Melville's inescapable heritage. Whether rejecting, preserving, or both, Melville made biblical images and ideas come alive in *Clarel*. Melville was an assiduous Bible reader, self-taught, and particularly sensitive to Hebraic thinking. By quoting the Bible so often, Melville invites the reader to reenter the literary and theological world of scripture. To read *Clarel* is to have one eye on the Bible. In fact, I suggest that readers of this study have both *Clarel* and the King James Bible open on the desk. Melville neither totally affirms nor totally rejects the wisdom and authority of biblical words but instead struggles to reconcile ancient biblical voices with his nineteenth-century narrative voices. Furthermore, whether identifying with or distancing himself from biblical texts, Melville's intertextual lover's quarrel with the Bible is really a quarrel over the nature, idea, and image of God.

The second methodological approach is to foreground the complexity of the narrator's voices in what Melville called "dramatic poetry" or "narrative verse."[5] Narrative voices in *Clarel* intertwine with characters' voices, show the other side of death and despair, and offer a theology of hope that many readers will see if sensitized to the complexity of Melville's narrative voices and to the obsessively dialogical nature of the poem. Not only the prevalence of biblical intertextuality but also the dialogical interaction between several diverse and divergent voices are the stylistic hallmarks of *Clarel*. It is more rewarding to read *Clarel* not as poetry, which some discourse theorists including Bahktin view as monological, but as narrative verse that contains the essential dialogical principle usually associated with prose fiction. *Clarel* also contains a narrative consciousness that is interested in bringing readers closer to its voices and closer to the divinity within the human heart. This phrase appropriately describes Melville's poetic exploration of divine immanence and, although derived from a combination of biblical, Christian, and Romantic traditions, expresses his own independent expansion and embellishment of a theology of hope.

The issue of Melville's narrator raises the biographical dilemma in Melville studies. Despite Melville's extraordinarily complex narratological art, which constantly changes a narrator's voices, tone, and distance from the story, many Melvilleans still equate the narrator's voice with Melville himself. Thus *Clarel*, for these critics, becomes a direct, unmediated, unedited source for biographical information on Herman Melville.[6] One would think that ever since Walter Bezanson's classic essay warning us that Ishmael is the center of *Moby-Dick* and urging us to distinguish between Melville and Ishmael as narrator, critics would not jump so quickly from text to Melville's personal life and back again.[7] Other critics such as James Duban and John Samson have extensively documented Melville's management of narrative voices and insist upon a separation between Melville the person and the various narrative voices and stances represented in his poems and fiction.[8] I have too much respect for Melville's complex imaginative art to claim that the characters or the narrator in *Clarel* unquestionably express the actual inner theological tensions of Melville's life. How much is biographical, how much the rhetoric of the artist? In other words, *Clarel* does not offer direct, unmediated access to the consciousness of Herman Melville.[9] Rather, *Clarel* testifies to a part of Melville's subjective theological world he explored as a literary artist and as a deeply thinking theologian.[10] We cannot go from text to autobiography and back as glibly as some scholars want to. *Clarel* is mediated to us via several narrative voices. Melville clearly resists the notion of one truth, of one voice, of one integrative, centered self throughout the poem. There are, however, consistent creative choices, consistent patterns of theological meaning, consistent commitments to certain truths that enable us to label them as Melvillean and help us trace a theological questioning that is represented in the poem. The most consistent commitment in the poem is to the exploration of the human phenomenon of faith.

The third methodological approach is theological, for *Clarel* is motivated by a concern for theological questions. This study wrestles with several of these questions. What image of God does Melville represent in the poem? How do the problems of theological doubt, undeserved suffering, and death affect the human relationship to God? Does the mysteriousness and unknowability of God—"How think to sound God's deeper heart!" (2.32.111)— imply the unbelievability of God?[11] Most important, what is the basis of faith? These questions are answered and explained within the context of biblical idioms, ideas, and metaphors and within the context of Melville's narrator, who is theologically central to *Clarel*.

Of course, the term "theology" is one of the most vexed abstractions in our language and raises questions of definition and the nature of theological language, not to mention whether one can infer a theology from a narrative poem. Melville did not pursue theology as a philosophical study of a divine object—God. In fact, the narrator and the character Rolfe express their disdain for theological abstractions and prooftexts: "Theology's scarce practical" (4.21.86) and "A paper pact, [the Constitution] with points abstruse / As theologic ones—profuse" (4.5.88–89). Thus "theology" as used in the poem (only once) and throughout this study does not refer to the propositional discourse usually associated with theology. As with Melville's narrator and the character Rolfe, for me theological language includes the narrative, the metaphorical, and the symbolic as well as the propositional. One can indeed infer a theological stance from Melville's literary choices and from an intertextual reading of the Bible and *Clarel*. The term "theology" in this study never refers to an a priori systematic theology. The Melvillean theology represented in the poem emerges from the narrator's and the characters' encounter with the mystery of God and is not systematic.

Melville's theological reflection offered in the poem does not so much take place in the domain of abstract thinking as existentially. I use "existentially" not in the technical sense, as used by existentialists, but as a generic term for the way we live and die. The theological reflection comes from the search for a faith based on human existence—the poem's depiction of concrete events, emotions, and situations: life, suffering, doubt, fear, love, and death. There are human beings who love God, who doubt God, and who deny God— Melville knew this as an existential fact.

Clarel is a poem motivated by concerns of doubt and faith and proceeds not from any concession to popular religion or theological dogma, but from the encounter between the divine and the human. In *Clarel*, faith is experiential, but deeply problematic because God is hidden and never speaks in the poem. Thus before discussing the question of faith, I first pursue the questions of God, doubt, suffering, and death in *Clarel*. Melville's search in *Clarel* is the most difficult of all searches: the quest for an answer to why humans suffer and die, a search for life and love in the face of God's hiddenness and silence. The question of the hiddenness or presence of God constitutes a severe critique of the starting point for orthodox theologies: the unquestioned assumption of the presence and accessibility of God. This certitude was not shared by Herman Melville—nor was it shared by the psalmists, prophets, and wisdom sages of the Hebrew Bible. The question of God's presence is the central theological and literary concern of *Clarel*. The God question does not take shape apart from the text but is a part of the very narrative fabric of *Clarel*.

This study is divided into five chapters. Chapter 1 illustrates that Melville's pilgrimage—"this hunt without one clew" (3.21.182)[12]—takes place within the context of a central biblical metaphor and idea of the Hebrew Bible: the hiddenness and silence of God. The idea of divine self-concealment is more than an image; it is the way Melville's creative consciousness experienced the encounter between the human and the divine. The key question that haunted Melville and called the poem into being is, What does the experience of a hidden, silent God do to faith and to self-understanding? Divine self-concealment produces an ambivalent response from human beings. To use Melville's own words in describing *Clarel*, a hidden God can either "intimidate" or "allure."[13] One can flee from a hidden God, blaming Him for His absence and for the human condition of undeserved suffering and death; or one can return to a hidden God, trying to find some theological or psychological basis for hope and faith. In other words, if the center of Melville's theological world view in *Clarel* is hollow—a silent, hidden God— then one can seek that God even more fully or flee that God even more resignedly. That is, Melville's pursuit of a hidden God does not necessarily lead to rejection, denial, or atheism, as Lawrance R. Thompson suggests in *Melville's Quarrel with God*. Chapter 1 traces the biblical metaphor and the theological resonance of divine hiddenness and silence and the effects of divine self-concealment: the ambiguity of God and the human limitations on language, knowledge, and truth. Most important, however, Chapter 1 also reveals that the human bears the divine image and is thus an *imitatio Dei* of divine hiddenness and silence. Human self-concealment in the poem reflects divine self-concealment.

Chapter 2 traces one response to the hidden God: a bold, obstinate questioning of God's purposes. The many questions in the poem are explained within the context of the biblical lament or protest to God as petitions to *Deus absconditus*: the question of "how long, how long" will God remain hidden implies that hiddenness has gone on long enough. The powerful laments of disillusionment and the theodicy protests against death and undeserved human suffering are the result of the disparity between God's promise of presence and God's fulfillment in hiddenness.

Chapter 3 explores another response to divine self-concealment: taking theological and intellectual offense at God, with reverent skepticism. Melville uses the biblical metaphor of wrestling, in particular Jacob's wrestling with an angel of God, as emblematic of the mind's wrestling with opposite thoughts, especially doubt and faith. As a theological metaphor, wrestling suggests that one may come to recognize a tested faith only after a heroic struggle with doubt. Chapter 3 presents the notion of a Melvillean God-wrestler who achieves disciplined self-control and tolerance toward other traditions within a unification of contrary thoughts. Chapter 3 suggests that in terms of poetic length, structure, genre, and emotional moods, Melville's *Clarel* is patterned after the Psalms. The one hundred and fifty cantos of *Clarel* make it a nineteenth-century American Psalter.

Chapters 1 through 3 describe a Melvillean *askesis* or dark night of the soul, for they trace the spiritual difficulties in responding to a hidden God. What balances human frustrations with a concealed God, with the protest of the lament, and with the difficulty of theological skepticism, however, is a cumulative emphasis on divine immanence—the divinity within the individual.

Chapter 4 is the pivot of this study and explores the complexity of *Clarel*'s narrative voices and characterization.[14] Melville's narrative voices are recontextualized within the biblical representation of Elijah's "still small voice," a voice that serves as an example of spiritual inwardness. Narrative voices suggest a hope in immortality and the sustaining possibility of a revelation of the divinity within the human heart. Melville's narrative voices offer a theology of hope that counters the themes of hiddenness, death, suffering, and disillusionment wrestled with in chapters 1 through 3. With the cumulative hope in the possibility of a responsiveness to God exemplified by the "still small" narrative voice of spiritual inwardness, Melville offers a metaphorical recommendation for faith—giving the human heart in love to a hidden God.

Chapter 5 attempts to define Melville's protest theism and to trace his curious love for the biblical metaphor and epithet of the heart. In essence, this last chapter answers the question of how one goes from the limits of divine hiddenness and silence to a renewed theistic relationship with God—how one maintains faith in the face of hiddenness. In *Clarel*, faith becomes useful if not true, and one surrenders one's heart to God out of need. The search for God in *Clarel* culminates in a theology of the heart: a stubborn desire to love a lonely God despite His hiddenness and silence.

*T*his study also seeks to correct several deficiencies in Melville scholarship on *Clarel*. A tone of defensive *apologia* still exists in Melville studies when discussing *Clarel*. Although authorities such as Robert Penn Warren have expressed admiration for *Clarel*, even love for such Civil War poems as "Shiloh," most critics still evaluate *Clarel* tentatively, especially when contrasted to the other major nineteenth-century American poems.[15] We read *Clarel* because it was written by the same man who wrote *Moby-Dick* and *Billy Budd*. Such reasoning hardly does justice to *Clarel*, literally a library of poems that Melville brooded over for almost twenty years. Throughout this book, I redirect the evaluation of Melville's *Clarel* away from aesthetic comparisons with his other works or with other American poets to a discussion of the biblical nature of Melville's theological reflection. In other words, I believe *Clarel* should be compared not to the poetry of Whitman and Dickinson but to texts truly parallel in form and content: the great theodicies of the Book of Job and the Apocryphal 4 Ezra (Second Esdras), the reverent skepticism of Ecclesiastes, the pain of Jeremiah's complaints, or the laments of the Psalms. *Clarel* will always evoke the scholarly curiosity of some Melvilleans and students of nineteenth-century faith and doubt, as does Matthew Arnold's *God and the Bible* or James Russell Lowell's *The Cathedral*. But *Clarel* might well be taught in seminaries and departments of religion, for it wrestles with the big questions of any theology, the questions of divinity, mortality, immortality, theodicy, doubt, and faith. The plot movement in *Clarel* starts with the search for the hidden God and ends with death overwhelming human existence. But between these two questions—the God question and the death question—the larger narrative world of *Clarel* (with its accompanying hopes and biblical voices and resonances) takes shape.

Another deficiency in Melville studies is simply the paucity of both literary criticism and theological exegesis of *Clarel*. Every page of *Moby-Dick* and *Billy Budd* has been explicated and recontextualized in hundreds of articles and scores of books. Although about twenty Melville scholars have devoted a part of or a whole chapter to *Clarel*, most discussions are too brief to cover adequately the full theological world of *Clarel*. The only extended studies of *Clarel* that dive deep into the interconnectedness of the poem are Walter E. Bezanson's introduction and notes to the Hendricks House edition of *Clarel* (1960; reprint, 1991); Joseph G. Knapp's monograph, *Tortured Synthesis: The Meaning of Melville's Clarel* (1971), William H. Shurr's two chapters in his book entitled *The Mystery of Iniquity: Melville as Poet, 1857–1891* (1972);

and Vincent Kenny's book-length study, *Herman Melville's Clarel: A Spiritual Autobiography* (1973).[16] Less than twenty adequately developed articles are in print.[17] By focusing an entire book on *Clarel*, I hope to do justice to the full depth and complexity of Melville's poem and to explore both sides of the poem's theological story: despair and hope, doubt and faith—its protest theism.

There are four interpretive obstacles that have blocked the critical apprehension and comprehension of Melville's representation of protest theism. (1) Most studies focus on Clarel—the main character—as the poem's main locus of meaning. To follow Clarel's fate is indeed to experience a dark, disappointing pilgrimage. Clarel learns little except suffering from his sojourn in the Holy Land; the reader, however, learns more. (2) Most critics also read the Epilogue of the poem as a tacked-on afterthought thematically different from the body of the poem. The hope and faith depicted in the Epilogue are, however, present throughout the poem.[18] (3) Many studies see the narrator obtrusively present in the Epilogue but fail to hear his many voices throughout the text recommending reverence, respect, and tolerance. (4) Finally, most critics do not recognize the extent of Melville's biblical imagination in *Clarel*, the depth of Melville's theological reflection, and the importance of the biblical metaphors, themes, and genres of hiddenness, lament, wrestling, inner voices, and the theology of the heart. *Clarel* points not to a definition of but to a direction toward God and faith.

As the title of this study suggests, my contribution to Melville studies is to place the arguments of Melville's biblically rich poem in the broadest possible biblical and theological contexts, to clarify and enrich its meaning and literary artistry. As the poem's narrator claims,

> Scripture, here recalled,
> The context less obscure may make. . . .
> (1.5.71–72)

❖

The Hiddenness and
Silence of God

But if in vain
One tries to comprehend a man,
How think to sound God's deeper heart!
—*Clarel*

Wherefore hidest thou thy face?
—Job

HERMAN MELVILLE WAS A GOD-CHASED and a God-chasing man. Melville represents in *Clarel* two theological motions, both away from God and toward God, that I call the paradox of divine distance. One can flee from God just as one can return to God, but both motions may form one circle. To be a distinct human being with independent thoughts and actions, one must go away from God, question God, even reject accepted beliefs. If, however, one flees too far from God, one is left with theological skepticism or even atheism. At the same time, the individual who flees God often feels the most intense deprivation: "like a lone dog that for a master cries" or like a "god-like mind without a god."[1] To have a center on which to release one's emotional feelings of awe and reverence, one must, however, turn to God or to nature and acknowledge the need for something greater than the human. The spiritual and emotional need for the divine may so allure a person that one tries to discover a faith in God. The theological paradox is that the human needs to be with the divine, but the divine may be hidden; the human may want to be independent from the divine, but God, often immanent within the human, is present. One flees from God to God. Even rebellion can be a theological search, and, quite often, it is only the near-unbeliever who thinks deeply about faith.

Many ancient and modern theologians have expressed this paradox of the urgent need to get to God combined with the desire for independent thinking. Such reflection produces the tension of faith and doubt in any theology. One of the more interesting delineations of this conflict of God-chasing and being God-chased, close to Melville in time and spirit, was written by Herman and Elizabeth Melville's Unitarian minister, Henry Whitney Bellows. In his 1859 address to the alumni of the Harvard Divinity School entitled "The Suspense of Faith," Bellows wrote:

> there are two motions of the human spirit in relation to God . . . a centrifugal and a centripetal motion—the motion that sends man away from God, to learn his freedom, to develope [sic] his personal powers and faculties, relieved of the over-awing and predominating presence of his Author; and the motion that draws him back to God, to receive the inspiration, nurture, and endowment, which he has become strong enough to hold.[2]

This self-emancipation away from God and the emancipation from self back to God is the oppositional, all-pervasive idea that actualizes *Clarel*'s narrative.

When Melville chased the unbearable hiddenness and mystery of God, he became profoundly troubled by the entire monotheistic tradition and, at the same time, questioned the assumptions of orthodox theology: the presence and accessibility of God. Monotheism makes demands on the human mind that are, like the tetragrammaton, ineffable. The idea of a monotheistic God that may manifest Himself mysteriously in nature or within human beings but is still a radical unity, or the idea of one God creating both good and evil, is an abstraction as inaccessible to some as particle physics is to others. To apprehend and to comprehend the one God by any normal human sense strains the imagination to its limits. We cannot see Him, touch Him, or hear Him; we cannot even make an accurate image of His likeness. We invent vague abstract words such as "omnipresent," "omniscient," and "omnipotent" to try to describe an unimaginable, almost inconceivable, concept, to try to describe something that by definition is indescribable and mysterious. Even poetic language fails to give an adequate image of God. Like the poet of Isaiah, Melville also encounters the limits of art when trying to describe God: "To whom then can you liken me, To whom can I be compared?" (Isaiah 40:25).

The biblical idea and image that helped Melville articulate the paradox of divine distance and the difficulties of monotheism is called, in Hebrew, *El Mistater* or *hester panim*, the God that hides himself or the hidden face of God. This biblical idea of divine self-concealment is found predominantly in the great repositories of Wisdom literature in the Hebrew Bible: Proverbs, Job, Psalms, and Ecclesiastes.[3] Melville read and quoted from these Wisdom books.[4]

Divine self-concealment has two different meanings in the Hebrew Bible. One is an expression of divine judgment and retribution as expressed in Isaiah 59:2: "but your iniquities have separated between you and your God, and your sins have hid his face from you, that he will not hear."[5] The other meaning—the one that captivated Melville—is related to the hiding of God's face as a specific attribute of God's nature. Isaiah also says, "verily, thou art a God that hides thyself" (45:15). Here the reflexive Hebrew verb *mistater* ("hides thyself") indicates that God's self-concealment is an attribute of His divinity. Such is the God of the Hebrew Bible: a God who hides Himself. Some may seek Him, but He will not be found; some may call upon Him, but He may not answer. Melville's problem is that of other God-chasers such as Job: "Behold, I go forward, but he is not there; and backward, but I cannot perceive him: On the left hand, where he doth work, but I cannot behold him: He hideth himself on the right hand, that I cannot see him" (Job 23:8–9). God is present without being unquestionably manifested. He is hidden without being completely inaccessible.

To find a clarification of God, to find Him in hiding, is at the heart of Melville's twenty-thousand-line poetic testimony to the relationship between the human and the divine. *Clarel* is an original application and development of the biblical idea and image of the hiddenness of God and of the secondary acknowledgment of the silence of God.[6] *Clarel* not only reveals the specific divine attributes of self-concealment and silence but also questions the effects of divine concealment: the ambiguity of a God of many faces and the human limitations on the knowledge of nature, science, language, history, and wisdom. If God's faces are hidden, His nature, His universe, and His purpose may also be hidden. In a sense, God plays hide-and-seek with His own creation. Most important, however, *Clarel* reveals the human as a mirror image of God's hiddenness and silence—an unusual *imitatio Dei*.[7]

"WHAT WENT YE OUT FOR TO SEE?": AN OVERVIEW OF *CLAREL* AS DRAMATIC *AGON*

The narrative design of *Clarel* is an archetypal quest in which some of the pilgrims look for God and the fulfillment of faith in the so-called Land of Promise—Palestine. The poem is divided into four parts that together contain one hundred and fifty cantos: (1) "Jerusalem," (2) "The Wilderness," (3) "Mar Saba," and (4) "Bethlehem." The four parts describe a nineteenth-century pilgrimage from the walls of Jerusalem to the Judean wilderness and to the Dead Sea, which is, however, very much alive with theological conversation. The pilgrimage is an outer quest that requires giving up comfort and safety, encountering bandits and solitude. Some never see Jerusalem again. Yet the outer quest is also an inner quest made up of questions, dialog, talking across the theological boundaries of three world religions, and coming back. The return from the Dead Sea takes the pilgrims to the Mar Saba monastery, to the Church of the Nativity in Bethlehem, and then back to the gates of Jerusalem. On a mythical plane, Melville teases the reader with the hope of finding *gnosis,* knowledge of self and of God. As in any hero quest, we expect the characters to learn something or achieve some victory. On the theological plane, Melville has written a dramatic *agon* of theological reflection, as the historically sanctioned holy spots of Palestine prompt dialog about faith, doubt, God, Christ, death, immortality, evil, freedom, Providence, divine immanence, Judaism, Catholicism, Protestantism, the Bible, suffering, sexuality, nature, America—just about everything Melville found theologically or ideologically troubling in his century. Life is a pilgrimage in *Clarel,* and the characters are set in dramatic situations that are designed to present an *agon* of questions, a dialog of oppositions, a deliberate intellectual and theological test of our ability to hold contesting ideas in the mind at once, rather than coming down hard in an absolutist way for any single voice or opinion. The dialogical nature of the poem suggests that the intent is not to let any one character act as a mouthpiece for Melville, but that all the voices combine to represent Melville's larger thematic concerns.

The quest is also a love story turned sour. The main character, Clarel, a Protestant and a lapsed student of theology, falls in love with a Jewish woman, Ruth. When Ruth's father, Nathan, is killed by hostile Arabs, she is sequestered and undergoes a period of mourning. Clarel is barred by custom and by an intolerant orthodox rabbi from seeing her and thus decides to join a ten-day pilgrimage to Jericho, the Jordan river, and down to the Dead Sea, only fourteen miles from Jerusalem, but a world away theologically. Pilgrimages, like life, lead to death, and when Clarel returns to the holy city, he finds Ruth and her mother, Agar, dead from grief and fever. In essence, the love story of Ruth and Clarel is disrupted by the quest for a larger love, the ceaseless striving of the human heart for a loving God. Ruth is conceptualized dramatically and narratively precisely in order to die. Her death is one last test to prepare the reader for the apprehension and comprehension of passionate protest theism. Clarel is also, like Ishmael in *Moby-Dick,* an orphan, cut off from parental love, as he loses romantic love and questions divine love.

The development of the pilgrimage quest is an *agon* among five important sets of characters. Of all the dramatis personae, the pilgrims who succeed in completing the pilgrimage are perhaps most important narratively: Clarel, Rolfe, Vine, and Derwent. Clarel is the archetypal student, one who sees, listens, learns, and then unlearns every word spoken by the other characters. He is at times naive, often asks from others more than they can give, makes judgments too quickly, is driven by impulses and attractions that he does not fully understand, and, like many young students, wants easy answers. Clarel's primary wisdom teachers or guides are Rolfe, Vine, and Derwent. Rolfe and Vine are the two "exceptional natures" of the poem (1.31.45) because of their power of human presence and their effect on Clarel. Rolfe, often read as a self-portrayal of Melville, has an intellectual love of God and religion. Rolfe understands that religious emotion produces love, virtue, and self-control, but he is quick to criticize man-made creeds and to realize that his century is an age of doubt. He is a reverent skeptic, a strong partisan of several view-points, and intellectually complex. Rolfe has a complete vision of self, not based upon the world, but "poised at self-center and mature" (4.3.125). Vine is far more reclusive and fastidious than Rolfe. Clarel is mysteriously attracted to Vine yet puzzled by his detachment and inscrutability. Derwent, although often viewed as a superficial optimist, is paradoxically capable of some of the poem's most insightful remarks about hope and the power of subjective truth. He is an English cleric who also tries to teach Clarel.[8] Both Derwent and Vine, although admirable wisdom guides for Clarel, finally have an incomplete vision of self.

*A*fter the survivors of the pilgrimage, the set of characters most central to the dramatic situation includes those men who cannot "get used / To seeing evil" and who suffer from a "private wrong outrageous": Mortmain, Ungar, and Celio (2.37.56–57; 1.11.26). Mortmain is an outcast from his family, a reformer who has tried to change the world, but is disillusioned by human evil and imperfection. Ungar is a veteran Confederate soldier acting as a mercenary in the Levant. His source of bitterness is the national calamity of the Civil War. Celio, a hunch-backed Italian youth and one of the poem's more heroic doubters, is obsessed with the Passion of Christ. Mortmain and Celio, like Clarel, have also been disappointed in romantic love. The three monomaniacs—Mortmain, Ungar, and Celio—have an incomplete vision of the self based excessively on the world and are constantly in danger of giving themselves up to despair and bitterness. There is also a set of believers in the poem, those who are secure in their faith: the Syrian, Dominican, and Francis-can monks. Although they are criticized by several characters, their need for faith earns the pilgrims' respect. Then there are the poem's social chucklers, easily dismissed intellectually but appealing for their geniality and joyous fatalism, those men who deny death and suffering: the Cypriote, Glaucon, the Lyonese, and the man from Lesbos (the Lesbian).

The last important set of characters is the zealots, those who are dogma-tists of mechanical science, of one religion, or of one ideology: Margoth, Nehemiah, and Nathan. Margoth's excessive zeal is for geology, and he can-not accept any notion of the divine or of transcendence. Nehemiah is an evangelical Christian who reads the Bible literally. Although kind and charita-ble, Nehemiah is a zealot for biblical authority and wants to convert the world. Nathan's obsession is Zionism; he is a convert to Judaism and brings his death upon himself by his racist comments about Arabs.

Also important is the Druze guide, who stands out as a figure of self-control and who is often cited by critics as representing endurance. The narrative is retold to us retrospectively by the most complex human presence in the poem: the narrator, whose moral perseverance as a witnessing survivor of the painful pilgrimage indicates both heroism and an admirable mind. The narrator's personal virtues of reverence (e.g., 4.9.37–46), tolerance (e.g., 4.18.12–19), and empathy for human suffering (e.g., 1.8.12–20; 4.35.21) are apparent in his many dialogical voices. Finally, the poem includes a host of minor characters: sailors, bankers, mercenaries, monks, Arabs, merchants, and memorable donkeys and horses.

Several canto sequences are key thematic indicators of the process of searching and inquiring that motivates the poem as a dramatic agon. Throughout *Clarel* are interpolated cantos in which the narrator pursues key themes: "The Sepulcher" (faith and doubt), "Nathan" (American theologies), "Of Rama" (divine immanence in the human heart), "Prelusive" (evil), "Symphonies" (a musical representation of faith and doubt). Although the entire poem is a dramatic dialog of contesting ideas, certain cantos are obsessively dialogical as two characters talk to and often past each other: "Derwent and Rolfe," "Ungar and Rolfe," "Derwent and Ungar," "Derwent and the Lesbian," "Vine and Clarel," "Rolfe and Derwent," "Clarel and Ruth." A sequence of cantos is devoted to Jews, to Catholicism, and to Protestantism. The two most intriguing sets of cantos about perception and about the question of America's continued corporate existence are the Palm cantos (part 3, cantos 24–30) and the American cantos (part 4, cantos 20–21). The Palm cantos illustrate various characters' theological and aesthetic perceptions of the St. Saba palm tree, often compared to the doubloon in *Moby-Dick*. The American cantos are devoted to Ungar's grim, pessimistic commentary on America, a nation that has become more *pluribus* than *unum* because it focuses on progress and profit rather than on Christian charity. Ungar's comments are obliquely analogous to Melville's "Supplement" to *Battle-Pieces*.

The narrative design, characters, and cantos of *Clarel* can be viewed as a gnostic pilgrimage quest for insight—a dramatic agon of trying to know oneself, others, and God. Rather than viewing their journey as an orthodox Christian pilgrimage involving sin and repentance, Melville's characters more often speak about illusion and knowledge. Along the way, we encounter apologists, advocates, relativists, skeptics, literalists, and atheists. Yet I call *Clarel* a gnostic dramatic agon because it offers not a single answer but a combination of answers in dialogical relationship to each other. The poem encourages the promise of searching more than the fulfillment of single answers. All doctrines, myths, and speculations are pursued as potential approaches to gnosis, yet without ever denying that there are certain truths that teach us how to approach God.

THE QUEST FOR THE INVISIBLE PRESENCE OF GOD

Unlike Milton's *Paradise Lost*, where God actually speaks to Adam in the celestial colloquy of book 8, the word of God is not given any place in Melville's *Clarel*. The sustaining possibility of God's presence, however, is pursued from the first canto to the Epilogue. God is searched for, discussed, questioned, arraigned, and even prayed to. The most obvious, yet significant, observation to make about Melville's poem and pilgrimage in Palestine— "this hunt without one clew" (3.21.182)—is that several characters have come to search for God. In fact, the key question in *Clarel* is first asked by the narrator: *"And can the Father Be?"* (1.3.136).[9] Clarel, for instance, in the very opening of the poem reveals that he has come to Judea specifically in search of Christ:

> Christ lived a Jew: and in Judea
> May linger any breath of Him?
> If nay, yet surely it is here
> One best may learn if all be dim.
> (1.7.33–36)

Clarel will find either traces of Christ's teachings or more reasons for doubt. In a dramatic dialog with Derwent and Mortmain about Christ, the heart, and comparative religion, Rolfe uses a daring anthropomorphism and implies that faith will come only when we can find God's footprints in the snow:

> for we, misled,
> We peer from brinks of all we know;
> Our eyes are blurred against the haze:
> Canst help us track in snow on snow
> The footprint of the Ancient of Days?
> (3.6.21–25)

With all of human knowledge, to track God is profoundly difficult, for his footprints are instantly hidden by fresh snow: "snow on snow."[10] When Derwent tries to explain and to accommodate faith to the younger Clarel in the key canto, "In Confidence," Derwent uses the image of being lost in a snowstorm when he tells Clarel that even a lamp of knowledge to answer all Clarel's questions would not change the human condition: "Still lost you'd be in blanks of snow" (3.21.240). A snowstorm is blinding (a "haze" 3.6.23) and cold. For Derwent, without Christ who "built a hearth," there is no warmth (3.21.245). When Mortmain returns from his vigil in the desert—

like Elijah returning from the "brook Cherith" and hearing a "voice aerial" (2.34.20, 22)—he asks: "What god invoke, for leave to unveil / That gulf whither tend these modern fears, / And deeps over which men crowd the sail?" (2.34.25–27).[11] Mortmain, unsure of God's presence, wants God to unveil the "gulf" of "modern fears" and the "deeps" of doubt which make up his life—the "impious years" (2.34.26, 24). And after the avalanche that ends part 2, "The Wilderness," the narrator asks about the source of the "fog-bow," "a thing of heaven" (2.39.151): "What works there from behind the veil?" (2.39.149). The hidden God, "in that silence sealed," works behind the veil (2.39.148).

As the search for the hidden God becomes more frustrating, the questioning begins to resemble an arraignment of God. In discussing the hidden sins of Sodom by the Dead Sea, Mortmain claims that the "Doom well imposed" took place "In some god's reign, some god long fled" (2.36.46–47). After the pilgrims leave the Dead Sea and are reminiscing about their trials in the safety of the Mar Saba monastery, Mortmain's questions become more subversive:

> Is God an omnipresent God?
> Is He in Siddim yonder? No?
> If anywhere He's disavowed
> How think to shun the final schism—
> Blind elements, flat atheism?
> (3.6.56–60)

Mortmain's question is parallel to Jeremiah's: "Is not the Lord in Zion?" (Jeremiah 8:19). Both prophets of doom conflate divine inaccessibility and human insensitivity toward God. Mortmain's questions of God's omnipresence (simply put as—is God here?) culminate in a prediction that if God is gone, hidden, or denied, atheism may be the result. When Rolfe describes the red city of Petra, he ponders whether the silent God will come out of the door carved in the ancient church of *El Deir*: "Thence will the god emerge, and speak?" (2.30.38). The answer is obvious to Rolfe: "We'd knock. An echo. Knock again— / Ay, knock forever: none requite" (2.30.54–55). Human beings can knock on the doors of divine silence all they want: the hidden God does not emerge. Like Saul struggling against the dictates of an inscrutable God throughout the first Book of Samuel, Rolfe learns of the silence and hiddenness of God.

No passage in *Clarel* can better convey the bitter sense of the tremendous distance between God's hiddenness and the human desire for divine presence than the prayer of the Syrian monk, a thin, ragged hermit who is seen by the pilgrims descending Mount Quarantania, where Jesus is supposed to have experienced his great struggle with Satan. His painful words are truly an Everyman's prayer to the hidden God:

> O God (I prayed), come through
> The cloud; hard task Thou settest man
> To know Thee; take me back again
> To nothing, or make clear my view!
>
> (2.18.133–36)

The Syrian monk believes that God is in the heavens but also knows that He is hidden, metaphorically, by clouds. The monk's desire for a theophany—his wish to see God appear—is so intense that he is willing to accept death rather than live without God's presence.[12] Knowledge of God may be a "hard task," yet it becomes communicative to the monk precisely at the point where the very limit of acquiring knowledge of God is experienced: divine self-concealment. What we know of God may really be what we know of the unknowable. By such a standard, the Syrian monk is one of the most knowledgeable characters in *Clarel*.

What must be remembered in *Clarel* is that the experience of encountering a hidden God is one of faith, for as Melville writes—the monk "prayed." There may be no sure supernatural sign of divinity in the poem, but in Melville's development of God's hiddenness, we are made to feel a theological event—the logic of God that defies human logic. To use Melville's favorite pun, it would be a grave error to dismiss the monk's prayer and vision on Quarantania as a subjective vision resulting from an "ecstasy of fast" (2.18.157). Subjective perceptions are true for the perceiver, and if we dismiss the monk, we must also dismiss, as Rolfe implies, another great biblical voice of despair: "construe then Jonah in despair" (2.18.158).

Not only human beings question and pray to the hidden God, but also Jesus questions God. By the Ecce Homo arch in Jerusalem, the narrator gives us Celio's interior monologue that becomes a universal statement of the human sense of personal abandonment and longing:

> But, crying out in death's eclipse,
> When rainbow none his eyes might see,
> Enlarged the margin for despair—
> *My God, my God, forsakest me?*
>
> (1.13.44–47)

Echoing the cries of Psalms 22:1 and the Gospels (Matthew 27:46 and Mark 15:34)—"My God, my God, why hast thou forsaken me?"—Jesus here confronts the silence and hiddenness of God. Celio and the narrator emphasize the suffering man named Jesus—"Yon Man it is this burden lays" (1.13.37)—in this passage rather than the Christ who died for humanity's sins. "Forsakest" has the connotation of abandonment, and Jesus, "Pain's Lord" (1.28.10), senses that his Father has left him.[13] At this point in the poem, Melville has Celio reflect on the reality of suffering rather than faith.[14] By not referring to the second half of Psalm 22, Melville ignores the hope and confidence of the psalmist and, instead, focuses on the cruelty of Christ's abandonment by God. Parallel to Christ's cry to the hidden God's aloofness, the narrator gives over Jerusalem's lament to the hidden God—an echo of Jesus' cry:

> Prediction and fulfillment met
> In faint appealings from the rod:
> Wherefore forever dost forget—
> For so long time *forsake*, O God?
> (1.22.19–22, emphasis mine)

This passage has its biblical roots in the dire warnings of God's destruction of the Israelite nation for their sin of forsaking Yahweh and serving other gods in chapters such as Isaiah 6 and Jeremiah 5. Melville gives a strong reinterpretation here by suggesting that God has forsaken Jerusalem rather than the people forsaking God, although the "despair alleged of sin" is mentioned (1.22.18). Clarel also echoes Jesus by using the pronoun "my" when he cries to God in his frustration over Derwent's notion of faith: "God, *my* God, / Sorely Thou triest me the clod!" (3.21.226–27, emphasis mine). And, finally, in a transliterated evocation of Jesus' Aramaic words on the cross, Mortmain utters the "cry of cries" (3.7.4): "ELOI LAMA SABACHTHANI!" (My God, why have you forsaken me—3.7.1). Clarel calls Jesus' words "the ghost's reproachful litany" (3.7.11), for Jesus, like Jerusalem, Clarel, and Mortmain, reproaches God for His hiddenness.

As Jesus cries to God, humankind cries to Christ in *Clarel*. But the human addresses a hidden Christ, as if some characters disbelieve the resurrection event, Hebraicize Christ to resemble a hidden God, and forget the importance of Easter: "Lilies and anthems which attest / The floral Easter holiday" (1.3.199–200). As the narrator helps us to follow imagination and the three Marys back from Golgotha to their empty room, they "Deem vain the promise now, and yet / Invoke him [Christ] who returns no call" (1.3.192–93). In the Church of the Holy Sepulcher, Clarel asks the same question about Jesus that was asked about God—where is Jesus: "Nay, is He fled?" (1.5.36). Mortmain's verse inscription on the rock by the Dead Sea also bemoans the withdrawn cross (Southern Cross and the Crucifixion Cross), which is analogous to an estranged God:

Emblazoned Bleak in austral skies—
A heaven remote, whose starry swarm
Like Science lights but cannot warm—
Translated Cross, hast thou withdrawn,
. . . .
Estranged, estranged: can friend prove so?
Aloft, aloof, a frigid sign:
                (2.31.50–53; 57–58)

Mortmain, bemoaning the loss of the "Slanting Cross" (2.31.44), engages in
an act of imagination which sums up in a single metaphorical judgment the
full complexity of God's presence and "aloof" hiddenness. Rolfe's lament for
the hidden Christ is as powerful as Celio's arraignment of Christ:

Whither hast fled, thou deity
So genial? In thy last and best,
Best avatar—so ripe in form—
Pure as the sleet—as roses warm—
Our earth's unmerited fair guest—
A god with peasants went abreast:
Man clasped a deity's offered hand.
                (2.21.63–69)

The fading of such a hopeful picture—man clasping Jesus' hand—gives Rolfe
the same anguished sense of abandonment by God: "Cut off, cut off! Canst
feel elate / While all the depths of Being moan" (2.21.92–93). Rolfe testifies
to the human need for God by lamenting his state of being cut off from God.
Numerous lament or complaint passages from the Psalms are analogous to
Rolfe's lament, such as Psalms 88:14: "Lord, why castest thou off my soul?
why hidest thou thy face from me?" Here the afflicted psalmist prays to the
hidden God just as Rolfe's "depths of Being," like the soul, biblical bearer of
the emotions, moan the distance between the human and the divine. In Psalm
88, one human response to the hidden God is a feeling of utter abandonment:
"Thy fierce wrath goeth over me; thy terrors have cut me off" (88:16). The
monk who plays the wandering Jew in the Mar Saba masque also laments his
abandonment: "My fate! / Cut off I am, made separate; / For man's embrace I
strive no more" (3.19.60–62). The wandering Jew is not only an archetype of
alienation, indicating that he is cut off from other people, but his words also
express a theological idiom: "Hence solitude / Elect I; in waste places brood /
More lonely than an only god" (3.19.75–77).[15] To be "cut off" in *Clarel*
means to be cut off from the human and from the divine, and even to feel as
lonely as the hidden God Himself.[16] To be "cut off" from God resembles the

condition of death. The particular anguish of a premature death also evokes a gesture of hiddenness from Clarel. When Clarel, by Ruth's grave, attempts to kiss her dead hand, his response is to hide his face—"But 'tis not she! and hid his face" (4.30.133)—a symbolic gesture that indicates "how estranged in face!" Ruth is (4.32.98), how cut off human beings are in death and in life when far from God.

What is most striking about the human response to the hidden God or the fled Christ in *Clarel* is that characters, such as Rolfe, address God or Christ at all. Why even cry to a hidden God? The lament of "cut off" testifies to the human need for God. At least Jesus and Clarel can use the pronoun "my"— "my God"—that suggests acknowledgment of and hope for God. For divine self-concealment in *Clarel* is not a completely negative idea. The human response to hiddenness indicates a remembrance of a first and a yearning for a second revelation of God's mysteriousness—a revelation that would hope-fully reveal the inscrutable mystery of human existence also. To declare the hiddenness of God, with His accompanying silence, is paradoxically a confes-sion of hope in the face of hiddenness. Melvillean hiddenness is not the notion of divine absence or the Nietzschean perception that God is dead. By crying to God, the human acknowledges the divine; by lamenting God's hiddenness, the human remembers divine presence. God's hiddenness can be interpreted as indifference, but it can also be seen as too mysterious to be clearly articulated by human words. God and creation may have something to say, but only few can hear it.

THE MANY FACES OF GOD

The hiddenness and silence of God (and Christ) cause the concept of God to become ambiguous. Just as one cannot think of any being without the possi-bility of its not being, one cannot contemplate the hidden God without the possibility of its presence or, at least, its return. Hiddenness implies presence. God in *Clarel* is, therefore, a pair of ideas. Whenever one experiences God, one experiences a multifaceted being, the many faces of God. God is mercy and judgment, beauty and terror, patience and wrath. During Celio's medita-tion on the historical Jesus and the Passion of Christ at the Ecce Homo arch, he views Christ as a many-faced God:

> Yea, thou through ages to accrue,
> Shalt the Medusa shield replace:
> In *beauty* and in *terror* too
> Shalt paralyze the nobler race—
> Smite or suspend, perplex, deter—
> Tortured, shalt prove a torturer.

> Whatever ribald Future be,
> Thee shall these heed, amaze their hearts with thee—
> Thy *white*, thy *red*, thy *fairness* and thy *tragedy*.
> (1.13.94–102, emphasis mine)

Here Christ is "beauty" and "terror," "white" and "red," "fairness" and "trag-edy." As the human is repelled and attracted by the hidden God or hidden Christ, we recognize the many faces of God, always experienced in pairs. Christ tortured mankind with an ideal dream, according to Celio, and was tortured in turn by mankind's unwillingness to sense His divinity. God and Christ are, as Gerard Manley Hopkins wrote in "The Wreck of the Deutsch-land," "lightning and love." Melville implies that the historical process of 1,800 years ("through ages to accrue") has not sufficed to realize the greater meanings of Christianity, and until human beings can understand a many-faced Christ and God ("The shark thou mad'st, yet claim'st the dove," 1.13.71 and Matthew 10:16), the ideals of Christian faith and consciousness may stay unrealized. Celio laments to Christ about the delayed Parousia and insists that not until Christ comes again will mankind's doubts about His identity and promise be answered:

> How long wilt make us still to doubt?
> How long?—'Tis eighteen cycles now—
> Enigma and evasion grow;
> And shall we never find thee out?
> (1.13.74–77)

How difficult it is, though, to understand, much less love, a many-faced God: what the narrator calls the "complex passion" (1.5.217).

The idea and image of a many-faced God or, in *Clarel*, a Hebraicized Christ has its roots in the Hebrew Bible. In the Book of Names, Exodus, the thirteen attributes of God's name are explicitly revealed: " . . . The Lord, The Lord God, merciful and gracious, longsuffering, and abundant in goodness and truth, Keeping mercy for thousands, forgiving iniquity and transgression and sin, and that will by no means clear the guilty; visiting the iniquity of the fathers upon the children, and upon the children's children, unto the third and to the fourth generation" (34:6–7). Here the ultimate mystery of God's nature includes both positive and negative faces, mercy and judgment. The God of Exodus is a jealous, possessive God, "For thou shalt worship no other god: for the Lord, whose name is Jealous, is a jealous God" (Exodus 34:14), yet a God of mercy who freed the Israelites from slavery in Egypt. The dual faces of God is also a constant theme throughout Deuteronomy where judg-ment is often juxtaposed to mercy: "For the Lord thy God is a consuming fire, even a jealous God" (4·24) versus "For the Lord thy God is a merciful God; he will not forsake thee, neither destroy thee, nor forget the covenant of thy fathers which he sware unto them" (4:31). In Hebrew, two different divine names, *El* and *Yahweh*, also suggest this duality. *El* is the name of God used by the patriarchs and suggests a distant and majestically austere God. *Yahweh*, the name of God given to Moses and all Israel in Egypt, suggests the closer presence of a God of mercy.

As the pilgrims look down upon the desolate wilderness of Siddim in part 3 and compare it with their green fields and orchards at home, nature's "variance" compels them to contemplate the many faces of nature and God and, ultimately, gnostic dualism and the problem of the two Testaments.

> At variance in their revery move
> The spleen of nature and her love:
> At variance, yet entangled too—
> Like wrestlers. Here in apt review
> They call to mind Abel and Cain—
> Ormuzd involved with Ahriman
> In deadly lock. Were those gods gone?
> Or under other names live on?
> The theme they started. 'Twas averred
> That, in old Gnostic pages blurred,
> Jehovah was construed to be
> Author of evil, yea, its god;
> And Christ divine his contrary:
> A god was held against a god,
> But Christ revered alone. Herefrom,
> If inference availeth aught
> (For still the topic pressed they home)
> The two-fold Testaments become
> Transmitters of Chaldaic thought
> By implication. If no more
> Those Gnostic heretics prevail
> Which shook the East from shore to shore,
> Their strife forgotten now and pale;
> Yet, with the sects, that old revolt
> Now reappears, if in assault
> Less frank: none say Jehovah's evil,
> None gainsay that he bears the rod;
> Scarce that; but there's dismission civil,
> And Jesus is the indulgent God.
> This change, this dusking change that slips

(Like the penumbra o'er the sun),
Over the faith transmitted down;
Foreshadows it complete eclipse?

(3.5.31–63)

Melville's poetic description of gnostic thought and its emphasis on the battle of the Bibles is an implied plea to end dualistic thinking. There is no sense in talking about a vengeful God of the Hebrew Bible over against a loving God of the Christian Bible. Jesus shows anger and vengeance in the New Testament (overturning the table of the money changers or, in Matthew 21:41, "He will miserably destroy those wicked men"), and God shows mercy in the Hebrew Bible (saving Jonah and Nineveh and God's patience with the stiff-necked Israelites). Furthermore, the pilgrims implicitly suggest a theological continuity and cohesiveness within both Testaments despite the supposed differences of a vengeful angry God versus a loving, compassionate Christ. In the passage just quoted, the narrator suggests a continuity based on contrasts: anger *and* love, works *and* faith, promise *and* fulfillment, covenant reciprocity *and* unilateral grace. Nature, the faces of God, and the two Testaments are different yet theologically united: "At variance, yet entangled too / Like wrestlers" (3.5.33–34). In the Bible, the multiplicity of the faces of God makes for an ambiguous God: "I am the Lord, and there is none else. I form the light, and create darkness: I make peace, and create evil: I the Lord do all these things" (Isaiah 45:6–7). Isaiah and Melville wish to stop all the foolish chatter about good versus evil (dualistic theology). They understand that under the notion of a single unitary God or Christ there is good and evil, presence and hiddenness, closeness and distance, cruelty and kindness. If dualism prevails, the narrator predicts the eclipse of faith (3.5.63).[17]

THE AMBIGUITY OF NATURE

One God must not be "held against" another God (3.5.44), just as nature's face of "spleen" is not really at variance with nature's other face of "love," for they too are "entangled," intertwined "like wrestlers" (3.5.31–34).[18] Nonhuman nature can be red in tooth in claw, often cruel and grotesque, from a human point of view. But nature is also filled with mercies and beauty and has often been viewed as a medium of God's immanence (such as the sacred trees associated with the patriarchs or the rustling, oracle-giving balsams that warned David). Any emphasis on one face of God or nature more than another would be false ("Christ revered alone" [3.5.45]). The concept of God in *Clarel* becomes a radical oneness uniting Jehovah's and Christ's traits. Moreover, whenever we experience God (or His manifestations), the ethical dualities of evil and good are combined into one radical unity, one braided cord: "Evil and good they braided play / Into one cord" (4.4.27–28). Just as there are Eden and Gethsemane, Christmas and Good Friday, God, nature, and man have good and evil within them.[19]

The difficulty of comprehending a many-faced and hidden God is compounded by the ambiguity of God's manifestations in nature. The idea that God's essence is hidden, inscrutable, and unknowable but his existence unquestioned is not an impossible notion for someone familiar with Jewish and Christian traditions. The claim, however, that all of creation is as unknowable as God's identity is much more alarming for a Christian or a Jew. *Clarel* indicates over and over again how utterly precarious is our grasp of any absolute meaning in God's creation—including God, nature, and humanity. After the burial of Nehemiah, part 2 of *Clarel* ends with a rush and a roar of a nearby avalanche. Then comes silence and the noiseless, mysterious appearance of the "fog-bow" (2.39.154). As soon as it appears, however, "It showed half spent— / Hovered and trembled, paled away, and—went" (2.39.160– 61). The universe of *Clarel* is unpredictable. An avalanche is followed by a fog-bow, just as in the Hebrew Bible the deluge that rendered life almost extinct is followed by a rainbow—a promise that the universe could be trusted. But the fog-bow in *Clarel* is too ephemeral to be interpreted as a renewed divine covenant and promise. Instead, we witness the gliding of God's manifestations from one form to another. Natural events in the Clarelian universe are not neutral in meaning, but they by no means make their meaning directly discernible to us. Nature confuses people, for it glides to and fro between natural evil and danger (avalanche) and symbolic good and promise (fog-bow). Just as one must wrestle with the dual faces of the hidden God and unite them, one must also encompass the gliding, ambiguous manifestations of God in nature. Creation may not be a second language to read and thereby know God; creation may be a cipher to puzzle over and thereby hide God: "What works there from behind the veil?" (2.39.149). We cannot lift the veil that separates the hidden God from His creation.

A veil of human limitations lies over all knowledge of nature in *Clarel*. By the river Jordan, the Dominican monk insists upon the human need for God, but that we cannot know God through the cosmic indifference of nature. Religious systems based on naturalism cannot give mankind the notion of a loving personal God and cannot offer hope or incentives to right conduct.

> Science but deals
> With Nature; Nature is not God;
> Never she answers our appeals,
> Or, if she do, but mocks the clod.
> Call to the echo—it returns
> The word you send; how thrive the ferns

About the ruined house of prayer
In woods; one shadow falleth yet
From Christian spire—Turk minaret:
Consider the indifference there.
'Tis so throughout. Shall Science then
Which solely dealeth with this thing
Named Nature, shall she ever bring
One solitary hope to men?
'Tis Abba Father that we seek,
Not the Artificer.

(2.25.144–59)

When claiming that nature is good, one makes an assertion of faith in the meaning of creation. One does not mean that nature, in the form of avalanches, sharks, and scorpions (all appear literally or figuratively in the poem), is good. For the actuality of nature is "indifference," like the "dead indifference of walls" of the iceberg in Melville's poem "The Berg": "Nature is not God; / Never she answers our appeals." If one claims to comprehend nature, nature simply "Fools the wise, makes wise the fools— / Every ruling overrules?" (4.26.325–26). If anything, Nature hides God, and the only way to approach God is to ignore God as "artificer" (2.25.159) and to seek Him as a personal God—God the "Father" (2.25.158).

Celio conflates the hiddenness of Christ, the indifference of nature, and his own skepticism toward the resurrection when he views the sun rise over Mount Olivet:

He breaks. Behold, thou orb supreme, [sun]
'Tis Olivet which thou ascendest—
The hill and legendary chapel;
Yet how indifferent thy beam!
Awe nor reverence pretendest:

. . . .

Knowest thou the Christ? believest in the dream?

(1.15.6–10, 13)

In a common enough pun, Celio asks the rising sun if it knows of the Son of God.

The Dominican monk also claims, in the Abba-Father passage, that science is as futile in the pursuit of knowledge of God as nature is, for science deals only with second causes—nature. In one of the dialogs in the Judean wilderness on the unknowability of God and the universe, Rolfe tries to moderate Derwent's admiration for science's eagles such as Newton:

O'ermuch
'Twould seem for man, a clod, to clutch
God's secret so, and on a slate
Cipher all out, and formulate
The universe.

(2.21.27–31)

Rolfe does not necessarily belittle what can be and has become known through science. He merely encourages a reticence toward any scientific claim of total illumination of the universe.

THE LIMITS OF WISDOM

The finest example of Melville's reiterated theme in *Clarel* of the limits imposed on the human search for complete knowledge and truth is Rolfe's image of the human mind bound inside a citadel:

Now first they tell
The human mind is free to range.
Enlargement—ay; but where's the change?
We're yet within the citadel—
May rove in bounds, and study out
The insuperable towers about.

(2.21.37–42)

Science and reason have little room for maneuvering in a universe where it is "the glory of God to conceal a thing" (Proverbs 25:2). Human science is surrounded by the "insuperable towers" of the inexplicable. In *Clarel*, one is not permitted to speak of what is known without also speaking of what cannot be known, for what is known is insignificant when compared with what is hidden.

Rolfe's intellectual humility in approaching the mysteries of the universe appeals to Clarel. After hearing Agath the timoneer's story comparing the Encantadas to Palestine, Clarel feels that human reason and language also cannot "solve the world!":

What may man know?
(Here pondered Clarel) let him rule—
Pull down, build up, creed, system, school,
And reason's endless battle wage,
Make and remake his verbiage—
But solve the world! Scarce that he'll do:

Too wild it is, too wonderful.
Since *this* world, then, can baffle so—
Our natural harbor—it were strange
If *that* alleged, which is afar,
Should not confound us when we range
In revery where its problems are.

(4.3.108–19)

Here, Melville reveals through Clarel the fundamental awareness of the limitations of human language and reason. Words are futile to get at the solution of this world or the next. As long as Clarel relies on the normal processes of reasoning, observation, and language, he will never find the meaning of this life or the possibility of a life to come. Clarel, like Koheleth (Ecclesiastes), is agitated by thoughts of eternity. Clarel's confusion is that human beings are aware of their ignorance of this world and of human mortality, yet, at the same time, aware of another "alleged" world that confounds the human mind. The semantic field of the key word "world" may include the sense of time, enigma, and hiddenness that the word "world" has in Ecclesiastes: "also he hath set the world in their heart, so that no man can find out the work that God maketh from the beginning to the end" (3:11). The human inability to know the future or to see a reasonable pattern of meaning in the world is related to the mysterious unknowability of the hidden God. The unknowability of the world is also expressed in Ecclesiastes 8:16–17:

> When I applied mine heart to know wisdom, and to see the business that is done upon the earth: (for also there is that neither day nor night seeth sleep with his eyes:) Then I beheld all the work of God, that a man cannot find out the work that is done under the sun: because though a man labour to seek it out, yet he shall not find it; yea farther; though a wise man think to know it, yet shall he not be able to find it.

Not only can human beings not discover the meaning of God's work done under the sun, but also Clarel and Ecclesiastes may be ironically reversing their own skepticism toward language by speaking so many words. I see a biblical kinship between Clarel's rejection of "verbiage" and Koheleth's famous cry: "of making many books there is no end; and much study is a weariness of the flesh" (Ecclesiastes 12:12). Elsewhere, Clarel even characterizes language as a "waste of words, that waste of all" (3.5.182).

In *Clarel*, human beings re-experience the truth that not everything is found in or by us; everything is not measured by human standards of rational certainty. History is yet another area where one asks, "What may man know?"

(4.3.109). The tenacious existence of the Jewish people, for example, troubles Clarel:

> *This* seems a deeper mystery;
> How Judah, Benjamin, live on—
> Unmixed into time's swamping sea
> So far can urge their Amazon.
> (1.2.47–50)

If Jewish history is a mystery, Christian history is a veritable haze. The small lamps within the Church of the Holy Sepulcher "make a haze of mystery: / The blur is spread of thousand years, / And Calvary's seen as through one's tears" (1.3.52–54). Melville shows us that within the Church of the Holy Sepulcher in Jerusalem and in many other historically sanctioned holy places in Palestine there is no pure sensation or objective historical perspective unencumbered by meanings inherited from history, including faith or doubt. The mysteriousness of Christian history is a haze of hiddenness that gives no sure perception other than, for the narrator, the sorrow of tears. When we try to understand the life of Jesus—the historical Jesus—and the early history of the Church of Jerusalem, we find an unbridgeable gulf between now and then:

> Nearing thee
> All footing fails us; history
> Shows there a gulf where bridge is none!
> In lapse of unrecorded time,
> Just after the apostles' prime
> (1.13.80–84)

Because history is, simply put, mystery, we cannot go back in time and know the real history of the appearance of the man called Jesus, for our knowledge of him comes from authors who lived after Jesus and knew him as divine through "the heart / Of heavenly love" (1.13.87–88).

Although absolute knowledge via science or history is beyond human capability, this limitation does little to repress the desire for knowledge. The quest for what Melville calls "wisdom" is so pressing that, even at the limits imposed on it, the lack of wisdom becomes a witness to the incomprehensibility of God and His universe. Rolfe seeks wisdom in Palestine: "Some lurking thing he hoped to gain— / Slip quite beyond the parrot-lore / Conventional, and—what attain?" (1.31.36–38). One answer to the narrator's rhetorical question is implied in Clarel's question: "And where is wisdom's recompense?" (4.2.178). All we know from *Clarel* is that to hunt for wisdom, we must dig down deep—"But deeper—deep as nature's mine"—into a person (2.4.136). Wisdom may not be found though. In the interpolated canto "Of Rama," the wisdom of the ideal god-men can be found if one digs: " 'Tis an open mine: / Dig; find ye gold, why, make it thine" (1.32.51–52). The narrator implies, however, that such wise men may exist only in the verse. The futility of digging for wisdom is a theme common to Hebrew Wisdom literature: "But where shall wisdom be found? and where is the place of understanding?" (Job 28:12). Again, in Job and *Clarel*, the world is a mystery, especially the nature of God and His creation. Human beings dig in the earth for precious stones, but no such mining can take us to the greatest treasure of all—divine wisdom.[20] The human ingenuity that enables us to find gold in the earth is unable to find wisdom. Ultimate knowledge of the human or the divine is not possible. As Melville writes, "But if in vain / One tries to comprehend a man, / How think to sound God's deeper heart!" (2.32.109–11). Ecclesiastes 7 also sounds this same theme of the inability to dig for wisdom:

> All this have I proved by wisdom: I said, I will be wise; but it was far from me. That which is far off, and exceeding deep, who can find it out? I applied mine heart to know, and to search, and to seek out wisdom, and the reason of things, and to know the wickedness of folly, even of foolishness and madness. (7:23–25)

Job and Ecclesiastes admit that the reason for the failure of human wisdom-searching is that absolute wisdom is of God. Human beings have no absolute knowledge of life's events, of God, or of themselves. As Mortmain says to the sinners of Sodom, "all's known / To Him" [God] (2.36.64–65).

Even if a person has gained wisdom, several pilgrims, like Ecclesiastes, can see no true advantage for the wise over the foolish or even over the insane. Rolfe thinks that Ungar is "wise" (4.23.32), and Derwent says that Mortmain has some "wisdom" (3.27.85), but Mortmain curses his own wisdom: "Wiser am I?—Curse on this store / Of knowledge!" (3.28.5–6). Rolfe implies that Mortmain may have taken the wild plunge into deserts and madness:

> See how the Swede
> Like any rustic *crazy* Tom,
> Bursting through every code and ward
> Of civilization, masque and fraud,
> Takes the *wild plunge*. . . .
> (2.16.110–14, emphasis mine)

The man from Lesbos also points out how close wisdom is to madness: "Wisdom? our Cyril is deemed wise. / In the East here, one who's lost his wits / For saint or sage they canonize" (3.27.86–88). Although folly is not a viable option for the searcher in *Clarel*, wisdom is at best ambiguous, at worst unattainable. Like Pip's insanity in *Moby-Dick*, which was "heaven's sense," wisdom may be only divine madness.

Melville's point is that even if a phenomenon can be explained by science, the mysteriousness prevails: "Science explains it [fountain of Siloam]. Bides no less / The true, innate mysteriousness" (1.28.108–9). For Melville and Ecclesiastes, true "wisdom is vain" (Melville's Civil War poem "The Conflict of Convictions"). In the words of Ecclesiastes: "And I gave my heart to know wisdom, and to know madness and folly: I perceived that this also is vexation of spirit. For in much wisdom is much grief: and he that increaseth knowledge increaseth sorrow" (1:17–18). The limits of knowledge and wisdom placed upon mankind by the nature of the hidden God and his ambiguous manifestations serve a critical function. They keep awake in us the awareness that the search for absolute knowledge—whether of history, nature, man, or God—is ultimately directed toward a God and universe in which mysteriousness predominates. The sphere in which mankind can make definitive, verifiable statements about God and His creation is an extremely limited one.

The search for the hidden God, along with the inability to search and find true wisdom, is the main gesture not only of *Clarel* but also of the Hebrew Bible. The seeking and finding (or not finding) of God is a major theme of the Bible. The movement of an everlasting, ever-defeated longing, yearning, and search for God and wisdom is the deep heart of Israel's story. In fact, one could argue that of all the metaphors in the Bible chosen by the biblical poets to describe the relationship between God and Israel—king and subject, shepherd and sheep, father and child—it is the metaphor of the lover and the beloved that is the very essence of the human-divine relationship:

> But if from thence thou shalt seek the Lord thy God, thou shalt find him, if thou seek him with all thy heart and with all thy soul (Deuteronomy 4:29). And thou shalt love the Lord thy God with all thine heart, and with all thy soul, and with all thy might (Deuteronomy 6:5). And she [Israel, allegorically] shall follow after her lovers, but she shall not overtake them; and she shall seek them, but shall not find them: then shall she say, I will go and return to my first husband [God]; for then was it better with me than now (Hosea 2:7). I will seek him whom my soul loveth: I sought him, but I found him not (Song of Songs 3:2); I [Israel] opened to my beloved; but my beloved [God] had withdrawn

himself, and was gone: my soul failed when he spake: I sought him, but I could not find him; I called him, but he gave me no answer (Song of Songs 5:6).

The Melvillean need to know God's presence and purpose and the desire to realize the ultimate mystery of the hidden God—no answer is given and the beloved is often not found—have their roots in the biblical voices of searching in Job, Ecclesiastes, Hosea, Deuteronomy, and the Song of Songs.

THE ESTRANGEMENT OF THE INNER SELF

The human limitation on knowledge, history, and wisdom can prompt one to take intellectual and theological offense at unexplained, ambiguous mysteries and to seek estrangement from God and creation. The same pattern of estrangement exists in one's relationship with another person: we sense the interior of another's consciousness; we want to communicate and hope to comprehend, yet often can do neither, and we are often aloof and estranged from one another. The estrangement and aloofness of the characters in *Clarel* do not suggest a biographical comment on Melville or a sociological comment on American society so much as a psychological and spiritual imperative: the hiddenness and silence of humanity.[21]

Characters in *Clarel* have a hidden, silent, inner self. Like Hawthorne's Reverend Hooper, the minister with the black veil, they are apart from others, hidden, expressing a guarded reserve in character and style. When traveling through "Latin lands" on his way to Palestine, Clarel experiences "clandestine," vexatious "inklings" that prompt him to examine his own hiddenness (1.1.73, 74, 72).

> These under-formings in the mind.
> Banked corals which ascend from far,
> But little heed men that they wind
> *Unseen, unheard*—till lo, the reef—
> The reef and breaker, wreck and grief.
> (1.1.75–79, emphasis mine)

The crux of Clarel's insight is not only that the inner mind has a subconscious aspect but also that the essence of the mind is hidden and silent. The reefs not only suggest danger—to ships or to ontological soul-searchers—but also a ring of protection for the unknowable mind. Vine's reclusive nature is also an unknowable hiddenness:

> Like to the nunnery's denizen
> His virgin soul communed with men
> But thro' the wicket. Was it clear
> This coyness bordered not on fear—
> Fear or an apprehensive sense?
> Not wholly seemed it diffidence
> Recluse. Nor less did strangely wind
> Ambiguous *elfishness* behind
> All that: an Ariel *unknown*.
>   (1.29.43–51, emphasis mine)

The narrator cannot quite understand why Vine's soul communes with others as if through a convent's gate. Is it fear or diffidence? When Vine is first seen by Nehemiah and Clarel at the Sepulcher of Kings, the narrator portrays Vine as one who is "secluded," "who would keep separate," but is "uncovered" when seen by others (1.28.44, 51, 37). The narrator attests to the ambiguity and unknowability of Vine's selfhood, what he calls "Ambiguous elfishness behind / All that: an Ariel unknown" (1.29.50–51). Vine is compared to an elf and to Ariel in Shakespeare's *The Tempest*. Just as Ariel could appear to some and remain hidden to others, an elf also connotes a sense of hiddenness—a little green man blending into the forest cover. Melville has a curious affection for the simile of elves in *Clarel*, for he often compares a character's selfhood to a "virgin elf" or "innocent if lawless elf" (2.24.2; 1.32.17). A character's inner self seems to be hidden in convents, hermitages, or forests like a nun, recluse, or elf: "Left in his hermitage of mind" (1.43.43). The Franciscan monk Salvaterra, who guides the pilgrims through the Church of the Nativity in Bethlehem, is also described as possessing an inner nature not readily uncovered by others: "Yet under quietude they mark / The slumbering of a vivid spark— / Excitable, if brought to test" (4.13.30–32). Even the stoic, taciturn Djalea has a hidden underside: "Yes, underneath a look sedate, / What throbs are known!" (4.29.28–29). In his futile attempt to penetrate Vine's inaccessibility, Clarel compares Vine to Guido's portrait of Beatrice Cenci and to a white-hot anchor hidden under the ashes of a forge:

> 'Twas Vine. He wore that nameless look
> About the mouth—so hard to brook—
> Which in the Cenci portrait shows,
> Lost in each copy, oil or print;
> Lost, or else slurred, as 'twere a hint
> Which if received, few might sustain:
>   . . . .

Reserves laid bare? and can it be?
The dock-yard forge's silent mound,
Played over by small nimble flame—
Raked open, lo, the anchor's found
In white-heat's alb.

(3.7.16–21, 28–32)

Guido's motive in creating Cenci's "nameless look" (like Vine's) may have
been purposely to hide or to obscure ("slurred") her inner nature and leave
only "a hint," which if caught by an observer is difficult "to sustain." Like
Clarel's under-formings in the mind, it may be safer not to rake open the
concealed inner self—the hot anchor—not to lay bare a person's "reserves."
Clarel slowly learns of the inaccessibility of human hiddenness. As Clarel says
of Rolfe by the Jordan river, "I cannot penetrate him" (2.27.10). No one can
truly know another in *Clarel*. Even Rolfe's maritime story in the canto "A
Sketch," based on Captain George Pollard's shipwreck and survival and implying that Nehemiah is a reformed, mellowed Ahab who accepts God's will,
does not explain Nehemiah: "It [the story] needed something more / Or else,
to penetrate the core" (3.2.24–25).[22]

Clarel is filled with isolated, reclusive characters not only because of the
topic and setting of part of the poem—celibate monks at Mar Saba and
Bethlehem—but also because secular, worldly people respond to life as
monks do. The canto in part 4 entitled "The Carpenter" is a miniature paradigm of human hiddenness. After an argument with a friend, the Carpenter
turns his home into a monastery, "grew familiar with the mouse," and never
comes out again until "feet foremost he was borne away" (3.2.53, 58). The
tale of the Carpenter is a story of physical withdrawal and hiddenness, in
which he rejects humankind and centers his life on God. But what must be
remembered is that Clarel retells this tale of hiddenness, just as Rolfe tells the
Pollard story in an attempt to understand the hidden nature of Nehemiah—
both sketches are examples of *Clarel* as a dramatic and dialogical agon. The
narrator gives a sea picture to help us understand Rolfe's response to Clarel's
redaction of the tale of the Carpenter: "As when upon a misty shore / The
watchful seaman marks a light / Blurred by the fog, uncertain quite" (3.2.59–
61). People are figuratively blurred by fog from one another, and as Clarel
says of Vine, the human heart is "a fountain sealed" (2.17.22).

Implied in human hiddenness is a sense of estrangement and loneliness,
what Melville called in his Mediterranean *Journal* (1856–57) the "genuine
Jonah feeling."[23] Celio's reserve estranges: "Though this still guarded a reserve / Which, not offending, part estranged" (1.12.16–17). Each person is
as solitary as a single "weed / Detached from vast Sargasso's mead" (2.17.32–

33) and can be "More lonely than an only God" (3.19.77). No matter how intimately one may come in contact with another, one still remains alone in one's innermost being because every personality has its unique hiddenness—loneliness is a part of personality. The Clarelian theme of disappointed love and failed communion indicates that people cannot overcome their loneliness through contact with others.[24] Both Celio and Mortmain have, at one time, been disappointed or even cheated by a woman (Celio's Beatrice, 1.12.80–85, and Mortmain's "unrenderable thing," 2.4.132–44). For Clarel, Ruth's death frustrates any attempt to "take thy wife; / Venture, and prove the soul of life, / And let fate drive" (4.29.104–6). Love as secular redemption in *Clarel* cannot be a substitute for love of God—both complex passions so difficult to attain in *Clarel*.[25]

Such disappointed love accentuates the need in *Clarel* for "the spiritual sympathy" that "transcends the social" (1.19.3–4). Clarel is certainly guilty of asking from others more than they can or even know how to give, but his "longing for solacement of mate" (1.2.12) is more of a spiritual need than any latent homosexuality. Critics who persist in seeing Clarel's attempt at making a human connection as a sign of the failure of heterosexual love and the hope for homosexual love ignore the poem's theme of spiritual sympathy.[26] He certainly is too demanding emotionally; however, to label him as homosexual, we must call every caring male character in the poem homosexual. Even Derwent experiences a need for spiritual and emotional communion:

> Yet, intervening even there,
> A touch he knew of gliding care:
> We loiterers whom life can please
> (Thought he) could we but find our mates
> Ever! but no; before the gates
> Of joy, lie some who carp and tease:
> Collisions of men's destinies!—
>
> (3.27.173–79)

Derwent's need to be "fraternal in love's overture" even causes him to be socially imperious—forcibly taking Rolfe's arm "as he would so transmit a charm" (4.23.77, 73). The deprivation that Derwent and Clarel experience is that of a person cut off from God. Both Rolfe and the monk who plays the wandering Jew lament their condition of being cut off (2.21.92; 3.19.61). Even when Clarel foresees the communion between men of "exceptional natures" (Rolfe and Vine), the narrator undercuts any hope for a permanent human relationship:

What now may hap? what outcome new
Elicited by contact true—
Frank, cordial contact of the twain?
Crude wonderment, and proved but vain.
If average mortals social be,
And yet but seldom truly meet,
Closing like halves of apple sweet—
How with the rarer in degree?
                              (1.31.50–57)

The characters in *Clarel* are like the Psalmist's simile comparing his loneliness, cut off from a hidden God, to a lone sparrow: "I watch, and am as a sparrow alone upon the house top" (Psalms 102:7).[27] Psalms 102:2 reads, "Hide not thy face from me in the day when I am in trouble, incline thine ear unto me: in the day when I call answer me speedily."

            But this single one [a sparrow]
Plaining upon a terrace nigh,
Was like the Psalmist's making moan
For loss of mate—forsaken quite,
Which on the house-top doth alight
And watches, and her lonely cry
No answer gets.—In sunny hight
Like dotting bees against the sky
What twitterers o'er the temple fly!
                              (1.38.19–25)

The narrator suggests that Clarel, like the Psalmist and the sparrow, is cut off from humanity and divinity. Here, Melville again selectively reinterprets biblical passages by suggesting that "no answer" is given as the bird-man flies over the Temple Mount. But Psalm 102, in fact, ends on praise and the reassurance of God's protective presence and power. The opening lament of Psalm 102 and *Clarel* make the search for God's face and voice parallel to the search for human companionship.

Even during what Bryan C. Short calls one of the poem's "epiphanic moments," when Rolfe, Derwent, and Vine sing the "Ave Maris Stella" together on the banks of the Jordan, any sense of communion is undercut by the fact that Nehemiah does not join in the singing (2.24.48–67).[28] When Clarel's desire for "communion true" (2.27.68) becomes so overwhelming that he hungers for Vine to be his spiritual "brother" (2.27.107), Vine's rebuke is the final summation of how solitary characters are in the poem.

Lives none can help ye; that believe.
Art thou the first soul tried by doubt?
Shalt prove the last? Go, live it out.
But for thy fonder dream of love
In man toward man—the soul's caress—
The negatives of flesh should prove
Analogies of non-cordialness
In spirit. . . .

(2.27.121–28)

The inability of males to become one flesh and the limits of bodily human existence serve as an analogy for the same inability of the characters to mingle spiritual sympathies together. As the narrator says in the canto "Passion Week," "the world is rent / With partings" (4.32.15–16).

In the psychological sphere, *Clarel* poses the question of not only how lonely and hidden human beings are from each other but also how the inner hidden life is deliberately not reflected in the outer life for the purpose of protective concealment. For example, when Vine withdraws into his silence and hiddenness—"Vine into his dumb castle went" (1.31.59)—his neutrality and withdrawal may be part of a premeditated, planned personality: "And neutral not without design" (1.31.65). Nehemiah's reserve is a deliberate attempt to conceal his past:

In this hid matter of his past
The saint evinced a guardful wit;
His waning energies seemed massed
Here, and but here, to keep the door.
At present his reserve of brow
Reproach in such sort did avow,
That Clarel never pressed him more.

(1.38.37–43)

The protective aloofness of a Vine that rebukes Clarel's advances is even present when Nehemiah sleeps or dreams. A person's countenance in *Clarel* is usually a mask, not a face, and is reminiscent of the undecipherability of the human face in the chapter "The Prairie" in *Moby-Dick*:

The face
Though tranced, struck not like trance of death
All rigid; not a masque like that,
Iced o'er, which none may penetrate,

Conjecturing of aught below.
Death freezes, but sleep thaws. And so
The inmate lay, some lines revealed—
Effaced, when life from sleep comes back.
And what their import? Be it sealed.
(1.22.101–9)[29]

Men and women are totally estranged in death ("estranged in face!" 4.32.98), "cut off" in life, and partially revealed, but "sealed," in sleep. Despite John Donne's famous assertion that no man is an island, Melville insists on the isolated hiddenness and silence of human beings. The human face is hidden to protect the virgin elfishness of the inner self. Only the fool seeks to reveal more than he should.

THE PARADOX OF RECIPROCAL DIVINITY

Human hiddenness, with its implied loneliness, estrangement, and self-protection, is more than a comment on the human condition in *Clarel*. The hidden human self has an ontological status—a divinity rooted in human nature. Human beings partake of the hiddenness of God, for God "created man in his own image, in the image of God created he him" (Genesis 1:27). *Deus absconditus* creates *homo absconditus* because the human bears the divine image. The key to Melville's theological reflection in *Clarel* is the reciprocal relationship between two hidden, divine subjects: human beings and God. This relationship is revealed in a very quiet sentence in part 4, canto 21, entitled "Ungar and Rolfe." In fact, cantos 20 and 21 might be called the American Cantos, for they contain a powerful dialog on and critique of America. In canto 21, Ungar has discerned on the walls of American civilization the same words of warning that appeared in the time of Daniel on the walls of Belshazzar's palace: "God hath numbered [the days of] thy kingdom and finished it" (Daniel 5:26). In a canto that has been called by C. Vann Woodward "the blackest commentary on the future of his country ever written by an American in the nineteenth century," Ungar claims that there is no hope for positive change in the distorted democracy and harsh industrialism of the New World with its penchant for leveling mediocrity and its devastating Civil War.[30] Ungar quietly says, "God is—man. / The human nature, the divine" (4.21.63–64). Ungar goes on to elaborate this thought more clearly: "For man, like God, abides the same" (4.21.71). Rolfe agrees—"Yes, God is God, and men are men" (4.21.76). Yet the curious syntactical sense of Ungar's quiet sentence ("God is—man. / The human nature, the divine") implies, because of the linking verb "is," that man is the complement of God and that "the divine" is the complement of "human nature." Every person is made in God's likeness as a matter of biblical cosmogonic legend. Here Ungar's extraordinary sentence points to the larger paradox of hiddenness: God is within us—immanence—and God is beyond us—transcendence. When one speaks of God creating the human in His image or of human beings as children of God, one speaks of closeness (immanence) yet, at the same time, of vast distance (transcendence).

Ungar's belief in reciprocal divinity also explains the practice of human self-concealment in the poem. A character's self-concealment is not only a psychological but also a theological need. Minds are protected by concealing reefs, walls, veils, masks, and burning ashes in the poem. The human mind, like God, hides its innermost nature and purpose, thereby putting up a wall between itself and others. Danger exists in trying to dig through the walls of one's innermost being. During Mortmain's mad dream when, like the fool in Ecclesiastes 4:5, he chews his own flesh, Rolfe warns of the danger in digging too deep to try to know the inner self:

> God help thee, and may such ice make
> Except against some solid? nay—
> But thou who mark'st, get thee away,
> Nor in such coals of Tartarus rake.
>   (3.15.28–31)

It is dangerous to dig beneath the coals of a Mortmain or lift the "veil / Of Sais" of a Djalea (3.15.90–91). Since the human bears the divine image, the inner human self is symbolic of the hidden nature of God. Since God is a many-faced Being in *Clarel*, wherever one encounters divinity, divine terror is nearby. Christ will bring peace and the sword and is responsible for the dove and the shark. The danger is that one can die in the pursuit of the ungraspable knowledge of divine immanence in man. "Few might sustain" the hidden "reserves laid bare," for example, in the portrait of Beatrice Cenci or in Vine's hidden "white-heat's alb" (3.7.21, 28, 32), and many may wreck themselves upon the "reef," upon the "under-formings in the mind" of men like Clarel (1.1.78, 75). God warns Moses in Exodus 33:20 of the danger in trying to reveal divine self-concealment: "Thou canst not see my face: for there shall no man see me, and live." Just as the extrinsic presence of God contains danger, so does the intrinsic presence of God in man contain a threat to all metaphysical searchers. To lift the veil that covers the face of man or God is extremely dangerous and implies the desire to become a God. Unlike Ahab's aggressive attempt to burst through walls and masks to get at the hidden essence of whale, *Clarel* insists upon caution and restraint when confronting the divine human. Divine hiddenness suggests human hiddenness: the call to search and that which endangers the search.

The dangers in trying to know the inner human self reinforce the limitations in knowing the divine self—the hidden nature and purpose of God. Forcing a revelation of the fragments of divinity hidden in the envelope of human flesh suggests the kind of metaphysical hubris that gives no answers. Milton's famous oxymoron in *Paradise Lost* of the "human face divine" implies that the human face is human and divine—not only the perceptually extrinsic human outline but also the cognitively intrinsic divine presence. One can reach out and attempt to grasp another as a knowable object, but if human nature is impossible to grasp, can one ever hope to know another human being? *Clarel* indicates that one cannot fully know the divinity within a human being and, thus, cannot fully love another. In *Clarel*, however, knowledge is not measured by reaching one's desired love object. There is psychological and theological validity in the very reaching out toward another. The ability to point in a direction is as respectable in *Clarel* as the ability to define an object. The pointing toward God, rather than a full grasp of God, is the acceptance of the limitations on human knowledge, of the inaccessibility of two divine, hidden subjects: the human and the divine.

Ungar's belief in reciprocal divinity is the revelation of both a divinity within humanity and the concept of *imitatio Dei* given a Melvillean twist. Each person bears God's image, including the divine attribute of hiddenness and silence and the danger of forcing a revelation of divine self-concealment.[31] Thus the human mode of divine presence—God hidden but present in every person—explains why characters in *Clarel*, as images of *Deus absconditus*, cannot become fellow companions: our divinity is hidden from ourselves and each other. Communion is not possible.

"A GOD HE WAS, BUT KNEW IT NOT"

The fullest and most interesting development of the divinity within the human is the interpolated canto "Of Rama," which describes the divinity of Rama, the Indian hero of the Hindu holy book *Ramayana*. The canto describes not only "etherial visitants of earth" (4.18.160) like Christ or Buddha but all men.[32]

> That Rama whom the Indian sung—
> A god he was, but knew it not
>
> . . . .
> Nor the divine in him bereaved,
> Though what that was he might not guess.
>   Live they who, like to Rama, led
> Unspotted from the world aside,
> Like Rama are discredited—

Like him, in outlawry abide?
May life and fable so agree?—
　　The innocent if lawless elf,
Etherial in virginity,
Retains the consciousness of self.
Though black frost nip, though white frost chill,
Nor white frost nor the black may kill
The patient root, the vernal sense
Surviving hard experience
As grass the winter. Even that curse
Which is the wormwood mixed with gall—
Better dependent on the worse—
Divine upon the animal—
That can not make such natures fall.
　　　　　　　　(1.32.1–2, 10–28)

The "Of Rama" canto is an ideal picture of God in being—divine immanence—and the pilgrims fall far short of this ideal. The narrator realizes the gulf between the ideal and the real when he asks teasingly, "Was ever earthborn wight like this? / Ay—in the verse, may be, he is" (1.32.55–56). The difference between the canto "Of Rama" and the rest of *Clarel* is analogous to that between the Gospel of John and the Synoptic Gospels. The Gospel of John focuses on the higher nature of Christ—the presence of the divine. As the existence of Jesus means more than what appears merely as the physical phenomenon called man, so does man in "Of Rama" contain more—the divinity within him—than what seems to be only his "animal" nature (1.32.27). The Synoptic Gospels portray the external phenomenon of the appearance of the man named Jesus, the appearance predicted by Jewish Messianism. The rest of the cantos of *Clarel*, like Matthew, Mark, and Luke, also portray the physical external phenomena of pilgrims in this world.

The ethereal virgin self of the god-man is a being that contains dual characteristics, just as the hidden God is an ambiguous multi-faced duality: "Though black frost nip, though white frost chill, / Nor white frost nor the black may kill / The patient root . . . " (1.32.20–22). The "patient root" is the intimation of immortality—"the vernal sense / Surviving hard experience / As grass the winter" (1.32.22–24)—as much as divine immanence, God in being. Even the animal side of human nature cannot deflect the divinity within: "Even that curse / . . . / Better dependent on the worse— / Divine upon the animal— / That can not make such natures fall" (1.32.24, 26–28). The narrator yearns for the ideal: the god-man's ability to transcend the limitations placed on the spirit by its material, physical nature. Perhaps, only then, may one come close to what Melville calls, in his Civil War poem

"Commemorative of a Naval Victory," the "ethereal spark": "There's a light and a shadow on every man / Who at last attains his lifted mark— / Nursing through night the ethereal spark."

The difficulty is that many individuals are not in touch with what Melville calls the "god within the breast" in his Civil War poem "A Meditation." Just as the Creator plays hide-and-seek with His created human image, human beings play hide-and-seek with their divinity. Derwent claims that we should be guided by the heart (*"she"*):

> Does *she* renounce the trust divine?
> Hide it she may, but scarce resign;
> Like to a casket buried deep
> Which, in a fine and fibrous throng,
> The rootlets of the forest keep—
> 'Tis tangled in her meshes strong.
> (4.18.79–84)

For Derwent, the heart is the seat of man's hidden divinity.[33]

THE DIALOG OF SILENCE

Accompanying human hiddenness—the image of divine hiddenness—is the notion of human silence. It may seem curious to talk of silence in a poem that is an almost endless dialog. Yet characters talk so much in *Clarel* only to find silence. Words get lost in the Tower of Babel that is *Clarel*. In fact, the primacy of dialog in the poem is replaced by the primacy of questions. If one enters into conversation or dialog with the premise that the speaker will communicate something, listen to something, and reveal or learn something—if dialog is seen as an attempt to clarify one's position, to persuade, or to advance mutual understanding—then dialog in *Clarel* is a failure. For dialog is often cut off in *Clarel*; ideas are left unfinished or not pursued. When Clarel challenges Rolfe's interpretation of the famous prooftext from Matthew and Hosea—*"Out / Of Egypt have I called my son"*—as evidence for a comparative approach to religions (Christ as avatar of Osiris, 1.31.217–31), Rolfe refuses to pursue the idea: "but then Hosea?—Nay, / We'll let it pass.—And fell delay / Of talk; they mused" (1.31.229–31). Derwent will often interrupt a dialog, even cut off someone's response, in order to change the subject. Derwent tries to dismiss themes by commenting on the landscape, almost as if to find solace in nature. When Rolfe discusses Mortmain's "wild plunge" into madness, Derwent quickly interrupts him and asks the pilgrims to observe the moon. Rolfe sits as one "rebuked" and then lets the subject of Mortmain drop: "No matter, . . . let it go" (2.16.126, 129). Derwent tries to avert Rolfe from his discussion of

Rome versus Atheism in the canto "Of Rome" by catching a tree branch and proposing an irrelevant botanical query: "What tree is this?" Rolfe's sarcastic answer is a condemnation of Derwent's refusal to pursue an idea: "The tree of knowledge, I dare say: / But you don't eat" (2.26.146–48). When Rolfe points out to Derwent that Christliness is higher than manliness, Derwent abruptly ends the dialog by pointing to the drapery (4.14.111). Rolfe, who genuinely respects Ungar, refuses to accept Derwent's critique of Ungar's business— war—with the curt reiteration of "may be" for each of Derwent's claims (4.23.46, 51). Dialog often fails in *Clarel* for lack of reciprocity.

Dialog often ends in silence or in a condemnation of words. After the Syrian monk tells of his vision and dialog with Satan the Adversary, Rolfe asks "Surely, not all we've heard: / Peace—solace—was in end conferred?" (2.18.150–51). The monk gives no answer and hastily leaves; Rolfe implies that the monk's vision was more than an ecstasy of fast; and Vine keeps his judgment silent. Clarel, admiring the Druze's quietude and silence, claims that Djalea would not "fall / In waste of words, that waste of all" (3.5.182). The word of God "shall stand forever" (Isaiah 40:8), but clearly, for Clarel, the word of man is an ephemeral waste. The futility of language and human reason to "solve the world" frustrates Clarel: "And reason's endless battle wage, / Make and remake his verbiage— / But solve the world! Scarce that he'll do" (4.3.110–12). Vine even builds a monument to the death of all words—a cairn:

> An object reared aloof by Vine
> In whim of silence, when debate
> Was held upon the cliff but late
> And ended where all words decline:
> A heap of stones in arid state.
> (3.7.79–83)

When Vine relapses into silence, the narrator says the pilgrims "saw / In silence the heart's shadow draw" (2.22.143–44). Silence hides words as well as the heart—the seat of divinity.

The silences, misdirections, and interruptions are all part of the dialogical nature of *Clarel*. Human silence, as reflected in the interruption of dialog and the waste of words, adds to the ambiguity of theological, historical, and psychological opinions in the poem. Melville does not lift a finger to guide the reader through this confusion of words unevenly balanced by silence. He lets the characters unfold their positions and lets the dialog end without conclusion, without consensus, one character contesting another, spoken statement to spoken statement, silence to speech, silence to silence. Only by allowing the narrator to comment on certain speeches and by having different characters repeat the same consistent image or idea does Melville indicate where the dialog's center of gravity lies.

And yet the perceptions of God as a creating Being who expresses Himself through hiddenness and silence and of the human as a created being who also expresses himself through hiddenness and silence were not sufficient for Melville. The true perception of the divine and the human is dependent upon something deeper and much more difficult to define. In *Clarel*, recognition of a God who seeks concealment is not enough without a particular psychological response to God: an emotional estrangement from or responsiveness to *Deus absconditus*. The human mind can take theological and psychological offense at the hidden God and the unknowable universe—a response that leads to estrangement—or it can stand open to hiddenness and ambiguity in a state of reverence and hope that may lead to a closer responsiveness to God.

Fleeing from and to God—the Melvillean paradox of divine distance—is part of a more complex paradox of freedom. The human is both created and creator, both bound and unbound. In *Clarel*, we are created in this world and bound by time, death, chance, suffering, hiddenness, and silence. Yet we are self-creators in this world and free, in the course of a lifetime, to choose to deny, to doubt, or to believe—to flee from or to return to God.

❖

Melville's Lament

The Theodicy Questions

How long wilt make us still to doubt?
How long?
—*Clarel*

O Lord, how long shall I cry and thou wilt not hear!
—Habakkuk 1:2

THE PRIMARY RESPONSE TO THE HIDDENNESS and silence of God is not only hiddenness and silence between human beings but also a bold questioning of God's purposes and human fate. God's hiddenness prompts questions. Since we cannot see or know God or each other, we ask the perennial biblical question of "O Lord, how long?" will presence and knowledge remain hidden. Although divine self-concealment in *Clarel* makes knowledge of God and the universe ambiguous and limited, the lack of answers does not weaken the human power to question God about His purposes in creating human beings. In essence, much of *Clarel* asks this question of God: What are you doing?

To read *Clarel* is to live in a world of ceaseless questions, to walk with Job, Jeremiah, Koheleth, and the psalmists, and to ask the questions that overwhelm human existence. To read *Clarel* is to search for meaning in the presence of doubt, suffering, and death. To read *Clarel* is to propose everlasting questions to a God who, like the Sphinx in the Epilogue, answers none.[1] About twenty-five percent of the poem's lines are questions, and many stem from the biblical genre of the lament. The most powerful Clarelian questions are also theodicy questions that protest against divine hiddenness, human disillusionment, undeserved suffering, theological doubt, persistent evil, and inescapable death. Reading *Clarel* as a biblical lament and theodicy reminds us that God is silent, that people are finite, and that any idealization of divine presence or human understanding is severely limited. Humanity cries out, but whether God is concerned about this cry of distress is the Melvillean question of questions.[2]

The questions of *Clarel* are actually laments that build and eventually overwhelm the reader until all of life is understood as a tragic yearning for the answers to several puzzling theodicy questions. Why is there undeserved human suffering, evil, and death in the presence of a hidden God? Does God speak to the way in which Clarelian characters live and die? And, most importantly, what is the possibility of faith in a hidden God?[3] When *Clarel* is read with its biblical co-texts—the Psalms of Lament, Job, Jeremiah, and Ecclesiastes—the Melvillean lament and the image of the hidden God are defined with greater clarity. All these biblical-Clarelian questions are inextricably intertwined with the question of what it means to be human, inseparable from the question of how we live and die.

The Melvillean lament is anchored in the biblical genre of the lament found predominantly in the Psalms and in Lamentations, but also in Jeremiah and in the theodicies of Job and Ecclesiastes. In the Psalms, for example, a lament is the psalmist's complaint or protest about his distress in tragic predicaments of helplessness, doubt, divine silence, or suffering, whenever he finds himself in "the valley of the shadow of death" (Psalms 23:4). Although the Psalms cover the full spectrum of emotions toward God, including confidence, thanksgiving, praise, and hope, many of the psalms are individual and communal cries for help: "Why standest thou afar off, O Lord? why hidest thou thyself in times of trouble?" (Psalms 10:1). Typically, the Psalms of Lament contain questions addressed to God asking why God has abandoned Israel as a nation or as individuals. The questions are never directly answered by God; instead, the psalmist usually will voice a radical emotional swing from despair over God's aloofness to sudden bursts of renewed hope for and thanksgiving in God's presence and protection. Under the duress of suffering, however, the psalmist can even raise the frightening possibility of "there is no God" (e.g., Psalms 14:1), although this line is always attributed to the wicked or foolish. Nevertheless, when the innocent suffer, the lament question turns into a theodicy question asked of God. In other words, when the innocent and the righteous suffer, then the righteousness, justice, and even the existence of God are questioned. If the righteousness, justice, and presence of God are questioned, then so, too, is faith in God. Thus the psalmist, in an individual lament, can pose a theodicy question concerning the traditional teachings about reward for the righteous and punishment for the wicked: "Verily I have cleansed my heart in vain, and washed my hands in innocency. For all the day long have I been plagued, and chastened every morning" (Psalms 73:13–14). In the communal lament of Psalm 44, God is blamed for breaking His covenant promise to the Israelites instead of blaming the wicked, wayward human heart for transgressing God's covenant:

But thou hast cast off, and put us to shame... Thou hast given us like sheep appointed for meat; and hast scattered us among the heathen. Thou sellest thy people for nought.... All this is come upon us; yet have we not forgotten thee, neither have we dealt falsely in thy covenant. (Psalms 44:9–17)

This communal lament or complaint genre, like *Clarel*, does not simply lament the presence of human suffering and death. The psalmist protests the wanton nature of this suffering and either blames God or man. In other words, the lament-protest is a large part of the biblical response to theodicy questions and to divine hiddenness:

Wherefore hidest thou thy face, and forgettest our affliction and our oppression? (Psalms 44:24). How long, Lord? wilt thou hide thyself for ever? shall thy wrath burn like fire? (Psalms 89:46). Lord, where are thy former lovingkindnesses, which thou swarest unto David in thy truth? (Psalms 89:49).

Perhaps the most anguished lament in the Psalter is Psalm 88:

O Lord God of my salvation, I have cried day and night before thee: Let my prayer come before thee: incline thine ear unto my cry; For my soul is full of troubles: and my life draweth nigh unto the grave . . . among the dead, like the slain that lie in the grave, whom thou rememberest no more: and they are cut off from thy hand. . . . Lord, I have called daily upon thee, I have stretched out my hand unto thee. . . . Lord, why castest thou off my soul? Why hidest thou thy face from me? I am afflicted and ready to die from my youth up: while I suffer thy terrors. . . . Lover and friend hast thou put far from me, and mine acquaintance into darkness. (Psalms 88:1–18)

Psalm 88 is just one of the biblical laments that captures the spirit of *Clarel* so well: a heart committed to the quest for faith, old enough to die from the moment of birth, and asking theodicy questions of a hidden God.

Biblical theodicy is concerned with the question of why do the foolish and the wise, the wicked and the just, all suffer the same fate. Does not faith promise that the righteous shall prosper and live while the wicked suffer and die? Job and Koheleth (the voice in Ecclesiastes) are haunted by the fact that God causes the suffering of the innocent along with the wicked: "He destroyeth the perfect and the wicked" (Job 9:22) and "there is a just man that perisheth in his righteousness, and there is a wicked man that prolongeth his life in his wickedness" (Ecclesiastes 7:15). Furthermore, how can we speak of human innocence and guilt, of righteousness and wickedness, if all human beings suffer the same fate: death (Ecclesiastes 2:14)?[4] The real problem in theodicies, such as Job, 4 Ezra (2 Esdras), Ecclesiastes, and *Clarel*, is the possibility that God is not just. Thus, whenever humans suffer and die in the Bible and in *Clarel*, the implied issue is not only human innocence or guilt but also divine innocence or guilt:

> I cry unto thee, and thou dost not hear me. . . . Thou art become cruel to me: with thy strong hand thou opposest thyself against me. . . . For I know that thou wilt bring me to death. . . . When I looked for good, then evil came unto me: and when I waited for light, there came darkness. (Job 30:20–31)

There is a great deal of evidence within the poem for Melville's recognition of the biblical lament. The driving force of the cry of the lament and of the theodicy questions in the Bible is the discrepancy between the divine promise of prosperity, life, and God's presence versus the fulfillment in suffering, death, and divine hiddenness.[5] In one of the most important lines of the poem, Melville also defines Clarel's lament, just like the biblical lament, as the discrepancy between the way things ought to be and the way things are. As Clarel says after Ruth's death, "Conviction is not gone / Though faith's gone: that which shall not be / It *ought* to be! (4.30.116–18). The protest that accompanies this state of tension—the disparity between promise and fulfillment, hope and realization, knowledge and mystery, question and answer—is the very heart of Melville's lament and of the Bible.

The Clarelian questions themselves are the best evidence for a Melvillean lament that is biblical in tone and genre and is a variation on the theme of Isaiah's "Lord, how long?" (6:11) and Habakkuk's "O Lord, how long shall I cry, and thou wilt not hear!" (1:2). Variations include the bold theodicy question to God in the Epilogue—"Wherefore ripen us to pain?" (4.35.21).[6] The silence of this unanswered question to God is parallel to Jesus' unanswered cry on the cross. Melville, like Job, offers no definitive answer to the why of pain and undeserved human suffering. "How long wilt make us still to doubt? / How long?" (1.13.74–75) is another lament for deliverance. So is the wandering Jew's question in the Mar Saba masque of "How long, how long?" (3.19.127), referring to his state of being cut off from humanity and God. There is a definite family resemblance to these Melvillean questions: a biblical lament form though in different thematic contexts. The lament becomes an overwhelming poetry of suffering and spiritual agony because humanity feels forsaken by God: "Wherefore forever dost forget— / For so long time forsake, O God?" (1.22.21–22). Wondering whether the estrangement from God will be forever—"Cut off, cut off" (Rolfe's lament, 2.21.92)—

Rolfe represents humanity's yearning for the presence of God that can turn to a resentful arraignment of God: a "thrust / Into the cloud" (3.21.70–71). Clarel cries "God my God, / Sorely Thou triest me the clod!" (3.21.226–27), and Mortmain gives over a machine-gun burst of questions in an extended diatribe that accuses Americans of an unchristian league between "Mammon and Democracy" (3.5.154). Ungar's laments take the form of judgments against human wickedness and suggest that humanity deserves God's hiddenness and silence (4.22). "The High Desert" canto is perhaps the most extreme example of a manic lament where the pilgrims lose themselves in over thirty questions as they sweep from subject to subject under "the clear vault of hollow heaven" (3.5.204).

THE JEREMIAH VOICE

The prophetic book Jeremiah and the book of Lamentations are two of the biblical voices that we hear most often in *Clarel*. They are, I suspect, a large part of Melville's fascination with questions, invocations, dirges, elegies, complaining diatribes, and threnodies—all of which appear in the poem. Melville knew of Jeremiah's association with the lament mode of expression (jeremiads) and his reputation as the author of the book of Lamentations: "Note what these *Lamentations* say; / The doom the prophet doth rehearse" (1.24.58–59). Elsewhere, when Vine quotes a passage from Lamentations, Rolfe says, "Thy word / Is Jeremiah's, and here well heard" (1.34.9–10). By tracing the voices of Jeremiah throughout the poem, I will establish Melville's particular attraction to Jeremiah, not to the prophet or historical figure but to the book as a biblical co-text for reading *Clarel*. In part 1, "Jerusalem," Melville either quotes or alludes to Lamentations and Jeremiah to convey the sense of God's abandonment of the historically sanctioned holy spots, Mount Zion and Jerusalem:

> How solitary on the hill
> Sitteth the city; and how still
> How still!
> (1.34.1–3; cf. Lamentations 1:1)
> *All that pass by clap their hands*
> *At thee; they hiss, and wag the head,*
> *Saying, Is this the city.*
> (1.24.61–63; cf. Lamentations 2:15)

From Jeremiah, Melville invokes the sound of the bride and groom no longer heard in the city: "Where voice of bridegroom, groom and bride / Is hushed" (1.7.21–22).[7] Jeremiah's voice is important here in establishing the atmosphere of not only divine abandonment but also social isolation in *Clarel*. Jeremiah was the prophet who took the oath of celibacy and even abstained from weddings and funerals. This allusion is used to establish the lack of human community in the poem. The cantos "By the Stone" and "They Tarry" (1.33 and 1.34) contain Rolfe's laments over Jerusalem and over "change irreverent" (1.34.36) and allude to the words of Jeremiah and Jesus in Luke 19:41–44. Both biblical books convey the mood of brooding over God's absence from the place of worship—Jerusalem—and the resulting separation between the human and the divine. This break in communication between God and man causes the human lament to God.[8]

The supreme example of Melville's use of biblical prophetic voices and images occurs in the canto that the narrator calls "a chant in Scripture character" (3.17.13).[9] Here, Melville strings together a series of allusions to Jeremiah, Lamentations, and Ezekiel in an attempt to illustrate both the prophetic images of doomsday and of restoration. Allusions such as Jeremiah cast into a dungeon (3.17.22), "ashes on the brow!" (3.17.33), "Oh, now each lover leaveth!" (3.17.36) and "A sword without—the pestilence within" (3.17.41)—all connote the prophetic rhetoric and images of doom, the wasteland images of burning, humiliation, divorce, death, and enslavement that describe the destruction of Jerusalem in Jeremiah and Ezekiel. For instance, the source of the allusion "Oh, now each lover leaveth!" is Jeremiah 30:14, "All thy lovers have forgotten thee; they seek thee not; for I have wounded thee with the wound of an enemy. . . ." The biblical love affair between God and Israel has turned sour because Israel has whored after other lovers and forsaken the Groom-God of Jeremiah. But the second half of the monks' chant focuses on the prophetic rhetoric and images of restoration in which the enemies of Israel will be overthrown: "the nations groan / At the jar of Bel and Babylon / In din of overthrow. / But Zion shall be built again!" (3.17.46–49). The restoration images that make up a little less than half of the images in the biblical prophetic books focus on life, not death, on planting and rebuilding, and on God's face of mercy rather than judgment: "His mercy shall remain: / In rivers flow forever, / Forever fall in rain!" (3.17.56–58). Melville intentionally rewrites a prophetic lament here, reinterpreting Lamentations by ending his chant on mercy rather than on judgment. This important biblical reinterpretation Melville will return to again in the Epilogue of hope. The deliberately antithetical images that Melville evokes from the Hebrew prophetic tradition become essentially Melville's own and are central to the theological reflection in *Clarel*: oppositions are constantly brought together, no image or thought is allowed to exist in the poem singly.[10]

Another reason for Melville's use of Jeremiah is that Jeremiah was the great prophet of the positive interpretation of the desert wanderings. Jeremiah reaffirms Israel's faith and loyalty, not backsliding, the new bride following the Groom-God unquestioningly: "Thus saith the Lord; I remember thee, the kindness of thy youth, the love of thine espousals, when thou [Israel] wentest after me in the wilderness, in a land that was not sown" (Jeremiah 2:2). Of course, Jeremiah has an equal number of lines that blame the Israelites for forsaking the Lord, but the point here is that Melville is aware of the theological choice of either blaming the wayward human heart (far more common) or blaming God for suffering and disappointment. The mysterious hiddenness and aloofness of God was a source of theological confusion: "Why is my pain perpetual, and my wound incurable, which refuseth to be healed? wilt thou be altogether unto me as a liar, and as waters that fail?" (Jeremiah 15:18). The polarity of God's many faces can imply a God who is Jeremiah's strength and refuge and a God who is a deceitful brook. The divine and the human can fail each other. We can blame God for His hiddenness and ambiguous nature, or we can blame our own humanity as the occasion to sin. The Melvillean lament does both.

The Melvillean protest-lament has two variations: an arraignment of God or an arraignment of humanity. Because there is no answer to the enigma of suffering and death, the generations of "tried humanity" (1.3.118), because Melville's God in *Clarel* is a hidden and silent God, the human response can be a lament that turns to a judgment either against God or against man. For example, Mortmain sees death as fit judgment for human evil and sees God as the warrior "God of Habakkuk" (3.1.169). Suffering and grief fuel Mortmain's furious jeremiads: "The craze of grief's intolerant fire / Unwearied and unweariable" (3.1.172–73). Since God is silent, people often feel that they did something wrong to deserve such silence. Therefore they judge themselves and others as guilty. Of course, there is much evidence of human ignorance and malice to justify the poem's accusative judgments against the human heart. A close look at Melville's three central protests of disillusionment, death, and suffering and at his presentation of the suffering of Jesus and Clarel reveals the presence of questions that act as laments in the poem.

We must remember that protests or laments against God and the theodicy questions about human fate, although often indicative of theological doubt, are still within the range of God's ear. If God were presumed to be dead or nonexistent, why would Melville bother lamenting at all? A quest presupposes something to be found; questions presuppose the possibility of answers. In other words, the presence of questions does not indicate a crisis of faith, but a crisis of knowledge of the universe and of a hidden God, a crisis of understanding born in the desire to know a God whose purpose is unfathomable and whose face cannot be seen.

UNFULFILLED ROMANCE

Melville's most powerful lament voiced throughout the poem is that life is "an unfulfilled romance" (2.1.13), a process of disillusionment that always takes place in a context of failure.[11] The disillusionment is most apparent when highly imaginative or hopeful dreams prove to be beyond the possibility of fulfillment. Nineteenth-century Zionism is a prime example of misguided idealism for Melville, a dream that is partially responsible for the stubbornness of Nathan and the deaths of Ruth and Agar:

> But ah, the dream to test by deed,
> To seek to handle the ideal
> And make a sentiment serve need:
> To try to realize the unreal!
> (1.27.67–70)

The real always falls far short of the ideal in *Clarel*, and anyone attempting to view Palestine through the eyes of the kings and prophets of the Bible will immediately experience the gap between the promise of "chanted Zion" and the fulfillment of deserts and graves:

> What solace from the desert win
> Far from known friends, familiar kin?
> How nearer God? The chanted Zion
> Showed graves, but graves to gasp and die on.
> (1.27.73–76)

Mortmain's disappointment after the failure of reform in Europe, Ungar's pain and disillusionment after the national calamity that was the American Civil War, Clarel's loss of his love Ruth, and the corruption and perversion of the original teachings of Jesus—all indicate that ideals are qualified by human frailty and experience: "Pure things men need adulterate / And so adapt them to the kind" (4.14.81–82).[12]

"Unfulfilled romance" goes beyond the disparity between the ideal and the real, for Melville demonstrates that all of life is also beyond the possibility of fulfillment. Experience—that condition of life as one lives it out before interpreting it with psychological or theological explanations and significance—is a wrenching of the human heart with all the anguish of disillusionment and dashed dreams. In fact, the only way one educates oneself in *Clarel* is by unlearning what was first learned: "Clarel, receptive, saw and heard, / Learning, unlearning, word by word" (2.14.51–52). Every experience leads to disillusionment. For example, any abandoned quarry can fulfill one's illusive dream of Jerusalem as well as the heap of stones that Jerusalem was in 1856:

> Abandoned quarry mid the hills
> Remote, as well one's dream fulfills
> Of what Jerusalem should be,
> As that vague heap, whose neutral tones
> Blend in with Nature's, helplessly:
> Stony metropolis of stone.
>
> (4.2.7–12)

Even the archaeological discovery of the red city of Petra eventually disappoints because human expectation is always raised too high.[13] Nothing can stand close scrutiny; Colchis (the home of the golden fleece) charms only from afar:

> But expectation's raised.
>   No more!
> 'Tis then when bluely blurred in shore,
> It looms through azure haze at sea—
> Then most 'tis Colchis charmeth ye.
> So ever, and *with all*!
>
> (2.30.24–29, emphasis mine)

The romance of the Ephraim mountains also requires an "unlearning" disillusionment: "Of Ephraim, stretched in purple pall. / Romance of mountains! But in end / What change the near approach could lend" (1.1.46–48).

When comparing the crusades to events of his own nineteenth century, the narrator identifies his age with "that round / Of disillusions which accrue / In this our day . . ." (1.4.19–21). The pilgrim experience shared by Clarel is also characterized by disappointment and pain: "And each face was a book / Of disappointment. Why weep'st thou? / Whom seekest?" (1.5.99–101). Clarel applies Jesus' question to Mary in John 20:15 to himself and to all disappointed pilgrims searching and weeping for the Jesus who has yet to come again. All pilgrimages lead to disappointment because after so much travel and trouble, "How nearer God?" (1.27.75).

The most poignant lament of experience as multiple disillusionment is Mortmain's personal history. In seeking "that uncreated Good" (2.4.49), Mortmain's "precocities of heart outran / The immaturities of brain" (2.4.52–53). When the cause of reform is undermined by traitors, "Experience with her sharper touch / Stung Mortmain" (2.4.60–61). Because of Mortmain's "thwarted aims of high design" (2.4.135), he is "chastised" into questioning human nature and its limitations just

Like those new-world discoverers bold
Ending in stony convent cold
Or dying hermits; as if they,
Chastised to Micah's mind austere,
Remorseful felt that ampler sway
Their lead had given for old career
Of human nature.

(2.4.121–27)

The discrepancy between the nineteenth-century ideal called progress and human corruption—"Malice divides with ignorance" (2.4.92)—prompts Mortmain to question his own theories and to judge the discovery of America as only opening "ampler" spheres for the "old career / Of human" evil. Mortmain's unfulfilled romance turns into a judgment against humanity.

Ungar's laments in the American cantos (part 4, cantos 20 and 21) illustrate an anthropological response to God's self-concealment: original sin. If God does not talk to human beings, does not show Himself to us, we must have done something terribly wrong. And, of course, the world is admittedly full of evil doings, so "wickedness" becomes Ungar's key thematic word in his judgment against humanity (4.22.19–20). Vine asks Ungar (punning on the opening verse of the fourth Gospel—"In the beginning was the Word. . . .") "Is wickedness the word?" (4.22.19). Ungar says yes and suggests that true wickedness is the sin of birth, our earthly existence: "What's implied / In that deep utterance decried / Which Christians labially confess— / *Be born anew?*" (4.22.38–41). All of Ungar's lament-questions warn of the folly of ignoring human evil as the cause of suffering and death: "All recognition they forego / Of Evil . . ." (4.20.100–101). What Ungar calls "a callousness in clay" (4.18.121) makes the human heart unreceptive to "etherial visitants of earth" such as Christ and Buddha (4.18.160). The only cure for the hard human heart, in Ungar's mind, is the grace of "a prior love [that] must steep / The spirit" (4.18.129–30) or the sanctions of the "deterring dart" of Mosaic Law (4.18.159).

Mortmain's life, Ungar's laments, and the other numerous examples of unfulfilled romance suggest that experience for Melville was disillusionment based on expectation. In fact, experience cannot be acquired without the "unlearning" of disillusionment. Although experience in *Clarel* is predominantly painful and disappointing, it is not totally negative because every encounter that goes against expectation teaches a person the limitations of human expectations. For Melville, an experienced person is not someone who has the knowledge to solve problems better the next time they are encountered. He is, however, someone who expects disillusionment and even prepares himself for it. Experienced people know the poverty of human knowledge when compared with the disillusioning experiences of life. Unfulfilled romance may be the key to the significance of life, not the undeveloped innocence that believes all possibilities will be realized. An innocent such as Nehemiah who believes in the literal fulfillment of all biblical prophecy— "Yea, friend in Christ, I hear them swell— / The trumpets of Immanuel!"—is corrected by the narrator with one succinct, staccato word: "Illusion" (1.20.43–45). The unfulfilled biblical romantic must also learn that freedom from disillusionment is an illusion.

The greatest promise that leads to the greatest unfulfillment and the severest protest in *Clarel* is the good put forth by Jesus. Melville interprets Jesus as a man who sensed that his hidden father had abandoned him—"*My God, my God, forsakest me?*" (1.13.47). By entering history as a man, Christ entered in a way that permitted rejection of him:

> Upbraider! we upbraid again;
> *Thee* [Christ] we upbraid; our pangs constrain
> Pathos itself to cruelty.
> Ere yet thy day no pledge was given
> Of homes and mansions in the heaven—
> Paternal homes reserved for us;
> Heart hoped it not, but lived content—
> Content with life's own discontent,
> Nor deemed that fate ere swerved for us:
> The natural law men let prevail;
> Then reason disallowed the state
> Of instinct's variance with fate.
> But thou—ah, see, in rack how pale
> Who did the world with throes convulse;
> Behold him—yea—behold the Man [Christ]
> Who warranted if not began
> The dream that drags out its repulse
>
> (1.13.48–64)

Here, the promise of good—salvation—disappoints, and Celio claims that Christ, though "tortured, shalt prove a torturer" (1.13.99) by teasing mankind with an unfulfilled dream. Since Jesus' promise of Parousia is still delayed, human suffering elicits the response of cruelty rather than pathos ("our pangs constrain / Pathos itself to cruelty"), and Christ's teachings are rejected. But rather than blame humanity for its unwillingness to sense Christ's divinity, Melville suggests that Christ's dream was so unrealistic that his promise is a kind of false advertising that only exacerbates humanity's "discontent" and makes of Christianity a "dream that drags out its repulse." The life of Jesus was a momentary pastoral Eden that ended with his death,[14] and the result of that promise of "a heaven's unclouded days" (1.13.40) has been that Christianity has lent itself to cruel distortions, and revelation has changed to confusion: "the heart / Of heavenly love, so sweet, so good, / Corrupt into the creeds malign" (1.13.87–89). The discrepancy between Christ's divine promise and the "creeds malign" demonstrates a heart-wrenching fall from the ideal to the real. This unfulfilled romance that was and is the life and teachings of Jesus prompts questions—a biblical lament for the hidden nature and purpose of God and Christ:

> How long wilt make us still to doubt?
> How long?—'Tis eighteen cycles now—
> Enigma and evasion grow;
> And shall we never find thee out?
> (1.13.74–77)

The lament of "How long?" implies that this state of doubt and disappointment has gone on long enough. The agony over the disparity between God's promise of presence and God's fulfillment in absence is really a lament turned to a judgment against God.

Rolfe agrees with Celio's accusation that the perversion of Jesus' teachings is not so much the result of human callousness as much as the nature of life as an unfulfilled romance:

> What dream they knew, that primal band
> Of gipsy Christians! But it died;
> Back rolled the world's effacing tide:
>
> . . . .
>
> But worse came—creeds, wars, stakes. Oh, men
> Made earth inhuman; yes, a den
> Worse for Christ's coming, since his love
> (Perverted) did but venom prove.
> (2.21.76–78, 83–86)

Jesus' promise of love and heaven was and is too much for the "world's effacing tide." Because the words of Jesus are too demanding morally for humanity to adopt, earth is "a den / Worse for Christ's coming." The moral extremity of Jesus' call—to repudiate profit and selfishness, to serve the community, not the self—prompts the falsehood and oppression that have spread over the world in the name of Christianity—"creeds, wars, stakes." Again, for Melville the "thwarted aims of high design" (2.4.135) lead to unfulfillment and resentment. Although the unfulfilled romance breeds disenchantment,

disillusionment, and even the murder of its dreamers, Melville does not question the nobility and worth of those dreams. There is a touch of envy in *Clarel*
for early Christianity, that "green" time when people dared to dream of
heaven (e.g., 2.21.112; 4.32.56–58). Although it is necessary to reject fulfilled romance in *Clarel*, it is false to deny completely the good fortune of
those who dream of it.

OF DEATH AND CLOSURE

Along with the lament of life as an unfulfilled romance, life is also characterized by its finitude and suffering. In a poem where six characters die in less
than ten days, where a mad monk demands the password "death" from
passersby, where Clarel has visions of the dead walking, where bells knell and
dirges are sung, death characterizes the work more than life, a death whose
meaning is hidden and silent.[15]

> And death?—Why beat the bush in thee?
> It is the cunningest mystery:
> Alive thou know'st not death; and, dead,
> Death thou'lt not know. . . .
> (2.18.120–23)

Thus Satan teaches the Syrian monk that it is not the universality of death that
troubles mankind but that no one understands what the silence of death
means. Death truly is what Melville calls the "silent negative."[16] The experience of silent death only prompts questions: What is the meaning of an
existence whose ultimate end is death? Since there is no definitive answer to
such a question, the divine seems even more silent in death. Melville faces this
question and the enigma of suffering with a dynamic, bold questioning—
without, however, renouncing hope.

If people could only be sure that they survive their own death, then mortality would not be so fearful. As Rolfe experiences the death and burial of
Nehemiah on the shores of the Dead Sea, he questions:

> But were it clear
> In nature or in lore devout
> That parted souls live on in cheer,
> Gladness would be—shut pathos out.
> His poor thin life: the end? no more?
> The end here by the Dead Sea shore?
> (2.39.80–85)

Of course, neither God nor nature can answer Rolfe's lament-questions. Nehemiah's death also compels the narrator to ask questions. Part 3, "Mar Saba," has its first twenty-four lines made up of six questions—"reveries" on immortality. All the narrator's questions or "exhalings" from the heart remain unanswered. The "why" lament over death is a poignant cry in *Clarel* that expects no specific answer although one is desperately sought. As the pilgrims overlook Mortmain's corpse, the narrator gives us their pained thoughts that portray the span of a human life:

> They refrain
> From aught but that dumb look that fell
> Identifying; feeling pain
> That such a heart could beat, and will—
> Aspire, yearn, suffer, baffled still,
> And end.
>
> (3.32.42–47)

The full stop after "end" emphasizes the finality of death but only after suffering. Even the death of Celio—who is relatively unknown to Clarel— compels the pilgrims to meditate on death: "Whom life held apart— / Life, whose cross-purposes make shy— / Death yields without reserve of heart / To meditation" (1.40.31–34).

Since the human is an animal whose flesh is the prophet of its own end, it is the frailty of the flesh that points toward death. In *Clarel*, "no flesh shall have peace" (Jeremiah 12:12). Christ's problem was not that he lived in "a troubled era too" (3.21.267) but that he entered history infleshed in a human body which threw off a shadow like any other human body: "And shared besides that problem gray / Which is forever and alway: / His person our own shadow threw" (3.21.268–70). Like King Lear, whose hand smells of mortality, Mortmain's hand (etymologically his name means "dead hand") reminds him of mortality.

> He, going, scanned
> The testimony of the hand
> Gnawed in the dream: "Yea, but 'tis here.
> Despair? nay, death; and what's death's cheer?
> Death means—the sea-beat gains the shore;
> He's home; his watch is called no more.
> So looks it. Not I tax thee, Death,
> With that, which might make Strength a trembler—
> While yet for me it scants no breath—
> That, quiet under sleepiest mound,

Thou art a dangerous dissembler;
That he whose evil is profound
In multiform of life's disguises,
Whom none dare check, and naught chastises,
And in his license thinks no bound—
For him thou hoardest strange surprises!"

                                                 (3.28.34–49)

For Mortmain, death can be a form of judgment against human wickedness, against those "whose evil is profound."

Despite the fact that some die peacefully—either out of "care for kin" or perhaps "peace within" (1.40.60, 59)—death is "drear" for "moderns" without theological certitude:

Ah, own! to moderns death is drear,
So drear: we die, we make no sign,
We acquiesce in any cheer—
No rite we seek, no rite decline.
Is't nonchalance of languid sense,
Or the last, last indifference?

                                                 (1.40.53–58)

Whether the human response to death is passive stoicism or mental insensitivity, some individuals cannot face "that ill word / Whose first is D and last is H" (2.3.50–51). The banker and his son-in-law, Glaucon, because they pursue pleasure and profit and refuse to contemplate death, will suffer the most from death's sudden "arrest."

Cosmetic-users scarce are bold
To face a skull. That sachem old
Whose wigwam is man's heart within—
How taciturn, and yet can speak,
Imparting more than books can win;
Not Pleasure's darling cares to seek
Such counselor: the worse he fares;
Since—heedless, taken unawares—
Arrest he finds. . . .

                                                 (2.12.32–40)

Since death, like an Indian chief in his wigwam, is within the human heart, it is not an intruder. Here, death and life are not opposites, and we see the intertwining of death in life. Later in the poem, Melville will offer metaphors suggesting that life is in death. Death seems to be a force within life, not merely the end of life.

Oblivious to "the hallelujah after pain" of Easter (4.33.21), Clarel, when confronting either a vision or the arrest of death, laments death. After seeing Ruth in death ("how estranged in face!") during his vision of the dead on Good Friday (4.32.98), Clarel appeals to God and the Holy Spirit: "Where, where now He who helpeth us, / The Comforter? . . . " (4.32.103–4). No human "cheer" can comfort Clarel, for his lament turned to mourning remains forever unanswered: "The cheer, so human, might not call / The maiden up; *Christ is arisen:* / But Ruth, may Ruth so burst the prison?" (4.33.64–66). Despite the assurance of Matthew 28:6, Ruth is not "arisen."

Death also prevents us from understanding God's ways and purposes. Standing next to the graves of Ruth and Agar, Clarel asks the most important lament of all when confronted with the hard fact of death: "Ruth? Agar?—*art thou God?* . . . " (4.30.86). Clarel questions the nature of God because he is limited by God's silence and hiddenness in the face of human death. The limit of human existence is the limit of our understanding of God. The problem of death is really the problem of God. "Art thou God" is not a prayer but a judgment, asking how can the human draw near the presence of God, how can the human see the face of God, how can the human understand the ways of God? Furthermore, how can the human embrace such a God in faith? In death, the human experiences God's withdrawal most painfully.

In Melville's journal entry at Constantinople, dated Sunday, December 14, 1856, he writes of an Armenian woman who, like Clarel, asks the lament-questions of God and death:

> Armenian funerals winding through the streets. Coffin covered with flowers borne on a bier. Wax candles borne on each side in daylight. Boys & men chanting alternately. Striking effect, winding through the narrow lanes.—Saw a burial. Armenian. Juggling and incantations of the priests—making signs &c.—Nearby, saw a woman over a new grave—no grass on it yet. Such abandonment of misery! Called to the dead, put her head down as close to it as possible; as if calling down a hatchway or cellar; besought—"Why don't you speak to me? My God!—It is I!—Ah, speak—but one word!—All deaf.—So much for consolation.—This woman & her cries haunt me horribly.—[17]

The Armenian widow from Melville's journal, along with Hamlet, no doubt influenced the depiction of Clarel's behavior at Ruth's grave and his question to God. Armenian funerals wind their way throughout the poem and serve as a poetic device to foregound the difficulty of maintaining faith in the face of human suffering and death. In death, God seems unmoved by, if not indifferent to, the human cry for divine communication and presence: "Ah, speak—but one word!" or "art thou God?" (4.30.86). The Armenian woman and Clarel do not know whether God is indifferent to human pain, impotent to change our mortality, or angry and thus inflicting suffering. The force and power of this Clarelian lament is a theodicy question put to God and to ourselves. Whenever we postulate a loving, merciful, just God and then encounter disease, undeserved suffering, accident, premature death, or evil, we raise the issue of divine guilt. In essence, God is condemned by the same ethical standards He has supposedly given to us. Suffering and death are very much an issue between the human and the divine and lie close to the very heart of Melville's theological reflection as he explores the death of Jesus, Ruth, Nathan, Celio, Nehemiah, Mortmain, and Agar. Of course, the lament and question to God in both instances are not powerful enough to change human fate. In the poem and in the Journal, the dead remain dead.

The significance of the death question in *Clarel* is that death is more than a fact of human existence, more than a distant event we encounter at the end of a life, more than an end which suddenly and unpredictably comes upon human beings, whether in illness, accident, war, or old age. Death in *Clarel* lingers constantly before the pilgrims. To be human is to live in and beneath the shadow of death. As soon as we are born, the Armenian mourners are in the street. From the moment of birth, we are old enough to suffer and to die. When dead, we are separated from others, from the world, from ourselves, and, most terrifying, from God.[18]

BEARING THE CROSS: THE NATURE OF SUFFERING

Human suffering—whether "ills by fate assigned" or "misrule of our selfish mind" (4.18.150, 151)—also prompts unanswerable protests or laments. A demoniac in the Lower Gihon valley suffers from "private wrong outrageous" and "glared at heaven" in a nonverbal lament against God (1.11.26, 32). The suffering and loneliness of Nehemiah prompt the narrator to give over a skein of successive questions:

> since seldom yet
> Lone liver was, or wanderer met,
> Except he closeted some pain
> Or memory thereof. But thence
> May be, was given him deeper sense
> Of all that travail life can lend,
> Which man may scarce articulate
> Better than herds which share. What end?
> How hope? turn whither? . . .
>
> (1.8.12–20)

The inability to articulate Nehemiah's suffering leads to repeated theodicy questions. If human and nonhuman life share the common fate of biological "pain," how can human beings have hope and turn to a supposedly good God who has left humanity alone in the face of suffering, illness, death, and injustice? The brief, two-word, staccato questions cause and convey the sense of brokenness in the human-divine relationship. When Derwent tries to win Clarel's confidence, he speaks of the necessity of struggling with suffering and questions:

> Shall everything then plain be made?
> Not that there's any ambuscade:
> In youth's first heat to think to know!
> For time 'tis well to bear a cross:
>   (3.21.141–44)

Derwent tells Clarel why bearing the cross of suffering and, in Clarel's case, doubt is so difficult: "we dote / To dream heaven drops a casting vote, / In these perplexities takes part!" (3.21.168–69). God does not act as arbitrator to our questions. God does not answer our questions. Many even suffer the same fate as Jesus but without the "assurance" of heaven:

> But how of them whose souls may claim
> Some link with Christ beyond the name,
> Which share the fate, but never share
> Aid or assurance, and nowhere
> Look for requital? Such there be;
> In by-lanes o'er the world ye see
> The Calvary-faces. . . .
>   (4.10.42–48)

At the end of the poem, Clarel is one of these "Calvary faces," a cross-bearer walking the Via Dolorosa, the hard way of suffering, questions, and perplexities.

Clarel laments life as a quest made up of questions, as a pilgrimage of cross-bearing that leads to suffering and death. "Many shall fall, nor few shall die" before Mecca is seen (1.5.179), and all will remember the desert wastes.

> With skeletons but part interred—
> Relics of men which friendless fell;
> Whose own hands, in last office, scooped
> Over their limbs the sand, but drooped.
>   (1.5.172–75)

In the canto "The Island," the narrator retells the timoneer's allegory that compares the Encantadas to Palestine and the giant tortoises to suffering pilgrims:

> The smoke-wrapped peak, the inland one
> Volcanic; this, within its shroud
> Streaked black and red, burns unrevealed;
> It burns by night—by day the cloud
> Shows leaden all, and dull and sealed.
>
> (4.3.8–12)

Although there is no strict allegory here, the God-volcano is similar to the mountain of God—Sinai. The island mountain is covered with the figurative presence of God, the pillar of fire by night and the cloud by day, that also covers mount Sinai and the portable Tabernacle in Exodus (13:21–22; 24:15–17). But the presence of Melville's God in *Clarel* is hidden, "unrevealed," "sealed." Around the volcano is the "loneness" (4.3.15) of the ocean and the "silence" (4.3.22) of the island thickets.[19] The island also has the appearance of the Via Dolorosa or the worn stone shrines in the Church of the Holy Sepulcher:

> And yet a wasted look it hath,
> As it were traveled ceaselessly—
> Century after century—
> The rock in places much worn down
> Like to some old, old kneeling-stone
> Before a shrine. . . .
>
> (4.3.29–34)

The shells of the dead tortoises are compared to the "old skulls of Anaks" surrounding "Golgotha" (4.3.55, 56), and the living tortoise searches for water as the pilgrim searches for faith in a spiritually arid world: "Searching, he creeps with laboring neck, / Each crevice tries, and long may seek: / Water he craves, where rain is none—" (4.3.75–77). A parallel text here is Amos:

> Behold the days come, saith the Lord God, that I will send a famine in the land, not a famine of bread, nor a thirst for water, but of hearing the words of the Lord: And they shall wander from sea to sea, and from the north even to the east, they shall run to and fro to seek the word of the Lord, and shall not find it. (8:11–12)

The pilgrim-tortoise's life is "a hundred years of pain / And pilgrimage here to and fro" (4.3.86–87), and when exhausted with searching for the hidden face and word of God, he drops down in a "feint of death" (4.3.97). As the timoneer says, "As here, few there would think to smile" (4.3.99); Palestine and the Encantadas are no places for human joy. The timoneer himself embodies the fate of a man chastised to "Dumb patience of mere animal, / Which better may abide life's fate / Than comprehend" (4.3.105–7). When the Encantadas-Palestine allegory is over, Clarel puts a lament-question to himself, to the readers, and to God: "What may man know?" (4.3.107).

The suffering of life's fate also chastises the willful mariner in "A Sketch" to be "meek and reconciled; / Patient . . . " (1.37.98–99). The only positive aspect of physical suffering in *Clarel* is a renewed sense of priorities. Suffering weans one away from the will, and a too self-assertive attitude is condemned in *Clarel*. Thus Margoth and the Elder—two intolerant egotists—do not complete the pilgrimage, for they are not worthy of the quest for God and, significantly, never ask any questions. The final apathy that suffering can bring truly frightens Clarel. The monk-custodian at the Garden of Gethsemane speaks of James's and Peter's sleep in Luke 22:45–46:

> Nay, but excess of feeling pressed
> Till ache to apathy was won.
> To Clarel 'twas no hollow word.
> Experience did proof afford.
> (1.30.78–81)

Even the camaraderie and revelry of a good dinner and drinks at Mar Saba can only make the pilgrims "imparadised / For term how brief" (3.11.248–49) before death and suffering interrupt their party. As they clink their cups, a wail comes up from the valley of Kedron—an invalid's cry or lament to Christ for mercy and deliverance. Hedonism as a response to the suffering of life is totally rejected by this cry of distress. Anyone exempt from suffering in *Clarel*, no matter how briefly he may brighten the atmosphere of the pilgrimage, is seen as spiritually undeveloped, like Glaucon or the Cypriot. Melville's judgment in *Moby-Dick* holds true in *Clarel*: "So, therefore, that mortal man who hath more of joy than sorrow in him, that mortal man cannot be true— not true, or undeveloped" ("The Try-Works").

The paradigm of suffering in *Clarel* is Jesus' cry of distress "ELOI LAMA SABACHTHANI!" (3.7.1)—a lament to God for God to come out of hiddenness to end Jesus' suffering. The reiteration of this lament twice in the poem (1.13.47) and Clarel's echo of Jesus' cry (3.21.226–27) indicate that Melville's emphasis is on the suffering Jesus, not the Christ who died for humankind's sins. Rather than emulating Christ for his self-sacrificial nature, Melville focuses on the despair and suffering of the human death of Jesus on the cross—not a suffering whose purpose may be known and comprehended

in or beyond time but a suffering whose purpose is as hidden as the God who
sends it.

The "cry of cries" of Jesus on the cross—"My God, my God, why hast
thou forsaken me?" (Matthew 27:46; Mark 15:34)—has spread, according
to Mortmain, through the human heart until the resurrection of Easter is
questioned as a dubious message:

> Nor gone
> For every heart, whate'er they say,
> The eclipse that cry of cries brought down,
> And clamors through the darkness blown.
> More wide for some it spreads in sway,
> Involves the lily of the Easter Day.
>
> A chance word of the Swede in place—
> Allusion to the anguished face,
> Recalled to Clarel now the cry,
> The ghost's reproachful litany.
>
> (3.7.3–12)

Jesus' cry is a lament that reproaches God for forsaking him.

The cross is a symbol of suffering without redemption for some of the
characters in *Clarel*. Rolfe prefers the Latin cross over the Greek cross because
of its verisimilitude to the cross that held the suffering Jesus: "The Latin cross
(by that name known) / Holds the true semblance; that's the one / Was lifted
up and knew the nail" (3.18.46–48). Mortmain's response to the death of
Jesus is that although Jesus may have found hope on the cross, mere mortal
vessels can only feel pity for Jesus' and mankind's fate and then question the
presence of God:

> Cling to His tree, and there find hope:
> Me it but makes a misanthrope.
> Makes? nay, but 'twould, did not the hate
> Dissolve in pity of the fate.—
> This legend, dream, and *fact* of life!
> The drooping hands [Christ's], the dancing feet
> [Lesbian's]
> Which in the endless series meet;
> And rumors of *No God* so rife!
>
> (3.28.13–20)

Mortmain's lament against the suffering of Jesus is turned back upon God,
for he implies that the very existence of God must be questioned: "And

rumors of *No God* so rife!" For Agath, the Greek timoneer, the cross on his tattoo is also a sign of suffering during life's "wreckful way":

> Little I thought
> (A heedless lad, scarce through youth's straits—
> How hopeful on the wreckful way)
> What meant this thing which here ye see,
> The bleeding man upon the tree;
> Since then I've felt it, and the fates.
>
> (4.2.74–79)

In the presence of intense suffering, hopes are wrecked in *Clarel*. How fitting that the suffering pilgrims should follow the Greek pilot's tattooed cross and star to Bethlehem—"follow the star on the tattooed man" (4.2.142)—the cross that symbolizes suffering.[20]

It is essential to understand how Melville radically transforms theological conventions here. In the Pauline tradition, the cross was the symbol of Jesus' suffering, but through which the human is redeemed. The cross for some of the Clarelian voices, however, becomes a symbol of natural suffering without cause—from Golgotha to a tattoo. The Pauline tradition taught that by Jesus' death God delivered Christians from sin; and if no blame can be attached to an all-powerful, all-knowing, all-benevolent God for allowing Jesus to die on the cross, logically no blame can be attached to the instrument God chose and directed to attain His divine ends. The cross becomes, in this context, a symbol of salvation, not suffering; Jesus' death, rather than the tragedy of murder or the cruelty of the incarnation, becomes the forgiveness of sin.

Although he never explicitly stated it, Melville probably believed that Jesus' cry of abandonment—his lament—on the cross should remain unanswered, just like Clarel's cry over Ruth's grave remains unanswered. Perhaps Christianity's error was its attempt to answer for God the lament of Jesus by proclaiming that Jesus had risen from the dead, by accepting responsibility for the death of Jesus in human sinfulness, and by seeing the death of Jesus as the vehicle for salvation. In *Clarel*, the death and suffering of Jesus are the final signs of what it is to be human—a reminder of the human condition of suffering and death.

Just as Melville will not answer Jesus' lament of forsakenness with the hope of resurrection and salvation, he will not answer Clarel's lament for the resurrection and salvation of Ruth (4.33.64–66). Despite Clarel's poignant dirge for Ruth, he is left during Passion week "alone" and "in film of sorrow without moan" (4.32.8, 3). Despite his outward calm, Clarel experiences "no peace" (4.32.38) and is "oblivious" (4.32.55) to the greater meaning of Palm

Sunday. All he can do is walk the Via Crucis, just as Jesus did, with the procession of sufferers including Jews, monks, slaves, Turks, exiles, Moslem dames, starving Edomites, and overworked camels: "Cross-bearers all, alike they tend / And follow, slowly follow on" (4.34.43–44). Dogma may divide humanity, but suffering unites it.

This procession of sufferers is no walk into clarity for Clarel. Although many critics see Clarel's endurance and tragic awareness as positive aspects of surviving, Clarel experiences no acceptance and no message of cloven tongues of fire on Pentecost.[21] He is left only with silence and a return into the "obscurer town" (4.34.56): "They wire the world—far under sea / They talk; but never comes to me / A message from beneath the stone" (4.34.51–53). The dead remain dead. Although Robert Penn Warren reads Clarel's end as an "acceptance of the necessity for action" and a return to the world of mankind,[22] Clarel merely walks back into hiddenness, back to the universal procession of sufferers. It is tempting to interpret Clarel's suffering as a possible salutary incentive to change his life, such as those who recover from illness often attest to, yet the hopeful reading of Clarel's suffering that Warren looks for exists in the future and is beyond the story line of the poem. Reading the end of Clarel's pilgrimage prior to the Epilogue of hope leaves the reader with little whereby to mitigate the harshness of hiddenness, silence, disillusionment, suffering, and death.

The dialogical relationship in *Clarel* between what ought to be and what is, between theological interpretation and the lament over experience—life suffered through—is intricate. If Clarel's life is an unfulfilled romance of disillusionment, death, and suffering, then perhaps Melville is suggesting that the only solution for the unfulfilled romance is to make it absolutely unfulfilled. A half-fulfilled romance seeks no solution in life. Like Job, Clarel suffers but lives. Only when disappointment and suffering are complete—close to despair—does the Epilogue's encouragement come to hope. As Heraclitus suggested, the way down is also the way up. The way up, however, is apparent only to the readers, not to Clarel.

SUFFERING AND THE NATURE OF GOD

What Melville does not do, however, is to justify suffering and loss as necessary conditions for achieving awareness or maturity. Suffering might not instruct. Melville does mention a vague, unnamed lesson that Clarel learns from Vine—"From Vine he caught new sense / Developed through fate's pertinence" (4.32.11–12). Clarel, however, only learns that life is a lament against human fate and God's purposes. The palliative notion that God delivers the afflicted through their affliction (Job 36:15), that human beings grow through suffering by their ethical power or inner pathos to overcome suffering, is exactly what Job and Melville argue against. Nor will Melville change from lament and protest to the ethic of stoicism, which carries the admonition to bear suffering with patience and self-resignation. There is no resignation in Clarel's Hamlet-like behavior at Ruth's grave nor in his lament of "Where, Where now He who helpeth us, / The Comforter?" (4.32.103–4). Nor is there patience in *"Christ is arisen:* / But Ruth, may Ruth so burst the prison?"; nor in "but never comes to me / A message from beneath the stone" (4.33.65–66; 4.34.52–53).

Behind the complaints and laments of unfulfilled romance, death, and suffering lies the fundamental question of the presence and nature of God. As Mortmain asks by the Dead Sea, "Is God an omnipresent God? / Is He in Siddim yonder?" (3.6.56–57). On the one hand, if God cannot provide the reason why humans suffer and die, then God would appear to be somehow responsible for human suffering and death. On the other hand, if God chooses to be so silent and hidden that characters such as Mortmain and Clarel question His very existence in the presence of suffering and death, then one face of that hidden God is further concealed by human suffering. When the reason for and purpose of that suffering is unknown to human beings, they can accept suffering on faith or protest and lament God's injustice, God's hiddenness, and God's silence. The deeper theological resonance of Melville's lament is that, insofar as the lament is a protest against God's silence, it is also a call to God to absolve Himself of His involvement in human suffering and death. Only God can put an end to the endless to-and-fro of questions: "The running battle of the star and clod / Shall run forever—if there be no God" (4.35.16–17). Only God can put human suffering into perspective. Only God can provide the context within which suffering and death is comprehensible or at least bearable.

Although they are grammatically otherwise, the questions put to the hidden God throughout the poem act as declarative reminders of human limitations and divine mystery. The questions in *Clarel*, even though God never speaks in the poem, perform the same function as God's question to Job: "Where wast thou when I laid the foundations of the earth?" (Job 38:4). Although Job experiences revelation, whereas Clarel does not, God's questions from the whirlwind teach Job that the cosmos does not correlate to any human view of morality, equity, or justice. The inscrutable God does not take away all pain, and the universe is not necessarily rational or reasonable and certainly does not answer the human lament over undeserved suffering and death: "Have the gates of death been opened unto thee? or hast thou seen the doors of the shadow of death?" (Job 38:17). The Jobian God certainly admits that the world is not perfect when He sarcastically challenges Job to destroy evil with his human hand:

Cast abroad the rage of thy [Job's] wrath; and behold every one that is proud, and abase him. Look on every one that is proud, and bring him low; and tread down the wicked in their place. . . . Then will I also confess unto thee that thine own right hand can save thee. (Job 40:11– 14)

But the presence of laments in the poem does not necessarily mean that God, hope, and faith are distortions or falsehoods. Creation's design may be too complex for the human mind that has no deep knowledge of creation. In Job and in *Clarel* so much is dark, incomplete, and unanswered, for such is the Jobian poet's and Melville's stance toward a mysterious, inscrutable God. Humankind is incapable of clear-cut answers when asking questions about God, suffering, or death: the greatest mysteries of the universe. Questions remain open and are simply joined to the next question. Questions unasked, however, are far worse than questions unanswered.

Melville circles around the laments against God, suffering, and death in the totality in which they can be experienced and admits that it is not in our power to understand them. No matter how we try to answer such unanswerable laments, they become lost again in mystery. Divine mystery has always been the theological handmaiden of human limitation. Rather than thinking that there is a hostile God in league with nature against a rebellious or even a resigned humanity and that all of human suffering and fate are attributed to such a hostile God or to a sinful humanity, the laments point again to a Melvillean response of limitation and awe before a mysterious God. More than limitation and mystery, questions indicate Melville's rejection of philosophical theology and its abstract conclusions. For Melville, God will not be found in answers, in any concession to popular religion or creed, but only in questions. In a sense, Melville's laments cry out with humankind in pain yet, at the same time, give God the freedom to be God in all his inexplicable mysteriousness: "For my thoughts are not your thoughts, neither are your ways my ways, saith the Lord" (Isaiah 55:8). The Melvillean lament implies that the inscrutable mystery of a transcendent God is the central basis for any faith. Melville had many fellow pilgrims in the Bible who had the courage to lament but maintained faith in mystery. Job, Koheleth, Jeremiah, and even Moses and Abraham doubted and painfully rejected accepted beliefs such as "the righteous will prosper."

Although the laments and questions of Job, Ecclesiastes, and *Clarel* remain unanswered, the passionate and persistent quest for the answers to these questions earns our respect. In a sense, the quest for God is our ability to ask questions. Even though Ecclesiastes suggests that this striving for knowledge of the world and of God's mysterious ways is vanity and a chasing after the wind, *Clarel*, Ecclesiastes, and Job also imply that we can no more stop asking questions about God, death, and suffering than we can stop being human (see Ecclesiastes 7:24–25). The passionate quest, the protesting lament made up of theodicy questions, inspired Melville to write a twenty-thousand-line poem to God. In the meanwhile, all one can do is lament: "How long, O Lord?"

❖

CHAPTER THREE

God-Wrestling

The Thematics and Poetics of "Contraries"

Content thee: in conclusion caught
Thou'lt find how thought's extremes agree—
The forethought clinched by afterthought,
The firstling by finality.
                                        —*Clarel*

Doubts of all things earthly, and intuitions of some
things heavenly; this combination makes neither believer nor infidel, but makes a man who regards
them both with equal eye.
                                        —*Moby-Dick*

MELVILLE'S PILGRIMS NOT ONLY LAMENT a life of unfulfilled romance, undeserved suffering, and unredeemed death, but they also struggle with the
seeming opposites of faith and doubt. Although the questions in *Clarel* indicate an interrogative mode of thinking and a language of intense suffering
biblically associated with the lament, Melville offers a metaphorical recommendation for the need to go beyond protest, beyond complaint, and beyond
doubt by wrestling with spiritual questions. The supreme spiritual God-
wrestler for Melville was Jacob.

The mysterious encounter of the patriarch Jacob with an angel of God was
of especial intertextual importance to Melville as an example of the painful
struggle between the human and the divine. As Jacob wrestled with the angel,
as Job wrestled with God—"but I will maintain mine own ways before him"
(Job 13:15)—Melville also wrestled with "contraries." Immersed in the ambiguity of human existence lived between opposite extremes, Melville explored
the intense oppositions involved in literary creativity and in God-wrestling in
his poem entitled "Art":

In placid hours well-pleased we dream
Of many a brave unbodied scheme.
But form to lend, pulsed life create,
What unlike things must meet and mate:

A flame to melt—a wind to freeze;
Sad patience—joyous energies;
Humility—yet pride and scorn;
Instinct and study; love and hate;
Audacity—reverence. These must mate,
And fuse with Jacob's mystic heart,
To wrestle with the angel—Art.[1]

Jacob is not only what William H. Shurr calls Melville's "figure for the poet," but he was also a prenatal wrestler; his name in Hebrew—*Ya'acov*—is said to mean he who grabs a heel (at birth): "And after that came his brother out, and his [Jacob's] hand took hold on Esau's heel . . . " (Genesis 25:26).[2] Jacob is best known, however, for his night wrestling at the Jabbok brook in Genesis 32:23–32. Before wrestling with the angel of God, Jacob crosses over the brook, leaves his family and possessions on one side, then crosses back, and is left alone with the divine wrestler: "And he took them, and sent them over the brook, and sent over that he had. And Jacob was left alone, and there wrestled a man with him until the breaking of the day" (Genesis 32:23–24). In "Art" and in *Clarel,* wrestling also involves the notion of crossing a threshold, of going from human-space to God-space, not merely a geographical space but a theological space. Certainly the characters in *Clarel* are wanderers, crossing various thresholds, in search of self and God. In addition to threshold-crossing, wrestling in Genesis, in "Art," and in *Clarel* includes the notion of embracing or joining. The great medieval midrashist Rashi wrote one of the most extraordinary philological insights into Jacob's God-wrestling when he pointed out that "to join" in Aramaic is related to "embrace" and "wrestle." Thus Rashi claimed that the mysterious being who wrestles with (or hugs) Jacob in Genesis 32:24 is anticipating Jacob's brotherly embrace or hug of Esau when they are reconciled a few verses later in Genesis 33:4. The same cognates are used in both verses. Melville knew and used a few Hebrew words, other than names of people and places in the Bible, such as *"Marah"* (2.34.63) and *"shekinah"* (4.9.46), but there is no definitive evidence that he had access to rabbinic biblical commentaries—*midrashim.* But even in Melville's King James English translation, wrestling as a metaphor has a semantic field that reaches out in several metaphorical and theological directions. Another metaphorical direction is that, after God-wrestling, one has the renewed hope of the sun rising: "And as he [Jacob] passed over Penuel the sun rose upon him, and he halted upon his thigh" (Genesis 32:31). Jacob's enigmatic encounter in the darkness on the banks of the Jabbok ends in life rather than in death. The angel of night or perhaps of death flees with the coming of the dawn, and the God-wrestler has seen a dangerous face of God—a God who wants human beings to resist Him. Of course, this hope is immediately qualified by the image of Jacob-Israel limping away in pain. I am suggesting that for Melville there was grounded in the idea and image of God-wrestling an entire metaphysics of God-searching, threshold-crossing, and the wrestling-joining of pain and hope. The fusing of Jacob and the divine angel in a wrestler's grip metaphorically illustrates the divine-human continuum in *Clarel* and implies that wrestling provides the way to an authentic and deeper experience of God, although at great personal risk and cost: "And he [the angel] said, Let me go, for the day breaketh. And he [Jacob] said, I will not let thee go, except thou bless me" (Genesis 32:26).

The theological crux of Jacob's agon with God's messenger and his subsequent injury in the hollow of the thigh is his endurance, his will to struggle with his unknown antagonist until he sees God face to face. Thus Jacob called the place of his struggle "Peniel: for I have seen God face to face, and my life is preserved" (Genesis 32:30). Jacob's wrestling suggests that a hidden God who is questioned, resisted, and wrestled against may eventually reveal Himself. Jacob's struggle, with his resulting injury, is the sign of both his heroism and his agony. An affirmation of life or faith or art—the blessing and the new name of Israel that Jacob receives from the angel—clearly, however, includes pain.

Read as a gateway into *Clarel*, Melville's metaphor of wrestling in "Art" is more important theologically than as a possible Melvillean theory of literary imagination perhaps similar to Coleridge's esemplastic power of the imagination to reconcile opposites defined in the first chapter of *Biographia Literaria*. Melville's series of sharp opposites such as "audacity—reverence" suggests that wrestling is a distinct Melvillean artistic, psychological, and theological metaphor. The experiences of literary creativity, of selfhood, and of theological reflection in *Clarel* take place in a world of burning contradictions, but these opposites must be "fused" according to "Art" and *Clarel* into a coalescence of thought. "Art" suggests the difficulty of holding two seemingly opposite necessities of truth in the mind and heart at once. The dualities of "Art" are not necessarily reconciled into one higher power but are held over against one another dialogically until fused within the heart—the seat of human emotions, understanding, selfhood, and divinity in *Clarel*. The "audacity" to question or to doubt seems antithetical to reverence until both are contemplated within the heart, within the self.

THE AGON

The intertextual relationship between Genesis 32, "Art," and *Clarel* is centered on the image and idea of God-wrestling (the etymological meaning of Jacob's new name—Israel), the quintessential Israelite and Melvillean experience.[3] Melville recontextualized Jacob's wrestling as a human metaphor for the struggle of the self with antithetical ideas or dualities. As a psychological metaphor, wrestling insists that the mind develop the ability to contemplate "thought's extremes" in what Melville called a "Pocahontas-wedding / Of contraries . . . " (2.18.141; 1.28.32–33). As a theological metaphor, wrestling suggests that we may come to recognize a need for faith only after a painful, but heroic, struggle with its assumed opposite—doubt. Melville's conviction was that one can achieve faith only after wrestling with doubt and darkness and then wresting a blessing or insight from the struggle. Furthermore, Melville's idea of wrestling in Clarel is a heroic struggle that goes against born-again enthusiasm. Spirituality comes after human struggle, hard work rather than supernatural intervention. True faith is a struggle from within, not a lightning bolt from without. The Melvillean God-wrestler can achieve a disciplined self-control—what Melville calls "ripeness"—whereby one demonstrates caution toward any claim of theological imperialism, absolute atheism, or overzealous enthusiasm. Most important, such self-control or ripeness teaches tolerance—a generous openness to other ideas, traditions, and mysteries rather than a hardening into dogmatism and orthodoxy or the failure of imagination that characterizes religious fundamentalism.[4]

In the metaphor and idea of wrestling with moral and theological contraries, we recognize the spirit of scripture. Stark "either/or" contraries are deeply biblical: life versus death, righteous versus wicked, wise versus foolish, spirit versus flesh, mercy versus judgment, faith versus doubt, presence versus hiddenness, heaven versus hell. Through self-development based on the fusing of opposites and on austere self-control, the ideal Melvillean God-wrestler in Clarel resembles the ideal sage who exhibits order and self-control as portrayed in Proverbs. Beyond the thematics of the poem, we realize that Clarel's poetic structure is also organized around such contraries: whole cantos are set in opposition, and within cantos are juxtaposed opposite emotional stances. Other than the episodic nature of the pilgrimage and the structural characteristic of biblical intertextuality, Clarel's primary principle of organization (seemingly so unsystematic) is based upon the biblical swings in emotion and opposite moods found in the Psalms and suggests that Melville regarded his poem as a nineteenth-century Psalter. In the Psalms, we find the primary inspiration for the structure, tone, and the number of cantos (150) of Clarel. Thus the wrestling with contraries is not only a thematic concern; the poetic structure of Clarel is itself complementary.[5] Or, as it says in Ecclesiasticus, the Wisdom of Jesus the Son of Sirach, an Apocryphal text Melville knew, "Look upon all the work of the Most High; they likewise are in pairs, one the opposite of the other" (33:15).[6]

In what are perhaps the most cryptic lines in Clarel, Melville suggests that after painful struggle two contrary ideas may actually "agree"—as if paradoxes can be resolved over time and after struggle:

Content thee: in conclusion *caught*
Thou'lt find how thought's extremes agree—
The forethought *clinched* by afterthought,
The firstling by finality.
                    (2.18.140–43, emphasis mine)

Although these mysterious words that "slipped into" the Syrian monk from an unidentified source (perhaps an inner divine voice) can be read eschatologically according to Stanley Brodwin—"truth will ultimately be verified in the fullness of time and that death will reveal immortality"—these lines also suggest that the contrast between extreme thoughts may be actually a coalescence.[7] The words "caught" and "clinched" connote the sense of wrestling with "thought's extremes," "firstling by finality." Throughout his painful debate with Satan, the monk struggles with contraries. He expresses his belief in God—"Faith bideth," "He is there"—yet, at the same time, recognizes that doubt accompanies faith: "But He, He *is*, though doubt attend" (2.18.111, 100, 124). Faith and doubt are clinched together in the monk's mind. He can contemplate at once the seemingly opposite thoughts of God's presence ("He is") and the painful awareness of His absence—"O God (I prayed), come through / The cloud; hard task Thou settest man / To know Thee . . . " (2.18.133–35). The monk not only has the ability to think of two unlike concepts at once but also possesses a range in his scale of thinking—a gradation between extreme thoughts, a "both/and" instead of an "either/or" thinking.

Throughout *Clarel*, Melville insists on a coalescence of opposites: a "Pocahontas-wedding / Of contraries . . . " (1.28.32–33). Here, the narrator refers to a carving above a tomb that paradoxically juxtaposes green palm leaves with death. The narrator interprets the incongruity of "bloom, / Involved in death . . . " (1.28.28–29) in terms of the ancient conflict between Athens and Jerusalem: the pastoral of Theocritus versus the terror of Joel (1.28.30–31) and in terms of Matthew Arnold's "Hellenic cheer, Hebraic grief" (1.28.34). The yoking together of Joel and Theocritus introduces yet another coalescence of opposites in the character and personality of Vine who makes his first appearance by the sculptured tomb: "A funeral man, yet richly fair" (1.28.42).

The wedding of contraries in the poem is part of Melville's broader interpretation of the multiple faces of God and nature. Just as God is a pair of ideas or faces in *Clarel*—hiddenness and presence, "beauty" and "terror" (1.13.96)—so, too, is nature a pair of faces, "spleen" and "love": "The spleen of nature and her love: / At variance, yet entangled too— / Like *wrestlers* . . . " (3.5.32–34, emphasis mine). Melville insists upon ending gnostic dualism—to see the oneness in multiplicity. Just as nature's face of "spleen" is not really at

"variance" with nature's other face of "love," for they are "entangled" like
wrestlers, one god must not be "held against" another god (3.5.44). In this
canto ("The High Desert," 3.5), Melville lists his contraries: Jehovah's wrath
and Jesus' mercy, Abel and Cain, Ormuzd and Ahriman. The concept of God
is a radical oneness that encompasses both Jehovah's traits and Christ's. Evil is
also united with its opposite, good, into one braided cord—"Evil and good
they braided play / Into one cord" (4.4.27–28)—like the harmonic coalescence of the strophe and antistrophe of the Armenian singers carrying their
bier to the graveyard.

If God is experienced as several pairs of opposing ideas in *Clarel*—mercy
and judgment, hiddenness and presence, good and evil—surely the human
made in the image of God will also express itself in combined dualities. The
god-men described in the canto "Of Rama," that ideal picture of the divine
within the human, possess dual characteristics: "Theirs be the thoughts that
dive and skim, / Theirs the spiced tears that overbrim, / And theirs the dimple
and the lightsome whim" (1.32.35–37). God-men are capable of deep-
diving, profound thought and lightly skimming, superficial thought; they
experience the "tears" of sadness and the "lightsome whim" of joy and humor.
The unusual wisdom and selfhood of god-men enable them to "tell / Of
riddles in the prosiest lot" (1.32.40–41), in other words, to express difficult
thought simply—to dive and to skim.

THE MANY SIDES OF DUALITY

Just as the silent Clarelian characters imitate God's hiddenness and silence,
several characters also express the dualities of God and god-men: those who
have learned the art of wrestling. The pious but thieving crusaders exemplify
the human "complex moods," for "in that age / Belief devout and bandit rage
/ Frequent were joined . . . " (1.4.11–13). The apparently incongruous characteristics of belief and bandit rage are joined together in a complex synthesis
called "man" (1.4.10).

The Dominican monk, the spokesman for Catholicism in the poem, has a
"certain lure" (2.26.59), an ability to persuade others because he too is a
unique combination of contraries. He calls himself a "Catholic Democrat" and
is able to reconcile "those terms" because any Catholic may "aspire to sit in
Peter's chair" (2.25.81, 84, 90). Although the Dominican wants nineteenth-
century Christians to return to the pious age of Hildebrand (2.26.39), the
monk is also well-versed in the modern, liberal age of reason: "This intellectual
man— / Half monk, half tribune, partisan" (2.26.53–54). He can "win over
men" because he is "disinterested" yet "earnest" in his cause, "pure" yet "liberal" of others' views (2.26.62, 60–61).

Vine also exhibits a controlled synthesis of opposite characteristics.[8] He is a

combination of austere strictness and sensuous voluptuousness: "in sort
Carthusian / Tho' born a Sybarite . . . " (1.29.38–39). Under his soft appearance lies austere self-control: "Under cheer / Of opulent softness, reigned
austere / Control of self . . . " (1.29.30–32). He "communed with men" but
only like a nun talking "thro' the wicket" (1.29.44–45). Vine combines
involvement and detachment in one self; some men are in the world but not
of it. When Vine discovers Nehemiah drowned by the shore of the Dead
Sea—certainly no nineteenth-century deathbed scene—he is able to control
his alarm at encountering death:

> Since many a prior revery grave
> Forearmed against alarm's control.
> To him, indeed, each lapse and end
> Meet—in harmonious method blend.
> (2.39.27–30)

Throughout his life, Vine forearmed himself against death's alarm by contemplating death along with life. Contemplating apparent opposites, here Vine
suggests that the end of a life is merely a temporal or spiritual lapse, and that
life and death intertwine in a "harmonious . . . blend."

Rolfe, perhaps preeminently, has an extraordinary ability to join together
antithetical ideas. He praises Christianity's hope of heaven in the canto "Of
The Many Mansions" and then attacks it as "Circe's fooling spell" (3.3.27).
Clarel, at one point, is so confused by Rolfe's synthesizing mind that he
would prefer a person who is a strong partisan of his own opinions rather
than the many-sided Rolfe:

> Better a partisan!
> Earnest he seems: can union be
> 'Twixt earnestness and levity?
> Or need at last in Rolfe confess
> Thy hollow, Manysidedness!
> (3.16.259–63)

Clarel cannot understand Rolfe's character that joins opposites such as "earnestness" and "levity." Clarel calls Rolfe "hollow," for he fails to understand
"Manysidedness"—not an inability to take a stand but a generous openness
to many sides with a zealous commitment to none.[9] Like the god-man in "Of
Rama," Rolfe's selfhood is expressed in pairs of characteristics. Earlier in the
pilgrimage, Clarel almost recognizes Rolfe's many-sidedness as a winning
trait:

> But he winneth yet
> Through taking qualities which join.
> Make these the character? the rest
> But rim? On Syracusan coin
> The barbarous letters shall invest
> The relievo's infinite of charm.
>   (2.10.239–44)

Like the "barbarous" letters that only accentuate the background on the coin, Rolfe's "bluntness" (2.10.238) brings out his positive qualities of kindness and tolerance.

Clarel's major character flaw, on the other hand, is precisely his inability to yoke two thoughts together. He cannot practice the Dominican's pure faith plus liberal tolerance, nor Vine's opposites of self, nor Rolfe's many-sidedness. The young student wants simple either/or answers, what he calls a "saving truth" (2.22.139). When Rolfe, Vine, and Derwent discuss two apostate Jews—the "visionary" Spinoza and "the blind man" Margoth—who are poles apart, Clarel must know who is right: "And whose the eye that sees aright, / If any? . . . " (2.22.128, 129–30). Clarel's insistence upon one final answer to unanswerable questions is alien to the pilgrims: "And none responded. 'Twas like night / Descending from the seats of light" (2.22.132–33). Because Clarel is "little versed / In men, their levities and tides / Unequal. . . . " (3.14.95–97), he cannot understand the pilgrims' revelry at Mar Saba that follows so soon after Nehemiah's death: "Are these the pilgrims late that heard / The wheeling desert vultures scream / Above the Man and Book interred" (3.14.116–18). Clarel's inability to maintain two propositions at once is like the youthful inexperience of an adolescent puzzled by the party after a funeral. The narrator, who continually reminds us of man's complex, oppositional moods, depicts the pilgrim-revelers as "problematic shapes" (3.14.138) "In linked caprice of festal air / Graved round the Greek sarcophagi" (3.14.139–40). As Melville writes in "Marquis De Grandvin" (*The Burgundy Club Sketches*), life is a "mingled brew," both "wine and brine." Confused by the antithetical themes of the Mar Saba masque—a dramatization of the alienated wandering Jew followed by a poem celebrating the sympathy between gods and humans during the Golden Age of Greece— Clarel wants to know who is right: Jerusalem or Athens, the terror of Joel or the joy of Greek sculpture and Titian's art.

> But Clarel, bantered by the song,
> Sad questioned, if in frames of thought
> And feeling, there be right and wrong;
> Whether the lesson Joel taught

Confute what from the marble's caught
In sylvan sculpture—Bacchant, faun,
Or shapes more lax by Titian drawn.
Such counter natures in mankind.

(3.20.32–39)

Clarel does not understand the "counter natures," the opposites within "mankind." Troubled by "the din of clashed belief" (3.21.98) in Palestine, Clarel searches for one right or wrong, "one secure retreat" (3.21.120). Security, however, will not come to Clarel until he too wrestles with the contraries of human existence.

REVERENT SKEPTICISM: COMMON DOUBT VERSUS HEROIC DOUBT

The greatest struggle within the self for Melville is the wrestling with theological doubt—reverent skepticism. In *Clarel*, an immersion in skeptical thought is necessary for a tested faith: to contend with doubt and belief at the same time. Such a struggle does not necessarily lead to atheism but may help one to a belief based on need rather than metaphysical or theological certitude. One thing is certain in *Clarel*: those who follow any dogma or creed without any wrestling with doubt are rejected as intolerant dogmatists, as undeveloped selves. The survivors of the pilgrimage other than Clarel—Rolfe, Vine, and Derwent—do not demonstrate any deep inner commitment to God, but they do respect tradition and faith. As reverent skeptics, they wrestle with doubt and faith, suspend their judgment, and demonstrate reverence, tolerance, and the need for faith and charity unsullied by sectarianism and dogmatism.

One reason *Clarel* and other major works by Melville are often misread is that, like Pierre Bayle and Montaigne, Melville comes to an indirect, qualified faith only after wrestling with skeptical disillusionment in both the fulfillment of God's promises and the limits of human knowledge. Melville is often read as anti-God or anti-faith because the coalescence of two contraries—doubt and faith—is incompatible for some thinkers. Thus critics such as Lawrance Thompson and T. Walter Herbert, Jr., say Melville veiled his agnosticism with irony; a critic such as John Seelye insists that Clarel's theological quest is futile and faith is extinguished.[10] The pilgrimage from skepticism to an indirect faith is no doubt an inconsistent journey but one that must be traveled. An uncritical faith unprepared by wrestling with doubt is not tenable in *Clarel*. A critical doubt that does not expose itself to the possibility of faith is also mere arrogance and dogmatism.

When Nathan searches for some belief worthy of commitment, he must first wrestle.

> Alone, and at Doubt's freezing pole
> He *wrestled* with the pristine forms
> Like the first man. By inner storms
> Held in solution, so his soul
> Ripened for hour of such control
> As shapes, concretes. . . .
>   (1.17.193–98, emphasis mine)

The poetic power of these lines indicates that such wrestling is heroic for Melville. The struggle is an internal battle—"inner storms"—and has a long intellectual tradition back to Adam, "the first man." Eventually, after man wrestles at the pole of doubt, he may achieve a ripened form of self-control— a way of handling the extremes of thought. Unfortunately, Nathan is a spiritual window-shopper and tries Christianity, Deism, Pantheism, and then the "recoil" (1.17.234) from doubt to extreme Zionism. Nathan's Jewish faith, however, is the radical "zeal" (1.17.241) of a proselyte—the fervor of a convert whose faith outdistances even the belief of Agar, his wife, who was born into the Jewish faith. Nathan's tragic flaw is his overzealousness, and his eventual murder, because of Nathan's stubborn refusal to return to the protection of the city, comes as no surprise. Zeal kills in *Clarel*.

Clarel must also wrestle with doubt: "So doubts invaded, found him out. / He strove with them; but they proved stout, / Nor would they down" (1.16.153–55). Rather than ending in self-control, Clarel's wrestling with doubt causes only vacillation: "Doubt had unhinged so, that her sway, / In minor things even, could retard / The will and purpose . . . " (4.16.109–11). Clarel is unable to "untwine the ravelment / Of doubts perplexed . . . " (1.5.45–46). Despite Clarel's weakness as a theological wrestler, the narrator stresses that even Clarel must pass through skeptical thought before reaching any conclusions: "shall Clarel too / Launch o'er *his* gulf, e'en Doubt, and woo / Remote conclusions?" (1.41.75–77). The narrator's rhetorical question implies that something is beyond doubt: perhaps atheism or faith, certainly pain. When Clarel reads Celio's journal, Clarel learns how some skeptics struggle heroically with doubt:

> A second self therein he found,
> But stronger—with the heart to brave
> All questions on that primal ground
> Laid bare by faith's receding wave.
>   (1.19.26–29)

Celio is a much stronger skeptic than Clarel because Celio has the courage to ask questions.

Clarel eventually learns, however, to cherish the interrogative, skeptical habit of mind despite its pain and uncertainty:

> But whither now, my heart? wouldst fly
> Each thing that keepeth not the pace
> Of *common uninquiring* life?
> What! fall back on clay commonplace?
> Yearnest for peace so? sick of *strife*?
> Yet how content thee with routine
> Worldly? how mix with tempers keen
> And narrow like the knife? how live
> At all, if once a fugitive
> From thy own nobler part, though pain
> Be portion inwrought with the gain?
> (4.28.74–84, emphasis mine)

Here, Clarel makes a most important distinction between the "common uninquiring life"—one without questions—and the "nobler part" of life—one with questions despite the accompanying "pain." Pilgrims may yearn for peace of mind, but there is no peace if the cost is an unexamined life; there is only a radical questioning of God and His purposes, a dialog between doubt and faith. Nathan's wrestling, Celio's brave questioning, Clarel's strife—all point toward a Melvillean understanding of reverent skepticism based on questioning. Doubt becomes a challenge to faith but, at the same time, a preparation for or a development of a tested faith.

Common doubt is to be distinguished from passionate doubt in *Clarel*. Because critics have centered on common doubt, they read doubt as a negative phenomenon in *Clarel*. Richard H. Fogle, for example, writes: "Doubt is a negative, which inevitably hampers [Clarel's] imagination by short-circuiting possible meanings and relationships."[11] The most interesting explication of common doubt belongs to Rolfe as he compares the age of Cicero to the nineteenth century:

>   doubt ran,
> Faith flagged; negations which sufficed
> Lawyer, priest, statesman, gentleman,
> Not yet being popularly prized,
> The augurs hence retained some state—
> Which served for the illiterate.
> Still, the decline so swiftly ran
> From stage to stage, that *To Believe*,
> Except for slave or artisan,

> Seemed heresy. Even doubts which met
> Horror at first, grew obsolete,
> And in a decade. To bereave
> Of founded trust in Sire Supreme,
> Was a vocation. . . .
>
> (1.31.237–50)

Common doubt—"popularly prized" by the masses—eventually leads to the "atheism" of Caesar, when "the gods were gone" (1.31.253, 255). Common doubt without some faith degenerates from indiscriminate skepticism to the negativity of cynicism and the dogmatism of atheism. Common doubt is as hard and unyielding as a complete deference to any dogma. Rolfe laments the pandemic spread of common doubt because it brings not only irreverence but also a leveling effect of mediocrity:

> Doubt's heavy hand
> Is set against us; and his brand
> Still warreth for his natural lord—
> King Common-Place—whose rule abhorred
> Yearly extends in vulgar sway,
>
> . . . .
>
> Ah, change irreverent—at odds
> With goodly customs, gracious gods.
>
> (1.34.20–24, 36–37)

The irreverence of common doubt threatens "goodly customs" and traditions. Common doubt can become so popular that belief itself becomes the minority response to God:

> *Doubt* late was an aristocrat;
> But now the barbers' clerks do swell
> In cast clothes of the infidel;
> The more then one can now *believe*,
> The more one's differenced, perceive,
> From ribald common-place. . . .
>
> (2.26.47–52)

Melville, however, ultimately negates this common, superficial agnosticism—that nineteenth-century neologism first used by Thomas Huxley—because some agnostics are content to give up the search for metaphysical truths. Although *Clarel* points to the limits of human knowledge, the limits of theological claims made by believers (see the cheats of "The Easter Fire,"

3.16, and "The Sepulcher," 1.2), the limits of truth claimed by any one religion (see references to comparative religion, e.g., 1.31.207–30), and the limits of religious explanations of physical phenomena (4.18.11–19), *Clarel* still does not dictate an agnostic position. Instead, Melville suggests another kind of doubt: a passionate, heroic doubt, where the true wrestler doubts but never gives up the search for *gnosis*.

The passionate doubter is, first of all, extremely earnest, like Rolfe who ironically claims to want to skim rather than to dive deep intellectually. After an earnest, passionate, forty-line lament about the hidden Christ, the unful-filled romance of early Christianity, and the limits of science, he clearly dem-onstrates a sense of ironic self-deprecation when he says, "this earnest way / I hate. Let doubt alone; best skim, / Not dive" (2.21.101–3). Elsewhere, the narrator, for instance, defends Celio's skepticism because it is a passionate doubt worthy of the same "martyr's leaf" as was the first Christian martyr, St. Stephen:

> If Leopardi, stoned by Grief
> A young St. Stephen of the Doubt,
> Might merit well the martyr's leaf;
> In these if *passion* held her claim,
> Let Celio pass, of breed the same.
> (1.14.3–7, emphasis mine)

Celio's earnest questioning, Clarel's eventual refutation of the "common uninquiring life," Nathan's early heroic wrestling—all are instances of a pas-sionate doubt that Melville admired and compared to the heroism of faith that inspires "swordsmen of the priestly sword / Wielded in spiritual fight" (2.26.67–68). Vine's admonition to Clarel earlier in the poem emphasizes that each person must struggle with doubt—to "live it out": "Lives none can help ye; that believe. / Art thou the first soul tried by doubt? / Shalt prove the last? Go, live it out" (2.27.121–23).

Those who do live it out are the heroic wrestlers who never give up their skeptical questioning, such as the "bold freethinking" Jews: Uriel Acosta, Heine, Mendelssohn, and Spinoza (2.22.55, "Concerning Hebrews"). From the very beginnings of faith, faith "leaned" or was questioned by doubters: "Faith's leaning tower was founded so: / Faith leaned from the beginning; yes / If slant, she holds her steadfastness" (2.22.59–61). Heroic doubters do not threaten the "steadfastness" of faith because they are men of passionate "con-viction," men of "sincerest minds" (2.22.99, 100), who question not to destroy religion but to understand, to know. Heroic doubters struggle through their doubt—whether Judaic or Christian—but do not change reli-gions, since all creeds are subject to the burning flames of doubt:

> Is't him [Mendelssohn] you cite? True spirit staid,
> He, though his honest heart was scourged
> By doubt Judaic, never laid
> His burden at Christ's door; he urged—
> Admit the mounting flames enfold
> My basement; wisely shall my feet
> The attic win, for safe retreat?
>
> (2.22.85–91)

Passionate, heroic doubters cry the anguished cry of doubt and skepticism voiced by mankind from Job to Hamlet: "I do not know."

> Ah, wherefore not at once name Job,
> In whom these Hamlets all conglobe.
> Own, own with me, and spare to feign,
> Doubt bleeds, nor Faith is free from pain!
> (3.21.301–4)

Doubt and faith, although seeming opposites, are juxtaposed in one sentence here because the relationship between doubt and faith in *Clarel* is not doubt against its opposite, faith, but doubt combined with its congruity, faith. Skepticism, for Melville, is not only heroic questioning but also wrestling with contrary ideas at once, as in *Moby-Dick*: "Doubts of all things earthly, and intuition of some things heavenly; this combination makes neither believer nor infidel, but makes a man who regards them both with equal eye."[12] Apropos of Hawthorne's famous evaluation of Melville as a man who "can neither believe nor be comfortable in his unbelief,"[13] Melville demonstrates the crux of skepticism in *Clarel*. If one concentrates only on one side of the evidence for God, one becomes an atheist. If one concentrates only on the other side of the evidence, one becomes an absolute believer. If, however, one accepts both sides together without any presuppositions, one becomes a Melvillean reverent skeptic, a God-wrestler. The will to believe and the will to doubt are both part of the faith-response in *Clarel*.

SKEPTICISM, FAITH, CONTROL: THE PROVERBIAL WISDOM OF THE "MIDDLE WAY"

It is essential to understand that in *Clarel* Melville is not following his Victorian contemporaries in England. Melville does not claim, as did Tennyson in *In Memoriam*, that "there lives more faith in honest doubt / Believe me, than in half the creeds" (96.11–12). Nor would he agree with Browning that doubt may "occasion still more faith" ("Bishop Blougram's Apology").[14] Melville, however, contends that there is a range to the scale of denial, doubt, and belief. There is heroic doubt in some believers and heroic belief in some doubters. Since people have a natural tendency to dogmatize, which gives peace of mind and answers, the shock value of skeptical thought is positive because it destroys the pretentiousness of absolute knowledge and the spiritual pride of theological certitude. Melville suggests that characters who begin with doubt may end in certainty, but the majority of those pilgrims who begin with certainty, will simply end in dogmatism. Although there are believers and atheists met along the journey, Melville does not allow absolute believers or atheists to finish the pilgrimage.

The narrator explains Clarel's attraction to Celio in terms of faith and doubt, where faith meets disbelief upon the common ground of skepticism:

> Mutual in approach may glide
> Minds which from poles adverse have come,
> Belief and unbelief? may doom
> Of doubt make such to coincide—
> Upon one frontier brought to dwell
>
> (1.15.54–58)

Doubt is an element of both the desire for faith and atheism and can make these seeming opposites coincide. The point is that the polar opposites of traditional Western theology do not exist on the theological scale of denial, doubt, and belief in *Clarel*. When Derwent chastises Clarel for his "buzzing doubts," Derwent advises Clarel to emulate Christ's grafting of two supposedly opposite faiths:

> In all respects did Christ indeed
> Credit the Jews' crab-apple creed
> Whereto he yet conformed? or so
> But use it, graft it with his slip
> From Paradise? . . .
>
> . . . .
> Be not extreme. Midway is best.
> Herein 'tis never as by Nile—
> From waste to garden but a stile.
> Betwixt rejection and belief,
> Shadings there are—degrees, in brief.
>
> (3.21.272–76, 278–82)

Although Jesus "conformed" to Judaism, he did not abide by or "credit" all of Jewish "creed." Instead Jesus as Christ combined Jewish law with the fulfillment of the new Christian hope—"Paradise": "Think not that I am come to destroy the law, or the prophets; I am not come to destroy, but to fulfill"

(Matthew 5:17). Derwent suggests that Clarel and Christians should think in terms of "both/and" rather than "either/or." One single point called "doubt" does not exist; a range of doubts or "shadings" exists between belief and rejection.

"Midway" (3.21.278) suggests that one travels on a rambling pilgrimage of disbelief, doubt, and belief all through life, and God, in fact, exists within the middle of the wandering way. As Melville writes in his Civil War poem "The Conflict of Convictions," the agon between the convictions of faith and doubt may be the middle way: "YEA AND NAY— / EACH HATH HIS SAY; / BUT GOD HE KEEPS THE MIDDLE WAY." The Melvillean middle way expressed by Derwent, by the narrator, and by other God-wrestlers such as Rolfe is not the bourgeois middle way, with its tendency toward safe mediocrity and the avoidance of all conflict. Like the Via Dolorosa, an uphill street in the middle of Jerusalem, the middle way is the hard way of wrestling, of balancing many viewpoints. The Melvillean middle way is the interstitial space where belief, doubt, and unbelief continually contend with each other and within the individual for the human heart. As a place between extremes, the threshold where opposites meet and cross, the middle way is where the simple "either/or" oppositions are undermined and then joined as "both/and" complements. Melville's theological middle way is his version of the marriage of heaven and hell, the Via Dolorosa, the road on which Jesus the God-man walked, joining heaven and earth. It is a very unsettling place to live, for it requires a passage from orthodox theological paths to the often heterodox middle way.

What Melville implies by juxtaposing and combining assumed contraries in the middle way is that a person may doubt, deny, or disapprove of much of what is communicated to him from his tradition and training without severing his spiritual need for faith. One's dissent may even contribute to the scope and depth of one's need for faith. A person may also believe and approve of much of what is communicated to him from his tradition and training without severing his need for skeptical thinking to temper the pretentiousness of his theological certitudes. One's very faith may contribute to the scope and depth of one's need for doubt, in order for a tested faith to take root.

If skepticism without faith degenerates into "flat atheism" (3.6.60), then faith without skepticism degenerates into a false, excessive zeal such as Nathan's unrealistic Zionism or Nehemiah's blind biblical literalism. Nathan's untempered Zionism breeds only intolerance and hatred:

> Nathan the Arabs here esteemed
> The same—slaves meriting the rod;
> And out he spake it; which bred hate
> The more imperiling his state.
>   (1.17.308–11)

The "zeal, furious zeal, and frenzying faith" of "Christian fakirs" [pun on fakers] (3.16.65, 72) during the fraudulent lighting of the Easter candles in the Church of the Holy Sepulcher turn into a riot in which many pilgrims are wounded or trampled to death. Zeal kills. Nehemiah even sleepwalks into the Dead Sea and drowns, while seeing the New Jerusalem in his dream. Water is always a source of dangerous revelation in Melville's works, and here, at the Dead Sea, theological conviction fails to accord with reality. Too much transcendence without some accompanying doubt, or at least protest, causes madness. Even the pure faith of the Franciscan monk Salvaterra—who along with the Syrian monk, the Dominican monk, and Nehemiah represent the impulse toward faith in the poem—suffers from too much transcendence:

> Ah, fervor bought too dear:
> The fingers clutching rope and cross;
> Life too intense; the cheek austere
> Deepening in hollow, waste and loss.
> (4.13.159–62)

Only the Syrian and the Dominican, because of their ability to wrestle with contraries, are respected by the narrator and by the pilgrims.

Those characters who are able to hold antithetical ideas at once and those who have two or more sides to their personalities have the best chance for developing Melvillean control or ripeness. Those who concentrate on only one side of the evidence—Nathan, Nehemiah, Salvaterra—may exhibit some austere control but only at the cost of their well-being or even their life. The ideal goal of all selfhood is control:

> By inner storms
> Held in solution, so his soul
> Ripened for hour of such control
> As shapes, concretes. . . .
> (1.17.195–98)

Although Nathan "ripened," he never achieves final ripeness, for he becomes overzealous and one-sided. Vine and Rolfe—"exceptional natures" (1.31.45)—however, do exhibit control of self: "Under cheer / Of opulent softness, reigned austere / Control of self . . . (1.29.31–33). Vine not only controls his sexual struggles but also balances the opposite sides of his character. He is Carthusian and Sybarite, involved and detached. Moreover, Vine demonstrates a "neutral frame— / Assumed. . . . " (1.30.86–87) that is the result of a controlled self: "And neutral not without design" (1.31.65). Vine has a premeditated character based on the recognition and control of opposite personality traits. Rolfe also combines both "a genial heart," and "a brain austere" (1.31.14) in one self that is "given to study" but also has lived outdoors, "a messmate of the elements" (1.31.16, 21). He even yokes together his frankness of expression, "indiscreet in honesty," with sensitivity, "frankly kind" (1.31.25, 23). Clarel sees in Rolfe "a gleam of oneness more than Vine's— / The irrelation of a weed / Detached from vast Sargasso's mead / And drifting where the clear sea shines" (2.17.31–34). Rolfe is separate from the mass yet still has a oneness in his multiplicity. Djalea, who is a symbol of composure and endurance according to Vincent Kenny, also controls his character extremes.[15] The Druze can listen to Nehemiah's reading of the Good Samaritan parable while still remaining alert to possible enemies, for he is "in patient self-control high bred" (2.9.43). When Djalea gives his succinct comment on the unknowability of God—"No God there is but God"—the narrator implies that he has the "passive self-control" of a Roman statue (3.15.115, 117). When the pilgrimage is over and Djalea is paid, he fantasizes about weaving the coins into the black hair of his beloved. At the same time, he exhibits his sexual self-control, his "governed hopes of rapture" (4.29.20). He demonstrates prudence, for he is not overly confident of his love—"For his the love not vainly sure" (4.29.25)—and combines the opposite characteristics of a man and a child: " 'Tis passion deep of man mature / For one who half a child remains" (4.29.26–27). He expresses yet another Pocahontas-wedding of opposites: "Yes, underneath a look sedate, / What throbs are known!" (4.29.28–29). Finally, the god-man in "Of Rama" serves as an exemplum for the control and balance of opposites. The god-man, who possesses the paradoxical Miltonian duality of "the human face divine," "retains the consciousness of self" (1.32.19) only because he is a coalescence of extremes. He is "innocent if lawless," "better dependent on the worse— / Divine upon the animal—," whose thoughts "dive and skim"—"theirs the spiced tears that overbrim / And theirs the dimple and the lightsome whim" (1.32.17, 26–27, 35, 36–37).[16]

   The biblical intertextual voice for this ideal picture of human self-control is the famous collection of Wisdom poems and gnomic maxims known as Proverbs. The very heart of Proverbs is the concept of self-control and order: restraining the emotions and the appetites, self-discipline. Proverbs teaches a life of austere, disciplined self-control, and especially of caution towards sexual passion and intemperate speech:

> Let her ["the wife of thy youth"] be as the loving hind and pleasant roe; let her breasts satisfy thee at all times; and be thou ravished always with her love. And why wilt thou, my son, be ravished with a strange woman, and embrace the bosom of a stranger? (Proverbs 5:19–20). A

wrathful man stirreth up strife: but he that is slow to anger appeaseth strife (Proverbs 15:18).

The prudential morality of Proverbs is very different from the absolute "either/or" moral rigor of the Mosaic Law found in books such as Deuteronomy (e.g., 30:15–20) or the extreme ethical "either/or" of a Prophet such as Isaiah (e.g., 1:16–20). Proverbs teaches a practical morality designed to fence in the boundaries against threatening experiences such as suffering, death, or illicit sexual passion by maintaining self-discipline and control within limits. Similarly, self-control is like a parental voice in *Clarel* governing Djalea's hope of sexual rapture and Vine's deliberately controlled response to Nehemiah's death. The poem's emphasis on self-control is Melville's attempt to maintain sanity in the face of disorder, whether religious, sexual, or psychological, in the face of the psychic dissolution caused by death, doubt, and suffering: "Take fast hold of instruction [or discipline]; let her not go: keep her; for she is thy life" (Proverbs 4:13). Part of self-control in Proverbs and in *Clarel* is a recognition, and then a crossing, of the so-called fundamental dichotomies or opposites of life: wisdom or folly, righteousness or wickedness. Sometimes these opposites are juxtaposed so closely together that the "either/or" nature of life seems to become a "both/and" coalescence of dichotomies: "Answer not a fool according to his folly, lest thou also be like unto him. Answer a fool according to his folly, lest he be wise in his own conceit" (Proverbs 26:4–5). One way to make peace with the disorder of life is first to recognize the complex dichotomies of existence and then to try to order this disorder by combining the extremes of human existence. To be wise in *Clarel* and in Proverbs is not only the practical sense of knowing what is and is not possible in this world. It is also the ability to live in a world that is filled with the pitfalls and temptations of all kinds of extremes and zealousness. Self-control is the practical response demonstrated by key Clarelian characters of keeping the middle way to avoid the extremes of zealousness: "Midway is best" (3.21.278).

THE MIDDLE WAY: FROM DISCIPLINE TO TOLERANCE

Since *Clarel* is a poem about the wedding of opposites, the notion that a hardening of an individual into a radical theological position is destructive (Nehemiah, Nathan) actually points to its opposite: the requisite indulgence and tolerance for the values and opinions of other people and traditions. One must not take emotional, intellectual, or theological offense at opposing viewpoints. The three survivors of the pilgrimage, other than Clarel, are conspicuously the most tolerant characters of the poem: Rolfe, Vine, and

Derwent. When Clarel is disarmed by Rolfe's frankness of opinion, Rolfe pleads: "Indulgence should with frankness mate; / Fraternal be: Ah, tolerate!" (3.16.214–15). "Indulgence" is consistently used by Melville to connote the openness to another's opinion no matter how incredulous or different it may be (2.25.82). Tolerance is one of the nonnegotiable values in the poem and denotes the ability to listen to an opposing world view and the attempt to understand it. Toleration is a touchstone to measure character. Even the most confirmed rationalist who has little patience for religious observance is tolerant. When Clarel watches from the walls the "spectacle" of a train of pilgrims entering the gates of Jerusalem, he notices some critical Americans—"rationalists" (1.41.59)—who bring up the rear of a column of votarists:

> The critic-coolness in their eyes
> Disclaims emotion's shallow sea;
> Or misapply they precept wise,
> *Nil admirari?* Or, may be,
> Rationalists these riders are,
> Men self-sufficing, insular.
> Nor less they show in grave degree
> *Tolerance* for each poor votary.
>   (1.41.55–62, emphasis mine)

Despite their critical viewpoint and their insensitivity to the "public reverence" (1.41.35) accorded to the religious leaders in the column, even rationalists, who do not show wonder or awe, show tolerance for theists. Rolfe and Derwent are even tolerant of the extreme religious literalism of Nehemiah. As Nehemiah attempts to remove physically the infinite number of stones on the pilgrims' path to prepare for the second coming of Christ, Derwent keeps his judgment silent: "but quick in heart / Conjecturing how it was, addressed / Some friendly words, and slid apart" (2.10.203–5). Rolfe's response to Nehemiah's zeal is not only tolerant but sympathetic to Christian hopes:

> And shall we say
> That this is craze? or but, in brief,
> Simplicity of plain belief?
> The early Christians, how did they?
> For His return looked any day.
>   (2.10.229–33)

Empiricism is also viewed as a form of literalism. Melville does not tolerate in *Clarel* any theological, atheistical, or empirical imperialism: an intolerance for others' religious attitudes or the arrogant belief in domains of certain knowledge. Margoth, the apostate "geologic Jew" (2.22.14), is the most insolent empiricist in the poem. He destroys the moral lesson of the story of Sodom with his geological proofs elevated to metaphysical truths, jeers at the Dominican, and mocks Catholicism ("Of Rome," 2.26). Even this most irreverent character is tolerated and even prayed for by Rolfe:

> Jew,
> We do forgive thee now thy scoff,
> Now that thou dim recedest off
> Forever. Fair hap to thee, Jew:
> Consolator whom thou disownest
> Attend thee in last hour lonest!
> (3.1.52–57)

The irritable, discourteous Elder is a Scotch Presbyterian who travels through Palestine with horse-pistols, a knife, and a surveyor's tape. He represents "sectarian intolerance" according to Walter E. Bezanson.[17] When the Elder leaves the pilgrimage without saying farewell because "he can't provoke a quarrel" with the indifferent desert, Vine restrains himself from making a "derisive comment" (2.10.135, 122), and the narrator, speaking for the pilgrims, wishes him peace:

> Well, peace with him go.
> If truth have painted heart but grim,
> None here hard measure meant for him;
> Nay, Haytian airs around him blow,
> And woo and win to cast behind
> The harsher and inclement mind.
> (2.10.123–28)

The opposite of the Elder's intolerance of religious rites and ornaments in the Church of the Holy Sepulcher—he calls Christ's tomb a "monkish" "raree-show" (2.10.148)—is the narrator's tolerance for the most imaginative religious legends:

> To view that legendary grot
> Whose milky chalkiness of vest
> Derived is (so the hinds allot)
> From droppings of Madonna's breast:
> A fairy tale: yet, grant it, due

To that creative love alone
Wherefrom the faun and cherub grew,
With genii good and Oberon.
(4.18.12–19)

Even the monomaniacs Mortmain and Ungar are tolerated and respected, though they often hurt the feelings of Derwent and others. After one of Mortmain's jeremiads, Vine remains still: "Respected he the Swede's wild will / As did the Swede Vine's ruled reserve" (3.3.46–47). During Mortmain's wildest moments, when he condemns human viciousness (2.3.180), Derwent, "the charitable priest" (2.3.173), bears with Mortmain and tries to calm him. The narrator praises Derwent's "Christian forbearance" and patience during Mortmain's "passion-fit" (3.6.152, 144). Clarel wants to know "how indeed the priest [Derwent] could show / Such strange forbearance . . . " (3.8.56–57), and Derwent answers that the source of his patience, tolerance, and forbearance is "Christian charity" (3.8.80). Even against Ungar, Derwent "forbore / To vent his grievance" (4.11.21–22).

Despite Derwent's optimism and latitudinarianism that so incense Mortmain and Ungar, Rolfe and the narrator admire Derwent for his tolerant middle way. Disturbed by the elaborate ornamentation on Christ's manger in the Church of the Star, Derwent, despite his supremely Protestant mind, courteously refrains from any brittle remarks:

He felt a secret impulse move
To start a humorous comment slant
Upon the monk, and sly reprove.
But no: I'll curb the Protestant
And modern in me—at least here
For time I'll curb it. Perish truth
If it but act the boor, in sooth,
Requiting courtesy with jeer;
For courteous is our guide, with grace
Of a pure heart.
(4.13.87–96)

Derwent shows the same Protestant toleration of Catholicism when he addresses the Dominican: "Brother, said Derwent friendly here, / I'm glad to know ye, glad to meet, / Even though, in part, your Rome seeks ends / Not mine . . . " (2.25.120–23). Derwent gives the final definition of tolerance in *Clarel* when he tries to calm Clarel's troubles over "the din of clashed belief" in Palestine (3.21.99):

Nor less let each tongue say its say;
Therefrom we truth elicit. Nay,
And with the worst, 'tis understood
We broader clergy think it good
No more to use censorious tone:
License to all. . . .

(3.21.91–96)

Although some overzealous enthusiasts believe that the ink on their Bible comes directly from heaven, and other atheistic imperialists jeer at the community of faith, the tolerant, reverent skeptic who can wrestle and balance antithetical ideas is the one capable of the most generous response to other people and ideas in *Clarel:* "License to all. . . . "

THE POETIC STRUCTURE OF CONTRARIES: THE AMERICAN BOOK OF PSALMS

The thematic struggle with contraries is reinforced by the poetic structure of contraries as we swing from canto to canto set in opposition or as we listen to a character's wild verbal reversals in thought and emotion. Clarelian characters commonly pivot from confidence to despair, from praise to protest, from acceptance to denial, and opposing scenes are often juxtaposed against each other with no logical transition.[18] These wild swings or reversals of contradictory psychological and theological moods are characteristic of the Psalms.

In addition to the sudden emotional reversals, the intertextual relationship between *Clarel* and the Psalter is suggested by the fact that *Clarel* contains 150 cantos, the same number of Psalms in the Psalter.[19] Furthermore, the Psalms, *psalmos* in Greek, were supposedly songs sung with musical accompaniment. *Clarel* has within it numerous musical forms: songs, hymns, symphonies, chants, recitatives, strophes and antistrophes, and dirges. If we keep in mind the literary form of the lament Psalm that is so extensively used in *Clarel* (discussed in Chapter 2), there is ample evidence to support the claim that Melville regarded his cantos as a nineteenth-century American Book of Psalms. How Melville reinterpreted Psalmic structure and mood after the passage of over 2,500 years, identifying with yet separating from the Psalms, is the intertextually difficult question to be explored here.

The effect of surprising emotional and structural reversals in the Hebrew Psalms can best be illustrated by a short Psalm with a sudden pivot from lament to praise, from fear to confidence:

How long wilt thou forget me, O Lord? for ever? how long wilt thou hide thy face from me? How long shall I take counsel in my soul, having sorrow in my heart daily? how long shall mine enemy be exalted over me? Consider and hear me, O Lord my God; lighten mine eyes, lest I sleep the sleep of death; Lest mine enemy say, I have prevailed against him; and those that trouble me rejoice when I am moved. *But* I have trusted in thy mercy; my heart shall rejoice in thy salvation. I will sing unto the Lord, because he hath dealt bountifully with me. (Psalm 13, emphasis mine)

The shock comes after the pivot word "But," and there is no preparation for this sudden reversal motivated by the psalmist's faith. Considering the greater number of lines devoted to complaint, the surprising turn to praise is emotionally unconvincing and, without the presupposition of faith, seems to indicate a speaker in psychological and theological disorder. But ancient Hebrew poetry is filled with such sudden emotional swings, a stylistic violence in the verse itself that might be explained by the violent social conditions of the time, by the paratactic nature of the Hebrew language, by the structural device of poetic parallelism, or by the sudden change in one's life when infused by the energy of faith. Melville's narrator, however, will give a very different reason for the sudden reversals and swings in mood and structure in *Clarel*: the nineteenth-century problem of doubt.

The main difference between *Clarel* and the Hebrew Psalms is that *Clarel* contains no steady reassurance of the presence of God and far fewer affirmations of faith and praise than the Psalms. Yet *Clarel* has the same structural juxtaposition of opposites as the Psalms. For instance, in the canto "Of the Many Mansions," Rolfe first admires the boldness of the Christian promise of good "against" the evil "experience" of this-worldly life: "boldly avow, / Against experience, the brood / Of Christian hopes" (3.3.16–18). In the next lines, however, Rolfe suddenly and surprisingly pivots, "But, changing . . . " (3.3.19), and attacks the Christian hope of heaven as "worse than Circe's fooling spell": "Here may the Gospel but the more / Operate like a perfidy?" (3.3.27,31–32). Such swings in thought and emotion demonstrate a structural principle of the poem: "illogical wild range / Of brain and heart's impulsive counterchange" (2.21.133–34). In the interpolated canto "Of Deserts," the Judean desert is described as hell: " 'Tis horror absolute—severe, / Dead, livid, honey-combed, dumb, fell— / A caked depopulated hell," but the opposite view is soon given: "But to pure hearts it [the desert] yields no fear; / And John, he found wild honey here" (2.11.66–68, 90–91). The image and idea of a desert wilderness is a coalescence of contrary connotations: the negative connotations of blastment, abandonment, and suffering along with the positive connotations of certain ascetic values of sanctuary, solitude, closeness to God, and strengthened faith. Another pair of cantos set in opposition is 1.5, in which the narrator mentions "the intersympathy of creeds" (1.5.207), followed by 1.6 in which feuding Christian sects are described as a "bickering family bereft / Was feud the heritage He [Jesus] left?" (1.6.40–41).

The songs, hymns, and poems within the poem are also organized in dichotomies, usually that of faith versus doubt. Within *Clarel* are poems written on rocks, on walls, in the lining of a trunk, on the walls of a hermit's cave; a salt-song sung at the Dead (Salt) Sea; drinking songs during the revelry at the Mar Saba monastery; funeral dirges; psalms sung during matins and evensong; an organ symphony; and even a monk's chant in biblical verses. *Clarel* is literally a chorus of voices. For example, Glaucon's song in "Flight of the Greeks" contrasts "the ruin and the wreck" of Achor with a pastoral grove of violets and birds (2.13.122–35). In a poem Clarel uncovers written on the plaster wall of his Jerusalem inn, the unknown poet juxtaposes the opposites of "Atheists and Vitriolists of doom" with his adoration of "the low lamps [of faith] flickering in Syria's Tomb" (1.41.106–15). These songs and poems within the poem strive, like the Melvillean God-wrestler, for a harmonic coalescence or balance of ideas, images, and sounds. The bridal unification, but not resolution, of opposites is attempted through the musical change from antiphony to harmony. The antiphonal form of several of the songs, poems, and entire cantos points to the poem's larger structure.

The most interesting antiphonal musical form is the chant sung by the men and boys of an Armenian funeral procession. The young maid "stretched on that Armenian bier" (1.43.25) is clearly a foreshadowing of the death of Ruth; however, the responsive voice striving for harmony but not yet achieving it is also an early attempt at harmonic coalescence that will be achieved later in the poem in "The Symphonies" canto:

> But, hark: responsive marching choirs,
> Robed men and boys, in rhythmic law
> A contest undetermined keep:
> Ay, as the bass in dolings deep
> The serious, solemn thought inspires—
> In unconcern of rallying sort
> The urchin-treble shrills retort;
> But, true to part imposed, again
> The beards dirge out.
>
> (1.43.31–39)

Later in the poem, the voices of the Armenian boys and men that make up Melville's antiphony are heard from again: "And heard the boys' light strophe free / Overborne by the men's antistrophe" (4.16.101–2). During Passion week, Clarel meets and hears the supposed opposite of the Armenian funeral procession: a Palm Sunday train of Armenian singers.

Ere long a cheerful choral strain
He hears; 'tis an Armenian train
Embowered in palms they bear, which (green,
And shifting oft) reveal the mien
Of flamens tall and singers young
. . . .
With the blest anthem, censers sway
Whose opal vapor, spiral borne,
Blends with the heavens' own azure Morn
Of Palms; for 'twas Palm Sunday bright,
                    (4.32.43–47, 51–54)

Immediately after this procession passes Clarel, who is "oblivious" (4.32.55) to its symbolic import, he sees, once again, the contrary Armenian funeral procession:

He saw the tapers—saw again
The censers, singers, and the wreath
And litter of the bride of death
Pass through the Broken Fountain's lane;
In treble shrill and bass how deep
The men and boys he heard again
The undetermined contest keep
About the bier—the bier Armenian."
                    (4.32.62–69)

From part 1, canto 43 to part 4, canto 32, Melville's antiphony of opposites—death versus resurrection, despair versus hope, funeral train versus Palm Sunday procession—fights for influence over Clarel.

The symbolic reconciliation of the antiphony of death versus life, of doubt versus faith, takes place in the organ-sea symphony that includes voices of debate, pain, and faith:

Hid organ-pipes unclose
A timid rill of slender sound,
Which gains in volume—grows, and flows
Gladsome in amplitude of bound.
Low murmurs creep. From either side
Tenor and treble interpose,
And talk across the expanding tide:
Debate, which in confusion merges—
Din and clamor, discord's hight:

Countering surges—paeans—dirges—
Mocks, and laughter light.
    But rolled in long ground-swell persistent,
A tone, an under-tone assails
And overpowers all near and distant;
Earnest and sternest, it prevails.
    Then terror, horror—wind and rain—
Accents of undetermined fear,
And voices as in shipwreck drear:
A sea, a sea of spirits in pain!
    The suppliant cries decrease—
The voices in their ferment cease:
One wave rolls over all and whelms to peace.
                        (4.15.39–60)

The "long ground-swell persistent" can be read as the sea of faith (e.g., Matthew Arnold's "Dover Beach") or the *cantus firmus* to which the minor melodies provide the counterpoint: dialog, "debate," and the suffering of "voices as in shipwreck drear." The ground swell of faith that begins as a timid rill before treble and tenor interpose and talk across its "expanding tide" (or *cantus firmus*) has an autonomy of its own in this organ-sea symphony as faith does in the poem, but clearly recognizes the musical presence of doubt and debate. The ideal harmonic goal is the coalescence of opposites: doubt and faith, dirges and laughter, tenor and treble, and pain and peace—or the overpowering of the minor melodies by the major melody of faith, a goal more easily achieved in the organ-sea symphony than in the poem. The narrator's long revery on immortality also includes a harmonic musical image that implies the transformation of pain to peace and the answer to unsolved mysteries:

Translated where the anthem's sung
Beyond the thunder, in a strain
Whose harmony unwinds and solves
Each mystery that life involves
                    (3.1.17–20)

In every possible narrative and structural way, Melville tries to change the stark "either/or" absolutism characteristic of the Law and the Prophets into the more flexible "both/and" balance of Proverbs. We saw this maneuver toward prudential morality in the description of the ideal God-wrestler who balances opposites, in the sudden pivot of the Psalm-like cantos, and here in the harmonic juxtaposition of opposite ideas that compels the reader to

consider them almost at once as in a stereoscopic vision. Such a view of the
opposites of doubt and faith or death and immortality is deeply biblical,
deeply musical, and deeply metaphorical. The prophetic books of the Bible
are famous for their ethical dimension: the command of "cease to do evil;
Learn to do well [good]" (Isaiah 1:16–17) requires a central stark "either/
or" ethical movement accompanied by powerful "either/or" images: red versus white, Babylon versus Jerusalem, whore versus bride, and garden versus
desert. In *Clarel*, many "either/or" constructs, such as desert versus town, are
blurred and crossed as one contrary is held together with another until they
are almost fused together:

> 'Twas yellow waste within as out,
> . . . The desert, see,
> It parts not here, but silently,
> Even like a leopard by our side,
> It seems to enter in with us—
> At home amid men's homes would glide.
>   (1.24.80–85)

THE PSALMIC SWING AND THE HEROIC IDEAL

Although the poem's biblical intertextuality is one of *Clarel*'s principles of
organization, it is still difficult, in part because of the insistent combining or
blurring of contraries, to perceive a clearly definable poetic structure. Certainly, there are some cantos that have effective, logical transitions between
them which were obviously planned that way. An example is the reference to
"Christ's moan" in 3.6.140 followed by the next canto opening with Christ's
actual cry on the cross, "ELOI LAMA SABACHTHANI!" (3.7.1). Another effective transition is the canto on Celio's skeptical questioning of the resurrection
(1.14) immediately followed by a pun and description of the rising sun-Son
in 1.15. There are several thematic groupings such as the Mar Saba Palm
cantos (3.25–26, 28–30) and Ungar's diatribes in the American cantos
(4.20–21). But too many cantos seem to be interpolated, distributed at
random throughout the poem. Even if one insists that the narrative flow of a
pilgrimage poem demands an essentially episodic sequence of cantos that
follows the geographic route of the pilgrims, the following cantos could easily
have been placed elsewhere: "Prelusive" (2.35), "Concerning Hebrews"
(2.22), "A Halt" (2.10), "Of Deserts" (2.11), or "Of Rama" (1.32). The
narrator adds to the reader's impression of an unsystematic structure by
opening many cantos without identifying the speaker or without orienting
the reader in any way except with a metaphorical introduction usually containing sea imagery (e.g., 3.3, 3.29, or 4.7). But the general arrangement charac-

terized by the Psalmic swing in contradictory emotions and moods provides the central coherence to the poem and its rendering of human experience. The narrator in the canto "The High Desert" reveals what I think Melville's motive is in setting cantos in a biblical context of oppositions. After a manic lament in which the pilgrims swing from question to question about the problem of the two Testaments, the gnostic view of Jesus versus Jehovah, and a terrifying vision of an American apocalypse brought about by overpopulation and the closing of the frontier, the narrator explains the lack of pattern and coherence in the canto:

> Thus they swept,
> Nor sequence held, consistent tone—
> Imagination wildering on
> Through vacant halls which faith once kept
> With ushers good.
> Themselves thus lost,
> At settled hearts they wonder most.
> (3.5.122–27)

Although there is a certain dynamism associated with reverent skeptics wrestling with doubt, questions, and theological mysteries, too much questioning can produce an unsettling state of disorder (common doubt). The pilgrims often range from one extreme position to another, like the temperature in a desert ranging between astonishing extremes of hot and cold. The Hebrew Psalms have been recontextualized thematically and structurally by Melville to express the insight that not very far behind the ideal image of the Melvillean God-wrestler, a person of antitheses and balance, order and control, is the image of vacillation of mood and mind, a sign of psychological and theological imbalance and disorder. Without faith's "ushers," imaginative doubters can get lost in "vacant halls." The metaphorical implication is that faith settles the heart and the imagination from the contradictory swings caused by overzealous doubt. If faith causes the emotional reversals in the Hebrew Psalms, doubt causes the swings in and between the cantos of *Clarel*. Too much transcendence or too much doubt can cause an illogical, almost schizophrenic, wandering in the mind, not the neither this or that, here or there, in the middle way, but the bewildered, aimless wandering in vacant halls. As we have seen, any zealot for faith or doubt—"A slave to one tyrannic whim" (1.23.77)—is rejected in *Clarel*. In fact, excessive zeal exemplifies a lack of self-control, a refusal to pursue the more balanced middle way, which like the Scot Elder's excessive irreverence, is compared to a javelin thrown too hard: "So fierce he hurled zeal's javelin home, / It drove beyond the mark—pierced Rome, / And plunged beyond, thro' enemy / To friend . . ." (2.1.80–83).

The "patient self-control" (2.9.43), however, expressed by pilgrims such as Rolfe, Vine, and Derwent implies some theological reserve and distance— never giving oneself too unreservedly to any one religious or skeptical form. Melville is suggesting here the reverse of that nineteenth-century shibboleth— evolution. *Homo religiosus* survives not by adapting but by maintaining a certain reserve. If one adapts too well or accepts too wholeheartedly any specific creed, dogma, or doubt, one will die spiritually when faith changes, when doubt is overcome—or go mad from too much transcendence or self-inflicted doubt. People understandably dogmatize, for they seek the security of final answers. People understandably question, for many religious assumptions no longer make sense to them. The cautious self-control, balance of opposites, and tolerance that Rolfe, Vine, Derwent, Djalea, and the god-men exhibit may seem rather unheroic by biblical standards, when compared with the heroic, painful protest and theodicy questions of the lament. But after wrestling, some people may achieve a quiet, watchful stance in order to gain understanding and tolerance: the composed, patient, self-controlled individual is very much a Melvillean ideal in *Clarel*. The tolerant self-control characteristic of God-wrestlers in *Clarel* is not measured against conventional social values—what Melville calls the "parlor-strain" of wisdom (2.21.130)—but by a character's loyalty to an idea of self that is personal and persevering and that eventually encompasses one's myriad oppositions. Contrarily, Melvillean wrestling does require extreme heroism to be continually open to unanswerable questions and to refuse the lure of simple answers, either for doubt or for faith. The wrestling with contraries, the control of self, the expression of tolerance, the refusal to become a zealot for any specific dogma, and the reserve of skepticism become a heroic obligation—the perseverance of undergoing a pilgrimage day after day for a lifetime.

❖

The Small Voice of Silence

The Narrative Voices

> That profound Silence, that only Voice of our
> God . . . how can a man get a Voice out of Silence?
> —*Pierre*

THE UNBEARABLE HIDDENNESS AND SILENCE of the divine and the human, the anxieties of questions and laments, and the spiritual wrestling with faith and doubt—all can be read negatively as Melville's *askesis* or the dark night of the soul. Chapters 1 through 3 of this study demonstrate the difficulty of a quest for the hidden God based on external rational evidence—proof for the mind and the senses. Pilgrims confront divine hiddenness and want ocular proof of God's presence. They question God's silence and want an answer discernible to the ears. They visit historically sanctioned holy places and look for the embodiment of the sacred, but they find the profane. They read words of scripture but find only exegetical disagreement. Some wrestle with abstract contraries but cannot find a resolution discernible to the rational mind. Yet such a dark reading ignores the paradoxical nature of the relationship between the human and the divine. A rival positive interpretation, however, is always implied in the dark journey of *askesis*. To call God "hidden," rather than absent or dead, is to invoke the sustaining possibility of a return of the divine presence. To question and to protest God is at least to acknowledge the possibility of a listening God. To wrestle heroically with contraries is an attempt to live through doubt to a tested faith and, at least, to maintain theological tolerance. Thus rival interpretations are paradoxically joined in Melville's image of a Pocahontas-wedding habit of mind. Does Melville, however, suggest any resolution to such paradoxically rival thoughts as faith and despair, protest and belief, or is Melville's theological reflection endlessly circular and indeterminate? Many critics see no resolution, no hope (other than endurance) and, therefore, conclude that Melville was also unable to represent poetically any basis for faith.[1] Chapters 4 and 5, however, will demonstrate a quest for hope and faith based on internal evidence: God is not revealed to the mind nor to the senses, but to the heart through the small voice of silence.

Although the security of hope and faith cannot be demonstrated in the events, setting, or characters of the poem, Melville does offer a convincing argument for hope and faith if one listens carefully to the poem's narrative voices. One of the most extraordinary passages in the Hebrew Bible, 1 Kings 19:11–13, serves as an intertextual gateway to understanding the narrative voices in *Clarel*. Here, on Mount Horeb, God's puzzling silence in earth, wind, and fire is a prelude to his surprising presence:

> And, behold, the Lord passed by, and a great and strong wind rent the mountains, and brake in pieces the rocks before the Lord; but the Lord was not in the wind: and after the wind an earthquake; but the Lord was not in the earthquake: And after the earthquake a fire, but the Lord was not in the fire: and after the fire *a still small voice*. And it was so, when Elijah heard it that he wrapped his face in his mantle, and went out, and stood in the entering in of the cave. (emphasis mine)

God reveals himself to Elijah, not in the wind, not in an earthquake, not in a fire, but in a "still small voice." A more accurate and literal translation of the Hebrew phrase *kol damama daka* would be a "thin voice of silence," the silent voice that was so dear to nineteenth-century Christians and that inspired the silent prayer of the Quakers. Elijah's encounter with divinity suggests that God does not manifest Himself in cataclysmic natural events, in the traditional symbols of divine power, but works quietly as a whisper. This paradoxical revelation of a silent God suggests an inner spiritual voice rather than an external physical voice that can be heard by the human ear. The Elijah passage invites us to reflect on God's existence not based on the clearly defined sensory perceptions of religious mysticism, but based on a paradoxical encounter with a silent voice.

Any student of the Bible, however, knows that there are other theophanies, such as God's appearance to Moses on Mount Sinai, where God is found not in silence but in fire, smoke, and a trumpeting voice (e.g., Exodus 19:18–19). Thus it is permissible to distinguish between outer and inner divine manifestations. Just as the eyes first see a person's outer characteristics before the heart feels the inner character, the external manifestations of wind, earthquake, and fire prepare the way for an inner revelation of God in silence—God's voice working intimately within Elijah's heart. After God's revelation in silence, Elijah wraps his face in his mantle. This bodily gesture is usually read as a sign of Elijah's reverence for the divine presence, like the seraphim covering their faces with their wings in the sixth chapter of Isaiah. Elijah's response of covering his face, however, suggests that God cannot be comprehended via any ocular or aural proof. The covering of the human face also suggests that Elijah, like Melville's pilgrims, is a reflection of a hidden God. The secret within the Elijah passage is that one's heart-hunger for the presence of God may enable one to touch the divinity within by listening to a divine manifestation revealed immanently within the human.

The question a Melville reader might ask at this point, however, is found in *Pierre:* "How can a man get a voice out of silence?" Elijah can truly hear silence only if he enters into the proper attitude toward God's presence in silence. Elijah's attitude can be summed up in the Hebrew word *kinah*, translated as "jealous" in 1 Kings 19:10: "I have been very jealous for the Lord God of hosts. . . ." More than the religious commitment that enables Elijah to fight Jezebel and the covenant-breakers, *kinah* (repeated twice for intensity in the Hebrew, first as a verb and then as a noun) also connotes the ardor, jealousy, and sense of possession between lovers. Elijah goes beyond the desire to see the face of the hidden God (as Moses wanted to in Exodus 33:17, 23) to the desire to know God in the heart as a lover would. In other words, Elijah's manner of experiencing this silent voice is from within. Rather than the traditional theological interpretation of God's voice working gently from without, 1 Kings 19:13 suggests that God's voice works intimately within Elijah's heart. Although the silent voice may have been external, it is only recognized as divine when it is internalized by the proper attitude toward God—jealous for the God revealed in the human heart. Elijah, whose name in Hebrew means "my God is Yahweh," has a possessive love for God and approaches God as God approached the people of Israel—as a lover to the beloved's lost heart. Elijah's jealous attitude indicates a state of mind in which aspects of a mysterious, silent God are revealed within the human, and one can thus experience not knee-knocking fear but reverence and love.

Elijah's theophany occurs significantly in a desert, in a place of isolation from the external world, in a place of ascetic withdrawal into one's own inner world. Solitude has always marked the encounter between the human and the divine. Elijah's small voice of silence can be read as a revelation of the presence of God, an inner voice often heard in isolation and often accompanied by dreams. The inner voice that the Elijah passage points to is the other side of divine silence. Even if skepticism brands the theophany as a subjective truth, it was taken as reality by Elijah. One's subjectivity becomes one's objectivity because the event, historically true or not, can still exert spiritual influence and affect the destiny of an individual or even of a whole community.

The character Elijah and his theophany on Mount Horeb help Melville's narrator contextualize his search for the presence of a hidden God. Elijah is the supreme example of the spiritual striving for a personal inner experience of God. Elijah's theophany is analogous to announcing the approach of a special presence in *Clarel:* an inner narrative voice.[2] The inner voice is a quiet unobtrusive revelation of the divinity within man. The narrator presents an inner voice that suggests the validity of subjective truth, the hope of immortality, and the possibility of spiritual peace. This inner voice that exists separate from character and event is a voice deliberately immanent in the world of *Clarel* and, by showing the other side of death and despair, prepares the reader for the impulse toward immortality and for the hope in the Epilogue. This theology of hope counters the themes of hiddenness, silence, death, suffering, and despair that most critics read from the poem.[3]

The narrator, by working within the text via four narrative voices, is the key to the poem's theology of hope.[4] Just as the three natural cataclysms— wind, earthquake, and fire—prepare the way for an inner theophany of the small voice of silence, Melville's (1) intrusive narrative voice, (2) participant narrative voice, and (3) reverent narrative voice prepare the way for the poem's (4) inner narrative voice of divine immanence. Listening to the four voices prepares one to understand a narrative consciousness that is interested in bringing readers close to the text and closer to the innermost part of a person, the divinity within.[5] These narrative voices are in an intricate dialogical relation to one another and to the characters' voices.

THE AUCTORIAL VOICE

The easiest and most prevalent narrative voice to apprehend and comprehend is the auctorial voice—the intrusive, organizing voice that, like a Victorian novelist, guides the reader and structures the poem. The speaker overtly organizes the narration by revealing its plan. Before allowing Celio and Clarel to meet, the organizing voice fills in more of Celio's background: "to make the sequel clear— / A crossing thread be first entwined" (1.12.2–3). The intrusive voice also edits the story-telling of the pilgrims for clarity or adds observations, such as in Nehemiah's story of Nathan:[6]

> a tangled thread,
> Which, cleared from snarl and ordered so,
> Follows transferred, with interflow
> Of much Nehemiah scarce might add.
> (1.16.201–4)

Interrupting the tale, the organizing voice often introduces interpolated cantos, such as "Of Rama," that resemble dramatic monologues with an implied listener, the reader: "The interval let be assigned / A niche for image of a novel mind" (1.31.292–93). Even the Palm cantos are overtly ordered: "Next meetly here behooves narrate / How fared they . . ." (3.26.65–66).

In addition to the usual elevated position of an omniscient narrator that enables him to describe the setting from an external perspective and to quote a character's dialog and inner thoughts, this narrator directly addresses the reader and even warns of difficult cantos ahead. Although the organizing voice may seem distant, by intruding into the narration it reveals an artificer at work, selecting his material and revealing his attitude toward his tale. If a reader's congenital optimism refuses to recognize the evil in humanity hinted at by Piranesi's black-and-white etchings, then he should skip the canto on Sodom and Gomorrah:

> For ye who green or gray retain
> Childhood's illusion, or but feign;
> As bride and suite let pass a bier—
> So pass the coming canto here.
>   (2.35.38–41)

After the banker and Glaucon, the idle rich, leave the pilgrimage because of their inability to face the desert and death—"Cosmetic-users scarce are bold / To face a skull. . . ." (2.12.32–33)—the organizing voice directly addresses the reader with a warning: "They fled. And thou? The way is dun; / Why further follow the Emir's son? [the Druze guide]" (2.13.112–13). The intrusive, organizing voice will also distance itself from a character and bitterly mock that character's primary trait. This distant voice mocks the excessive idealism and apocalypticism of Ungar's jeremiads with the stoic resignation of a narrator who has suffered much and who realizes that there can be spiritual pride even in one's pain: "Perchance its vanity he knew, / At least suspected. What to do? / Time cares not to avenge your smarts" (4.5.190–92). The narrator interrupts his account of the Black Jew's personal history with a parenthetical sting implying that the narrator cannot be sure of the truth of a character's word: "(If question of his word be none)" (1.2.23).

The auctorial voice often achieves an ironic distance from its own narration and mocks its creation with a cavalier attitude that is a combination of insecurity and aloofness. The candor, however, in explaining its juxtaposition of certain cantos and apologizing for poetical inadequacies has the ultimate effect of revealing the narrator as a human artificer engaged in the conscious and self-conscious work of literary creativity. For example, the narrator apologizes for the juxtaposition of a canto about Cyril's obsession with death next to a canto about the light-hearted, irreverent Lesbian. The narrative voice justifies its strategy:

Here, then, a page's slender shell
Is thick enough to set between
The graver moral, lighter mien—
The student and the cap-and-bell.
'Tis nature.

(3.25.4–8)

The intrusive voice also appeals directly for "license" (3.10.97) and apologizes for the mechanics of the verse and pleads for tolerance:

Because if here in many a place
The rhyme—much like the knight indeed—
Abjure brave ornament, 'twill plead
Just reason, and appeal for grace.

(1.4.30–33)

This voice will even apologize for its characterization of Margoth, as if any
Jewish reader might suspect anti-Semitism toward a thoroughly offensive
character whose only Jewishness is an accident of birth:

Perverse, if stigma then survive,
Elsewhere let such in satire thrive—
Not here. Quite other end is won
In picturing Margoth, fallen son
Of Judah. Him may Gabriel mend.

(2.20.16–20)

This voice is clearly far from an effaced narrator merely working his fictional
camera upon the world. By revealing his concern that he might be branded
anti-Jewish, by showing his insecurity about his rhyme scheme, and by justify-
ing the juxtaposition of cantos that illustrate dramatic emotional swings, the
organizing voice paradoxically reveals itself as sympathetically human.

The limitations of this intrusive human voice, however, are revealed in its
inconsistent omniscience. The auctorial voice often cannot give a character's
innermost thoughts in its own words, as if it does not know a character's
mind completely. Bezanson states that the narrator's "ability to read and voice
unspoken thoughts of the characters does not extend to an assured sense of
what is meant by them."[7] In *Clarel*, human nature is above understanding and
has an exact resemblance to the incomprehensibility of divine nature: "But if
in vain / One tries to comprehend a man, / How think to sound God's deeper
heart!" (2.32.109–11). For example, just before Celio and Clarel almost meet
in "Under the Minaret," the supposedly omniscient voice is unsure of the

meaning of Clarel's "mien" and Celio's "responsive look" (1.15.50, 51). When Clarel attempts to mingle sympathies with the introspective, reticent Vine, the organizing voice is not sure of the meaning of Vine's rebuke of Clarel:

> Does Vine's rebukeful dusking say—
> Why, on this vernal bank to-day,
> Why bring oblations of thy pain
> To one who hath his share? . . .
> (2.27.116–19)

After the narrative voice suggests that Vine's words to Clarel may have been "Go, live it out" (2.27.123), the voice then indicates that Vine's conceit of love between men as "negatives of flesh" implying "analogies of non-cordialness / In spirit" (2.27.126–28) may have been Clarel's "dream of vain surmise" (2.27.129). Narratological skepticism becomes an obligation in these difficult cantos as we ask the questions of who speaks and who sees. Are these Vine's words, the narrator's thoughts, or Clarel's surmises? This clearly non-omniscient voice cannot even offer a definitive interpretation of one character's opinion of another. Instead, we are given a choice of multiple possibilities. Vine infers from Rolfe's intensity that Rolfe is

> an ocean-waste
> Of earnestness without a buoy:
> An inference which afterward
> Acquaintance led him to discard
> *Or* modify, *or* not employ.
> (1.31.201–5, emphasis mine)

Speech itself is an uncertain form of communication for this narrative voice. When Vine chides Rolfe for his soliloquies—"hard for a fountain to refrain" (1.31.267)—the voice conveys only what Vine's comment is not—"no envy in the strain" (1.31.269)—not what his comment is—"Was that but irony?" (1.31.268). This unreliable voice often will not even speculate on a character's response, leaving the reader instead with a question—"But Clarel, what thought he?" (3.13.46). This intrusive voice will often add little qualifiers to its interpretation of characters that only increase ambiguity: "Such thought, or something near akin, / Touched Clarel . . ." (4.2.23–24).

This same organizing narrative voice will often employ hypothetical dialog, a dialog of "as if," when projecting thought or speech. After comparing Jove's tomb in Crete with Christ's tomb in Jerusalem, the voice says: "Such,

among thronging thoughts, *may* stir / In pilgrim pressing thro' the lane"
(1.3.12–13, emphasis mine). The pilgrim remains unidentified, and it is
unclear whether the pilgrim had such thoughts or the narrator had them. The
narrator often only conjectures what a character might say, as when Djalea's
words are introduced by "as he should say" (4.1.65). The hypothetical words
that follow are clearly the narrator's, not Djalea's. The hypothetical dialog
illustrates that characters are often merely voices for the narrator's own
words. This limitation on an intrusive, organizing narrator's omniscience
demonstrates that character is less important than the narrator's voices as
indicators of the main meaning in the poem.

The organizing voice often leaves a speaker's identity unknown—merely
tagging the character and his speech with "one said" (4.12.6). The long
revery on immortality that opens part 3, "Mar Saba," is identified merely as
"exhalings" from the "heart" "of one there by the moundless bed" (3.1.25,
26, 27). This narrative strategy is not unwitting. The narrator, when he wants
to, can and does give a specific referent to the pronoun "one": "But one there
was (and Clarel he)" (4.29.42). The use of "one" to indicate the nonspe-
cificity of character (see 4.9.17) demonstrates the narrator's purposeful ambiguity: Is this a pilgrim speaking or the narrator become character? The narrator is willful in not identifying the source of the revery about Baldwin and
Godfrey in the Church of the Star and again uses only the tag "one"
(4.13.69), insisting that "not Derwent's was that revery" (4.13.83; see also
2.36.21). Eventually it becomes clear that "one" not only denotes an unidentified character but also foreshadows the fusing of character and narrator.

The intrusive voice often delays the identification of a character's unmediated speech. We are led to assume that the narrator is speaking, and then,
many lines later, the narrator adds a tag such as "he mused" or "he said." For
example, the canto "The Pillow" reads like another of the many narrator's
monologues until, in the last three lines, the narrator adds the unconvincing
"buzzed thoughts! To Rolfe they came in doze" (4.8.28). In a moving passage on Celio's heroic skepticism, his premature death, and the question of
immortality, the words read as if they were the narrator's. Then comes the
much delayed remark: "Clarel, through him these reveries ran" (1.19.44).

The limitation on the omniscience of the intrusive voice, the unidentified
speakers, and the delayed identification of characters—all demonstrate the
unconvincing authority of character as the main indicator of meaning in
Clarel. Not only do characters such as Celio, Mortmain, and Ungar act as a
"composite picture," according to Vincent Kenny, emerging "as a single
character in their final meaning of the poem," but all the main characters "are
the embodiments of ideas, important only so long as they function as vehicles
for the ideas."[8] Characters often echo each other's ideas like variations on a
theme. For instance, Mortmain and Ungar both emphasize the evil within the

human heart (see the cantos "Sodom" and "Of Wickedness the Word"). Clarelian characters are also expendable and interchangeable, as one is replaced by another throughout the pilgrimage:

> For, ah, with chill at heart they mind
> Two now forever left behind.
> But as men drop, replacements rule:
> Though fleeting be each part assigned,
> The eternal ranks of life keep full:
> So here—if but in small degree—
> Recruits for fallen ones atone;
> The Arnaut and pilgrim from the sea
> The muster joining; also one
> In military undress dun—
> A stranger quite.
>
> (4.1.32–42)

Here, Ungar (the "stranger quite") replaces the dead Mortmain, and Agath replaces the buried Nehemiah (Agath even rides Nehemiah's mule), as the pilgrimage continues from Mar Saba to Bethlehem. The point is that *Clarel*, then, is not so much a dramatic poem with original characters as a poem of ideas given primarily by the various narrative voices; and characters are time and again overwhelmed by the thoughts and language of an intrusive narrative voice. Here, Melville seems to have foreshadowed T. S. Eliot's technique of using the Tiresias voice in *The Waste Land* to modulate, subvert, and even transform into the other characters' voices.

The non-omniscient organizing narrative voice insistently suggests a sailor; numerous sea metaphors and nautical scenes not only frame the cantos (4.7.1–14) but are also dispersed throughout the text (see 1.1.152–55; 1.12.67–68; 3.21.4–10; 4.9.39–46). Not surprisingly, Agath, a sailor, also uses sea metaphors. When other characters use sea metaphors, however, it appears that the narrator is working intrusively from within the text to make his presence known. Either several of the characters have a nautical imagination or the characters are refracted voices of the narrator. Although it is possible that Derwent, Clarel, and the monk in the Mar Saba masque all have acquired time at sea, it is not probable, and when Derwent (in 2.4.150–55), Clarel (in 3.21.112–18), and the Mar Saba monk (in 3.19.136–38) use extended sea metaphors, character again seems transformed by the thoughts and language of an auctorial narrative voice.

Although the intrusive voice, by revealing its artificer's hand at work and its limited omniscience, does seem more human, this voice is still the most distant narrative voice of the poem. This auctorial voice acts as a contrast to a closer, participant voice that is far more convincing and important in its relation to character.

THE PARTICIPANT VOICE

The participant voice in *Clarel* demonstrates that literature is an act of identification. It attempts to present the world through another character's eyes by coming close to the character. In the canto "The Wall of Wail," the voice changes back and forth from third-person to first-person narration, as if the narrator not only gives us the inner thoughts of the praying Jews but is also one of them:

> To be restored! *we* wait, long wait!
> *They* call to count their pristine state
> On this same ground: . . .
> .   .   .   .
> So happy *they*; such Judah's prime.
> But *we*, the remnant, lo, *we* pale;
> Cast from the Temple, here *we* wail—
> (1.16.100–102, 113–15, emphasis mine)

The lines given in first-person plural are not tagged in any way, such as with quotation marks, to indicate direct speech but are freely interpolated in the middle of a typical third-person omniscient narration. Although we cannot depend on punctuation or italicization alone for meaning in the erratic grammatical world of *Clarel*, Melville can and does give clear directions when he wants to indicate direct speech (see the quotation marks and the "he urged" tag in lines 1.16.141–42). The narrator changes his narrative voice to indicate his identification with the Jews. An even more startling example of a third-person to first-person change in the narration occurs in "The High Desert." The participant narrative voice begins the passage on gnostic dualism (3.5.27–63) by using the third-person pronoun "they" (line 47) or the demonstrative "these" (line 27) but then changes to the first-person plural pronoun "we" in line 84. This inconsistency in point of view gradually causes a dialogical unification of the characters and the narrator, whereby, as in Whitman's poems, the narrator's ego is projected into other consciousnesses. The effect of such character-narrator unity is to have the narrator participate in the lives of the characters. After numerous parenthetical "he muses" (e.g., 3.6.159) interrupting mediated third-person narrative sequences, after so much inconsistency in point of view, the reader begins to hear characters as voices of the narrator. Rather than an omniscient narrator giving us a character's thoughts in the character's words, the character's thoughts sound like

the narrator's thoughts and the "(he mused)" appears as an afterthought. Of
course, theorists would claim that in any narrative the character's words are
really the narrator's words since the entire text is mediated—retold by a
fallible human being, who can be unreliable. In *Clarel*, however, the ability of
the narrator to unite with character suggests a deliberate narrative strategy:
the narrative voices working from within the text are more convincing dramatically and more important thematically than individualized characters.

This narrative voice goes beyond participating to interrupting the character's words with caring, guiding remarks. In Bethlehem, Ungar meditates
alone upon the "Eastern skies." In a poignant wish fulfillment, the participant
voice hopes Ungar will kiss the heavens (a gesture out of character for Ungar)
and then addresses Ungar directly with an imperative "look up":

> How might his hand not go to mouth
> In kiss adoring ye, bright zones?
> Look up: the age, the age forget—
> There's something to look up to yet!
> (4.7.97–100)

When Clarel puzzles over the nature of warriors such as Ungar and the
Arnaut and suspects that both good men and mercenaries may reach heaven,
he asks, "And where is wisdom's recompense?" (4.2.178). The participant
voice addresses Clarel directly and hopes for a change in Clarel's heart: "So
willful! but 'tis loss and smart, / Clarel, in thy dissolving heart. / Will't form
anew?" (4.2.185–87). The participant narrative voice works from within the
text via an empathetic narrative technique to counter the lack of communion
between characters.

THE REVERENT VOICE

Closely related to the participant level of narrative, but not necessarily identifying or empathizing with the characters, is a reverent voice that is respectful
of religious legends and traditions.[9] This voice is a forerunner of the speaker
in the Epilogue who, according to Bezanson, talks "like a compassionate
father . . . to his hurt son."[10] This sympathetic voice also understands and
accepts the validity (not the verification) of subjective truth over any historical proof. In *Clarel*, subjective truth is a way of possessing knowledge as valid
as any based on reason or revelation. This voice speaks as if there are whole
areas of life that cannot be experienced until one believes in them first. The
importance of subjective truth in *Clarel* is that it leads to the understanding of
an inner voice, of a God who works within the human heart. Interrupting
Clarel's and Nehemiah's view of the Coenaculum, the reverent voice admits

that even if Christ's words at the last Passover supper were a "dream," they still guide mankind: "Ah, / They be above us like a star, / Those Paschal words" (1.26.54–56). Religious legends, more than any scientific discovery, give the hope that the human can grasp the divine:

> Those legends which, be it confessed,
> Did nearer bring to them the sky—
> Did nearer woo it to their hope
> Of all that seers and saints avow—
> Than Galileo's telescope
> Can bid it unto prosing Science now.
>   (1.35.110–15)

The legends that comfort the narrator are the same "Traditions beautiful and old / Which with maternal arms enfold / Millions, else orphaned and made poor" (2.1.85–87). If legends and traditions such as the star that guided the three kings to Bethlehem are mere fables, the reverent voice can only "lament the foundered Star" (4.1.18). The question of the objective truth or falsehood of a legend is a futile question "which none may prove" (1.14.66): "such ties, so deep, / Endear the spot, or false or true / As an historic site; . . ." (1.3.112–14). The narrator respects traditions, false or true, for they have the power to make history and to move the "hearts of some" (1.3.119).

Sympathy for subjective truth is best expressed in a conflation of "dream mixed with legend and event" (1.10.68) that describes Nehemiah's religious illusions. Religious traditions are not branded as delusions—as something proven false or wrong—but as personal, subjective illusions. Characters such as Nehemiah, the Dominican, the Syrian monk, and Salvaterra go very far on illusions and prefer them to a faithless reality. They create their own reality. The narrator readily admits that one's imagination has the power to glean truth from fables and legends: "Thy wings, Imagination, span / Ideal truth in fable's seat" (2.35.18–19). Mortmain voices the narrator's acceptance of subjective truth by describing Christ's death as "This legend, dream, and *fact* of life!" (3.28.17). In *Clarel*, whether a religious event was a dream, a legend, or a fact is unimportant, just as it makes no difference whether the small voice of silence was a projection of Elijah's subjective perception of God or an actual miraculous theophany in which God was silent but spoke. Derwent best explains why one cannot "undo" any dream, legend, or fact once it is taken as a historical event by millions or seen as a subjective perception by one:

> Well then, Madonna's but a dream,
> The Manger and the Crib. So deem;
> So be it; but undo it! Nay,

Little avails what sages say:
Tell Romeo that Juliet's eyes
Are chemical; e'en analyze
The iris; show 'tis albumen—
Gluten—fish-jelly mere. What then?
To Romeo it is still love's sky:
He loves: enough! Though Faith no doubt
Seem insubstantial as a sigh,
Never ween that 'tis a water-spout
Dissolving, dropping into dew
At pistol-shot. . . .

                    (4.18.94–107)

Although the portrayal of Derwent's character is as a superficial optimist, his remarks are often profound. This inconsistency between character portrayal and meaningful speech is caused by the narrator's thoughts projected through a character's words. In Romeo's mind, Juliet's eyes are the incarnation of love, despite their chemical makeup. Love may be blind from an analytical point of view, but the lover creates his own perception of his beloved, and it is "enough" that he loves. So, too, with the man of faith; it is his subjective faith and presuppositions that prepare him to believe. Melville is not at all troubled by the necessity for the subjective human lenses to supplement science with poetry.

THE INNER VOICE

The emphasis on subjective truth in *Clarel* not only prepares for a sympathetic understanding of the various dream visions in the poem such as Mortmain's palm vision of the Paraclete but also prepares carefully for the acceptance of an inner voice, a voice of subjective truth often associated with death and sleep. When Nehemiah sleeps, certain character lines are revealed upon his face. Looking at Nehemiah's face, but not understanding the "sealed" importance of it, Clarel feels like "Eliphaz the Temanite / When passed the vision ere it spake" (1.22.111–12). In Job 4:13, Eliphaz experienced "thoughts from the visions of the night, when deep sleep falleth on men." When a spirit passed before him, an image was seen but "there was silence, and I heard a voice, saying; . . ." (4:16). The word of God comes only after silence, just as in the Elijah passage. The narrator is clearly familiar with the silent encounter with the divine nature. According to Job, the vision of an inner voice can come in a deep sleep and in *Clarel* is suggested by the appearance of Nehemiah's face.

In nineteenth-century theories of physiognomy, the human face, if studied closely, could reveal the divinity within. Agath's experienced face is covered "with wrinkles of cabala text" and reveals not only suffering, "trial undergone," but also "a beauty grave pertained / To him, part such as is ordained / To Eld [God]; . . ." (3.12.34, 36, 37–39). Divine immanence is the Jamesian figure in the carpet of *Clarel*. Readers are constantly reminded of the possibility that God-like men are among us—unknown to both us and them. Mortmain suggests that if human wickedness is understood, then it is humanly understandable that Christ was crucified and that we are probably still crucifying the Christ-like individuals among us: "This day, with some of earthly race, / May passion similar go on?" (2.3.150–51). God working within the human heart is also demonstrated by Melville's use of the term "Eld" to denote God (1.3.160) and character: Don Hannibal is called the "limb-lopped Eld of Mexico" (4.25.20; see also Melville's use of "Eld" in his poem "The New Ancient of Days," line 13).

The most important and suggestive evidence for Melville's passionate belief in divine immanence is, however, "Of Rama," that important canto on man-God and God-man to which we have several times referred before. Here, Melville explicitly states that Rama, and men like him, "never the Holy Spirit grieved, / Nor the divine in him bereaved, / Though what that was he might not guess" (1.32.9–11). The divinity within the human heart is associated here with a particular manifestation of God—the Holy Spirit that is also addressed in Mortmain's death-sleep. Here, theological uncertainty is paralleled by psychological uncertainty. The divinity hidden within is protected by our inability to grasp it, yet we nevertheless sense its presence: "May life and fable so agree?" (1.32.16). If the reader accepts the evidence of divine immanence and the validity of personal subjective truth, the answer is yes.

The presence of a still small voice within is not surprising in a poem that presents incorporeal spirits (see the two spirits hovering over Mortmain in 2.36.116–28), dream visions, and personal calls from heaven (see Habibi's call to "write" in 3.27.114–16). The inner voice presented by the narrator seems to exist separately from the characters and the narrator but is actually a voice immanent in the human as well as in the poem. The tale in "The Carpenter" describes a man hurt by a friend's reckless word, who then becomes, like Emily Dickinson or Alice James, a nineteenth-century recluse. In the middle of the night, he lies awake and hears a voice: *"Me love; fear only man"* (3.2.48). The words are italicized and suggest a voice that is not the direct speech or thought of the Carpenter. The voice prompts the Carpenter to remove himself from human evil or "aggressive energy" (3.2.69) and to love God. Nehemiah also hears a voice in his vision of the New Jerusalem, "a great voice" (2.38.28) whose italicized words claim that *"no more is death"* and that *"eternity"* is available (2.38.29, 31). Although Nehemiah's self-transcendence causes him to sleepwalk to his death, in *Clarel*'s world of subjective truth, the reader cannot be certain that Nehemiah's yearning to unite with God and his vision of "faith fulfilled" (2.38.40) in eternity remain unachieved. Other records of inner voices include the voice that speculates on the nature of immortality and that comes from within the "heart" of an unidentified pilgrim by the grave of Nehemiah (really a narrative voice uniting with "one"):

> Translated where the anthem's sung
> Beyond the thunder, in a strain
> Whose harmony unwinds and solves
> Each mystery that life involves;
> There shall the Tree whereon He hung,
> The olive wood, leaf out again—
> Again leaf out, and endless reign
> Type of the peace that buds from sinless pain?
> (3.1.17–24)

Here, the narrative record of an inner voice—exhalings from the heart—gives a very different view of Christ's Passion than that which Celio, Mortmain, and Rolfe give. Some people can experience the cross as a sign of eternal mystery—not as God's silence toward and abandonment of Jesus but as "peace" and "harmony." Like the Hebrew Bible, *Clarel* has within it a dialogical reflex of self-criticism whereby one character's accepted belief is painfully (but not definitively) rejected by another's or by the narrator's. Just as the heterodox Wisdom books of Job and Ecclesiastes reject the belief articulated in Proverbs that the righteous always prosper, Clarelian reverent skeptics openly voice their objections to and uncertainties about orthodox faith. Clarelian believers, however, will often criticize incessant skepticism. Another example of an inner voice of subjective truth is heard in the canto "The Pillow," in which nameless "wandering voices" (4.8.5) proclaim that the old myths are dead. Such myths or "fables" and the silent voices that predict their demise come from within, "From man's deep nature" (4.8.9): "But never word / Aerial by mortal heard, / Rumors that vast eclipse; . . ." (4.8.11–13). One must not, however, arrogantly assert faith's "eclipse." The adjective "aerial" reminds us of Elijah's still small voice referred to elsewhere as "voice aerial" (2.34.22).

The most mysterious example of the inner voice occurs during the Syrian monk's debate with Satan on the possibility of understanding death and eventually finding spiritual peace—a canto we have looked at in Chapters 1 and 3 in different contexts. After the monk prays for God to reveal himself, he hears a whisper:

Then stole the whisper intermitting,
Like tenon into mortice fitting
It slipped into the frame of me:
Content thee: in conclusion caught
Thou'lt find how thought's extremes agree—
The forethought clinched by afterthought,
The firstling by finality.

                    (2.18.137–43)

Since the whispering voice slips into the monk, the identity of the source of these words—satanic, divine, or the monk—is ambiguous. The monk may eventually think these enigmatic words on the agreement of opposites, but the narrative voice suggests that the words are internalized within him: "It slipped into the frame of me." The monk, however, believes that the voice within is divine, for he says "His will be done!" (2.18.145).[11]

Inner narrative voices are associated with the sustaining possibility of hope in immortality and the possibility of inner peace. The narrative record of inner voices is important as an underlying motif that culminates in the Epilogue of hope and immortality. The inner voices reveal that the Epilogue is not a contradiction of the poem but a continuation of the poem's affirmation of subjective truths. The inner voices in *Clarel* suggest that portents from God come not as miraculous events but as whispers intimating immortality. They are trial flights at perceiving salvation, intuitions of the eternal that counteract dialogically the poem's themes of lament, suffering, and divine hiddenness.

THE STILL SMALL VOICE: "NO INCOMPLETION'S HEAVEN ORDAINED"

The narrator's awareness of death combined with the characters' reactions to the death of Nehemiah and Mortmain prepare for the tenability of immortality in *Clarel*. Paradoxically, the eternal quality of life presented throughout *Clarel* is always present in the sphere of mortality. Although the narrator does not know the nature of the "new emotion" that quells Clarel's doubts and vacillations, "one thing" is "clear" to the narrator: "Stays not the prime of June or youth: / At flood that tide makes haste to ebb" (4.29.50, 61, 62–63). It is understandable that critics are overwhelmed by the atmosphere of death in *Clarel*—particularly by the narrator's description of the valleys around Jerusalem entombed within a casket universe:

The valley slept—
Obscure, in monitory dream

> Oppressive, roofed with awful skies
> Whose stars like silver nail-heads gleam
> Which stud some lid over lifeless eyes.
> (4.29.148–52)

Despite such imagery and the multiple deaths in the poem, there is a twin constellation of despair and hope when encountering death. *"Despair"* and *"Hope"* are Cyril's two passwords for those who go by his Mar Saba cave (3.28.34, 32). Derwent's reaction to Nehemiah's death is a "faintly" uttered *"Resurget"*—a hope in the resurrection of the dead. Vine hopes for peace— *"In pace."* Rolfe can only protest to God and nature with his series of laments: "the end? no more?" (2.39.68, 69, 84). The narrator united with the unidentified "one," however, can hope that, countering death, in heaven "there peace after strife be given" (3.1.4). The cross can be a "type of the peace that buds from sinless pain" (3.1.24) rather than a sign of death and the unanswered cry of Jesus. In *Clarel*, life can be insane (Cyril, Habibi), meaningless (Margoth), lonely (cut off like Celio), or life can be created anew.

Melville suggests, through his narrative voices, that renewed life may come from change or incompletion:

> How then? Is death the book's fly-page?
> Is no hereafter? If there be,
> Death foots what record? how forestalls
> Acquittance in eternity?
> Advance too, and through age on age?
> Here the tree lies not as it falls;
> For howsoe'er in words of man
> The word and will of God be feigned,
> No incompletion's heaven ordained.
> (1.19.35–43)

Although these words are supposedly Clarel's reveries as given by the narrator, the indirect, mediated language, the delayed identification, and the narrator-character unity point to these thoughts being the narrator's. "Here the tree lies not as it falls" implies some kind of change—either the tree moves or it rots away. The passage contradicts its biblical co-text in Ecclesiastes 11:3, where the laws of nature are fixed:

> If the clouds be full of rain, they empty
> themselves upon the earth: and
> if the tree fall toward the south, or
> toward the north, in the place where
> the tree falleth, there it shall be.

By changing the meaning of the biblical verse, the narrator leaves the question of immortality open: "No incompletion [is] heaven ordained." If incompletion is not ordained, the line suggests that completion may come after death.

The theological rationale for such radical reinterpretation of biblical co-texts is also given in this revelatory insight into Melville's view of scriptural authority: "For howsoe'er in words of man / The word and will of God be feigned" (1.19.42–43). God is never present to us, but always present through human words, mediated to us through language. For Melville, the Bible was clearly written by human beings for human beings. A vast distance exists between the divine "word and will" and human interpretation, "words of man." Not only can divine purposes be misinterpreted by humans but also divine will can be "feigned" by humans or misrepresented. The possibility of misinterpretation suggests that perhaps we are misguided in seeing the fulfillment of human existence in mortality rather than in the divine promise of the "completion" of immortality.

One such completion after death may be ecological: the return of the body to the land. In the canto "Nathan," the narrator describes the trees shading the Indian burial mounds:

> With trees he saw them crowned, which drew
> From the red sagamores of eld
> Entombed within, the vital gum
> Which green kept each mausoleum.
> (1.17.63–66)

The "vital gum" from the Indians' decaying bodies keeps the trees alive and green. Since Easter occurs in the spring, the narrator suggests that the resurrection of Christ is also accompanied by a similar assurance of the reawakening of nature:

> Since Nature times the same delight,
> And rises with the Emerging One;
> Her passion-week, her winter mood
> She slips, with crape from off the Rood.
> (4.33.27–30)

Rolfe also associates death with the color green and with the feeling of peace: "Into the green land of the dead / Where he encamps and peace is shed" (here, he refers to the disaster-prone mariner in "A Sketch," 1.37.22–23). Rolfe even wants palm trees planted by his grave, so "green my grave shall be" (2.15.34).[12]

The completion after death is also the human truth that good deeds live on after one's death: "A good deed lives, the doer low" (2.15.4). The narrator, speaking for the pilgrims ("they" 3.2.2–4), also questions the organic relationship between goodness ("virtues") and immortality:

> Those virtues which his meekness knew,
> Marked these indeed but wreckful wane
> Of strength, or the organic man?
> The hardy hemlock, if subdued,
> Decays to violets in the wood,
> Which put forth from the sodden stem:
> His virtues, might they breed like them? [Nehemiah's]
> (3.2.11–17)

Again, Melville will reinterpret biblical prooftexts:

> For there is hope of a tree, if it be cut down, that it will sprout again, and that the tender branch thereof will not cease. Though the root thereof wax old in the earth and the stock thereof die in the ground; Yet through the scent of water it will bud, and bring forth boughs like a plant. But man dieth, and wasteth away: yea, man giveth up the ghost, and where is he?" (Job 14:7–10)

In Job, the tree cut down that renews itself from its roots is a metaphoric foil for the irrevocability of death. Like the fallen tree, Melville uses the hemlock to suggest that the change after death comes as virtues that live on in organic immortality. The implication is that if one hemlock can decay and thereby fertilize many violets, then one good deed may in turn "breed" a myriad of human kindnesses.

Mortmain's death and its accompanying record of the inner voice as a psychological revelation of the spirit of God best illuminate the nature of the other side of death. Mortmain's encounter with the St. Saba palm tree enables him to transcend himself from the mortmain (his name means "dead hand") of despair to the relief (living palm) of peace. The canto "Mortmain and the Palm" is as close as the reader gets to the peace promised by immortality. The palm represents not only what Bowen calls "the promise of life beyond death"[13] but also peace beyond calm: "O martyr's scepter, type of peace, [the palm] / And trouble glorified to calm!" (3.30.72–73). The narrator also has Clarel describe the celibate monk of Mar Saba as sharing with the palm "heaven on earth in gracious calm" (3.31.18). Heaven is associated with "liquid calm" in *Clarel* (1.7.62). Death can also be accompanied by "Peace":

the name of Death's daughter in the poem (1.28.94). When Vine comes across Nehemiah's corpse, he, too, recognizes death as "calm":

> Here is balm:
> Repose is snowed upon repose—
> Sleep upon sleep; it is the calm
> And incantation of the close.
> (2.39.31–34)

Vine's last line resembles Shakespeare's image of death as "the music at the close":

> O, but they say the tongues of dying men
> Enforce attention like deep harmony:
>
> . . . .
>
> More are men's ends marked than their lives before:
> The setting sun, and music at the close,
> (*Richard II*, 2.1.1–3, 11–12)

Mortmain's healing sleep of the dead does "enforce attention like deep harmony." Mortmain's Palm canto opens in his direct speech with a variation on the Plinlimmon theme from *Pierre*: "the true lore / Is impotent for earth . . ." (3.28.8–9). Chronometrical values seem antithetical to horological realities. Mortmain prepares for an engagement with the subjective truth of dreams by claiming that despite "rumors of *No God* so rife!" the Christ story is a "legend, dream, and *fact* of life!" (3.28.20, 17). Chronometrical dreams may now include horological facts regardless of whether objectively true. Mortmain's encounter with Cyril then brings us to the nadir of despair. Mortmain gazes at his chewed hand—sign of his mortality—and gives his soliloquy on death as judgment and chastisement of man. Immediately after Mortmain's revery on death, he encounters the "holy Palm" (3.28.50) and thus begins his transcendence from the depths of misanthropy and despair.

After looking at the palm that eases pain, Mortmain goes into a "dream" where "he felt as floated up in cheer / Of saint borne heavenward from the bier" (3.28.69, 70–71). Just as Elijah was also taken up to heaven, Mortmain experiences an ascent to God; however, Mortmain's ascent is really an inner quest into the spirit within. Just as Elijah is addressed not by an angel at the mouth of the cave but by the divine within himself, Mortmain is inspired (literally and figuratively) by the palm with the spirit of God. Just as Elijah, fleeing from Jezebel, falls asleep under a rotem tree, where an angel wakes and feeds him, Mortmain falls into a healing sleep of the dead and, though not awakened, is assured by the spirit of God represented by an "angel-tree" (3.28.83)—the St. Saba palm.

Melville represents Mortmain's inspiration by using the concentrated richness of biblical allusion. Mortmain first thinks of the angel Gabriel when the palm is associated with the annunciation: "That lily-rod which Gabriel bore / To Mary, kneeling her before, / Announcing a God . . ." (3.28.58–60). In Islam, the spirit of God is also identified with the angel Gabriel. The narrator continues to prepare for the coming of the spirit from within via the common biblical conflation of spirit, wind, and breath that runs throughout the Hebrew Bible: "Sensitive he to a *spirit*'s touch. / A *wind* awakened him—a *breath*" (3.28.78–79, emphasis mine). The Hebrew word *ruah* (literally, wind) is a rich metaphorical word that also means "spirit." Wind is the most common metaphor used in the Hebrew Bible to describe the spirit of God— God's manifestation of inner assurance revealed within the human: "Whither shall I go from thy spirit [*ruah*]?" (Psalms 139:7). The word "breath" in Hebrew, *neshama*, is often juxtaposed to "wind," *ruah*: "All the while my breath is in me, and the spirit [*ruah*] of God is in my nostrils" (Job 27:3). Melville's deliberate juxtaposition of "spirit," "wind," and "breath" within two lines clearly suggests that the spirit-wind-breath that manifests itself in breathing through the nostrils is the same breath of the spirit of God. Mortmain's invocation to the palm adds another allusion to Melville's version of the ways of the spirit: "Comfort me then, thou Paraclete!" (3.28.91). The Paraclete is the Holy Spirit translated as "Comforter" in the King James Bible: "And I will pray the Father, and he shall give you another Comforter, that he may abide with you for ever" (John 14:16). The workings of the spirit are hidden to the eye, for they come from within: "for he dwelleth with you, and shall be in you" (John 14:17). The word "Paraclete" occurs only in John where, significantly, eternal life is presupposed. Furthermore, according to Galatians 4:4–6, once the spirit enters human hearts, then they can cry out to God: "God hath sent forth the Spirit of his son into your hearts, crying Abba, Father." As the Dominican rightly says, " 'Tis Abba Father that we seek" (2.25.158). Perhaps, Melville is suggesting that about the acts of God, adults speak as children. The mystery that Melville's narrator gropes after here is the spirit of God—not only a Christocentric view of the spirit but also a general immanence of God's spirit working within the human heart: a nonsectarian assurance combining Islamic, Hebraic, and Christian allusions. Implicit in Mortmain's experience under the palm tree is that if salvation occurs, it will only occur when the spirit of God penetrates the human heart.

The inner voice within Mortmain's Palm canto is documented by the narrator as a call from the angel-tree to Mortmain's heart: *"Come over! be— forever be / As in the trance . . ."* (3.28.85–86). Mortmain describes his encounter with the spirit as "the lull late mine beneath thy lee, / Then, then renew, and seal the calm" (3.28.92–93). The words "calm," "lull," and "still" (3.28.81) suggest what the narrator calls "a quietude beyond mere calm" (3.32.21). The effect of the inner voice symbolized by the palm's spirit or "genius" (3.32.34) and recorded by the inner narrative voice is to receive the gift of Melvillean peace and quietude—to see death as a release. The dead are "quick wafted where the palm-boughs sway / In Saint John's heaven . . ." (3.32.37–38). The eagle feather found resting on the dead Mortmain's lips may, as Merlin Bowen suggests, be a "token of a higher wisdom than earth's."[14] The image may add to our envy of a Mortmain who dies simply and quietly as if he knows he is dying assured of peace—peace as a spiritual attitude, not merely the absence of conflict. A more secure reading of the symbolic scene of a feather on the lips that completes the images and allusions of the spirit-breath of God would indicate that the experience of death is compared to being breathless. One of the biblical bearers of life is the breath; death is when the spirit-breath is taken away, figuratively returned to God, when a feather can rest on the breathless mouth: "To test if breath remain, none tries: / On those thin lips a feather lies" (3.32.31–32). The narrator often uses the word "breathed" as a theological metonymy for a character "talked" or spoke.

Mortmain's breathless death sleep is related to Jacob's dream vision in Genesis 28:12, 19. The line of steps leading up to the palm is called a "long Bethelstair of ledges brown / Sloping as from the heaven let down" (3.30.135–36; see also 3.32.23, 53). As in Jacob's dream, where angels ascend and descend from heaven, the "steps" imply that the encounter with the palm is a Bethel-bridge between the divine and the human, a spiritual assurance that any place of dreaming may be "the gate of heaven" (Genesis 28:17).

One may speculate why Melville reserves this gift of peace and calm in death for Mortmain of all the characters. The narrator says about Nehemiah, "Man sinless is revered by man / Thro' all the forms which creeds may lend" (1.8.74–75). Mortmain deserves the gift of peace, for although Zoima and her fellow spirit question, "But may a sinless nature win / Those deeps he knows" (2.36.120–21), Zoima answers:

> Sin shuns that way;
> Sin acts the sin, but flees the thought
> That sweeps the abyss that sin has wrought.
> Innocent be the heart and true—
> Howe'er it feed on bitter bread.
> (2.36.121–25)

The fact that Mortmain thinks long and deep about sin demonstrates his innocence and, thus, his worthiness to receive the Melvillean gift of peace.

THE VOICED SILENCE OF HOPE: THE PROBLEM OF THE EPILOGUE

The recognition of several narrative voices; the apprehension of the importance of the narrator as a conveyer of meaning more than character, events, and scenes; the comprehension of Mortmain's revelation of the spirit; the presence of inner voices, of the divine spirit working within the human—all are prerequisites for understanding Melville's Epilogue. Most *Clarel* scholars have questioned what seems to be a contradiction between the despair of the poem and the hope of the Epilogue. Melville says no so many times in the poem that the tentative yes shocks readers as an uneven balance. We know that Melville rejected theological certainties and refused any easy philosophy of compensation. Why, then, the hope in the end?

The reason many critics read from *Clarel* mostly bitterness, despair, suffering, and agnosticism is that they concentrate their reading on character, event, and setting. An even bleaker reading will result if we mistake the main character, Clarel, as the primary indicator of meaning, despite the title. As I mentioned in the introduction, the title refers to the search for and clarification of *El*, the Hebrew and Canaanite word for God, as much as to the character Clarel. Like Kierkegaard's knight of faith retracing the road to Mount Moriah, Clarel retraces the Via Dolorosa, a "middle" road of pain, paradox, despair, suffering, forsakenness, and death. Clarel is living death by the time he "vanishes in the obscurer town" (4.34.56). Clarel learns nothing from Mortmain's death, learns nothing of hope and little of faith. In fact, only the careful reader-interpreter learns what Clarel never learns: that the narrative voices and the intimations of hope and immortality throughout the poem argue against Clarel's experience of despair and death and prepare the way for the human voice of hope in the Epilogue. The Epilogue is not an isolated event.

Clarel's end—his personal disappointment in not finding both human and divine love—is tragic, but it does not indicate a tragic world view of despair and faithlessness. Clarel's experience is only an occurrence within the much larger theological world of *Clarel*. To claim, as Kenny does, that Clarel is a quester who "is defeated without any hope extended for the reader to plunge back into earth's conflicts"[15] is to fail to perceive the evidence for hope, salvation, and peace offered via biblical co-texts, metaphors, and narrative voices throughout the poem. To claim, as John Seelye does, that the pilgrimage is futile—"the voyage out is a complete circle, a static configuration and the surviving travelers return unchanged"[16]—again ignores the reader's response and the burning theological oppositions in the poem that are always expressed, sooner or later, in pairs.

Clarel does project the lessons of endurance. That four characters finish the theologically and psychologically exhausting pilgrimage is remarkable. As Bowen writes, "Merely to persist, like Saba's green palm rising from the sterile rock, is itself a kind of affirmation of life in the face of its oppo-site. . . ."[17] It comes as no surprise, then, that certain critics (e.g., Kenny[18]) are drawn to the stoic resignation, endurance, and self-possession of the Druze guide, Djalea. The theme of survival, however, does not mitigate the harsh-ness of divine self-concealment and death. Melville wants the reader, via the narrator, to choose hope, affirmation, and the divinity within to counter the hiddenness and silence of God. The Epilogue of *Clarel* is similar to the ending of Lamentations, where 5:21 ends with the hope of return and renewal, but 5:22, the last line of the book, ends in rejection and despair. When reading Lamentations, Jews traditionally switch the order of these last sentences to emphasize that the end of a thing must be hope.

The theology of hope does not appear in the poem *ex nihilo*. In the third canto—"The Sepulcher"—the narrator wonders

> Who might foretell from such dismay
> Of blank recoilings, all the blest
> Lilies and anthems which attest
> The floral Easter holiday?
>   (1.3.197–200)

Such a foreshadowing of the end that may surprise—the Epilogue—is voiced by the same reverent narrative voice that speaks in "The Sepulcher," the Epilogue, and elsewhere. Throughout the poem, there is within faith the twin constellations of hope and despair. Both are honored. Human life is lived between "the harps of heaven and dreary gongs of hell" (4.35.13), between faith and doubt, between "Hope's hill" (the Mount of Olives) and the "pit Despair" (the Dead Sea) (1.36.53).

Hope is often a hope in immortality. The most persistent spokesman for hope in the poem is Derwent. Even in the Garden of Gethsemane—the site of Jesus' betrayal—Derwent insists upon "a hope to man, a cheerful hope" (2.3.126). Derwent is correct when he implies that even the bitter Mortmain should hope:

> There's none so far astray,
> Detached, abandoned, as might seem,
> As to exclude the hope, the dream
> Of fair redemption. One fine day
> I saw at sea, by bit of deck—
> Weedy—adrift from far away—

The dolphin in his gambol light
Through showery spray, arch into sight:
He flung a rainbow o'er that wreck.
(2.4.147–155)

Dolphins and rainbows form an image cluster in the poem that also represents redemption and immortality. The Armenian train bearing palms during Palm Sunday is also described as "a rainbow throng. / Like dolphins off Madeira seen" (4.32.48–49). Dolphins are signs of redemption and immortality and were perhaps associated in Melville's mind with the Neoplatonic legends of dolphins carrying dead spirits on their backs to heaven. Whatever the source, dolphins as air-breathing, water-swimming creatures are a perfect metaphorical representation of human life lived in the tension between two worlds: heaven and earth, faith and doubt, immortality and death. The metaphorical cluster of rainbow, palm, and dolphins, along with the validity of subjective truth, acts as powerful counterevidence to the despair and death in the poem. Derwent's insistence upon hope is truly "the only way" offered, and Derwent's emphasis on hope and the heart "seems to affirm that . . . we do well to hope."[19]

Although Clarel is "oblivious quite" (4.32.55) of the green palms that the Armenians bear on Palm Sunday, the hope of immortality is still present in the poem. If Parousia is delayed, we can still hope in the face of our unknowing, in the light of new possibilities that we cannot predict. The participant narrative voice empathizes with Clarel's estrangement from the dead—Nehemiah, Celio, Mortmain, Nathan, Agar and Ruth—and asks for evidence of the Comforter—the Paraclete as the spirit of God that Mortmain invokes before his death: "Where, where now He who helpeth us, / The Comforter?—Tell, Erebus!" (4.32.103–4). The question does not deny the presence of the Comforter as helper but only insists that the death question must remain open because no one has returned from the abode of the dead—"Erebus." Dying characters have, however, testified to the deliverance from the mortmain (the dead hand) of despair.

On Easter Sunday, the narrator indicates that hope does not deny the reality of human suffering and death but suggests that they are inevitable and indispensable conditions for what may follow:

The hallelujah after pain,
Which in all tongues of Christendom
Still through the ages has rehearsed
That Best, the outcome of the Worst.
(4.33.21–24)

Certainly, the message of hope has been a central idea in Christianity ever since the death of Jesus. The whole content of Christian faith is directed toward the end, the *telos*. The Christian faith is distinguished from other religions because in it faith and hope are inseparable. Faith gives a foundation to hope; hope gives a content to faith. The theology of hope formulates a theology of waiting for the "Worst" to be over.

Waiting for the end, the last moment, the fullness of time, is the point of hope. The reverent narrative voice of the psalm-like Epilogue insists that we never can understand life only by the appearance of the moment. We keep the end in sight, look to the end of life, and are left waiting to understand the end of God's ways with man:

> But through such strange illusions have they passed
> Who in life's pilgrimage have baffled striven—
> Even death may prove unreal at the last,
> And stoics be astounded into heaven.
>
> (4.35.23–26)

Certainly one of the strangest "illusions" has been the record of inner voices presented by the narrator in *Clarel*. The inner voice heard by Mortmain under the St. Saba palm tree implied that "death may prove unreal at the last"—the unreality of death at the end of a life. The completion at life's end, the organic immortality offered by change, the immortality of good deeds, the calm achieved by Mortmain—all emphasize that our body's fate will not puncture our mind's dream of immortality, that death occurs in a dream-illusion.[20]

Part of the tentativeness that readers sense in the Epilogue comes from a freedom to let God be God and an insistence that one wait for the end of a life. The Epilogue's "pro and con" noticed by Bezanson and others does not continue into the last line of the poem, which is in the imperative: "And prove that death but routs life into victory."[21] The poem's last word is "victory," perhaps connoting Melville's theological synopsis of the Victorian age, an imaginative victory over the nineteenth-century antagonist common doubt, and a victory over Melville's personal fear of annihilation. The Epilogue, however, should not be seen as an editorial move by Melville that finally places the poem under an umbrella of special revelatory faith in immortality or on a canonically correct theological perspective. In *Clarel*, salvation is not simple and comes from the depths of the heart. The Epilogue is the result of a twenty-thousand-line pluralistic theological hunt that finds death *and* immortality; attraction to Judaism, Catholicism, *and* Protestantism; despair *and* hope in a theological interrelationship. The constant hopping back and forth between the voice of despair and the voice of hope does not occur just for the sake of theological openness, however. The narrative does end on hope.

Melville's method of narrative voices that subsume character encourages one to complete the incomplete, to gather fragmentary evidence and subjective truths into a structure of hope: the weighing of things probable that are not impossible. Thus Melville invites the reader to accept interpretations that satisfy the need to believe and the need to hope, even if not proved by any objective observations. By forcing us to draw inferences from only partial and subjective evidence of voices heard within the heart, Melville enables us to live the experience of faith—"the substance of things hoped for, the evidence of things not seen" (1.7.68 and Hebrews 11:1). Melville thus extends the narrative into the reader's life. By purposely writing an Epilogue that generally negates the despair of the poem, Melville prompts us to return to the text and, as we reread, to listen for the fragmentary voices of hope—intimations of immortality—in the body of the poem. Each age finds voices from the past or from within that it feels best reveals what God is doing now. Melville found the small voice of silence.

CHAPTER FIVE

❖

The Unsatisfied Heart

Protest Theism

Faith, what's that?
—*Moby-Dick*

Who is this that pledged his heart to approach unto
me? saith the Lord
—Jeremiah 30:21

IN A LETTER TO NATHANIEL HAWTHORNE (April 1851), Melville wrote:
"Take God out of the dictionary, and you would have Him in the street."[1]
Even if one were to expunge the word "God" from the language, the "*Being*"
that the word represents would still survive.[2] Melville's statement suggests
that at the everyday base of human existence—in the streets—is a leaning of
the human toward the divine, an impulse of the created toward the Creator.
As Rolfe testifies, even if the antitheistic cry of "God is not" were "demonstrable," the "ghost would haunt, nor could be laid" (1.31.194, 196). In the
human heart, God would still live.

The ability to think of God implies a relationship to God. I have been
arguing that in the loom of theological thought that is *Clarel*, the experience
of faith, not only doubt, is the interlaced thread in the weave. Melville's
representation of faith, however, is not the Calvinistic notion of a definite
knowledge of God that indicates the one true religion, nor is it the Roman
Catholic notion of the one true Church. Melville has no interest in the five
points, the thirty-nine articles, the ninety-five theses, or even in the various
discrepancies in theological doctrines and dogmas. Melville never claims that
only one belief is true; he treats all beliefs, legends, and myths tolerantly in an
"intersympathy of creeds" (1.5.207). But Melville does represent in *Clarel* an
experiential faith. Although philosophical questions are asked—the challenge
of science and reason to belief, the challenge of natural laws to supernatural
miracles, the challenge of evolution to creation—*Clarel* is more concerned

with the actual human experience of faith. And such an experience cannot be dismissed with the word "subjectivity," implying that belief is dependent only upon one's perspective and presuppositions. The hiddenness of God, the protest of the lament, theological doubt, and even intimations of a divine voice immanent within—all are experienced events in *Clarel*. Melville's theological reflection comes from the poem's depiction and interpretation of these events, emotions, narrative voices, metaphors, and biblical co-texts.

The experiential faith represented in *Clarel* is what I call protest theism. Protest theism is a descriptive phrase reflecting the conviction that Herman Melville was neither an agnostic nor an atheist; rather, he was concerned in *Clarel* with finding the limits within which a nonsectarian faith is possible and life endures meaningfully. Protest theism is a response to God that allows the human to protest against the physical and spiritual limits imposed upon the human by the divine: undeserved suffering, death, divine self-concealment, and the presence of doubt. Melville's protest theism daringly reminds God of His promises, judicially tries God for His breach of promise—*inquisitio Dei*—and reverently upbraids God for his failure to remove the shadows of natural and spiritual evil from the human heart. Evil is any necessity that harms human beings or poses a threat to faith: illness, pain, death, violence, and especially, the suffering of the righteous at the hands of God. Protest theism continuously questions the nature of God's absolute love, justice, and goodness, prompted by the agonizing disparity between God's biblical promise of presence, protection, and peace and God's fulfillment in absence, suffering, and war. Protest theism is a protest against human fate—exemplified at its basic level by Clarel crying over Ruth's grave. But this protest, this lament, is not embodied and enacted in the absence of faith. Thus, the word "theism." Melville's theism can be defined as a meaningful responsiveness to God, which includes but goes beyond protest. How does one go, however, from the protest against divine hiddenness to a relationship with God?

Although flashes of divine immanence like inner voices and reverent voices of hope and peace do provide evidence for faith in the poem, the real basis for theism in *Clarel* is human need. Need evokes responsiveness; responsiveness evokes relationship. Faith in God is a permanent and fundamental need of human life in *Clarel*. Melville's poetic representation of faith does not rest on any sort of divine revelation or grace; nor on any assent to sectarian creed or dogma such as whether faith is under voluntary control of the will, of divine grace, or based on supernatural signs; nor on any metaphysical speculation such as the argument from design. In addition to the traditional rewards that faith promises, such as the eschatological claim of immortality and the psychological claim of inner peace (both represented in the poem), Melville adds the promise of the ethical imperative: human beings need faith to maintain ethical control over their actions.

Faith, therefore, becomes ethically useful, if not empirically true, and the human becomes *homo religiosus*. *Clarel* demonstrates not only a responsiveness to God but also a responsiveness to the world based on reverence—amazement and awe rather than arrogance and self-sufficiency. Without faith, reverence and charity would end, and civilization would run out of control. *Clarel* also asks how to sustain faith in the face of hypocrisy and theological corruption during America's nineteenth-century crisis of belief—a time of radical doubt. By viewing time and faith as cyclical, Melville suggests the possibility of a return to God. Faith is also an aesthetic and literary phenomenon in *Clarel*; it is linked to imagination because poets need religion to supply material for literary creativity. In turn, imagination helps one feel faith empathically. Faith and imagination elevate the profane to the sacred. Literary art represents the theological insights of protest theism that so completely saturate *Clarel*.

Melville's key to experiencing and maintaining protest theism is based on a biblical theology of the heart that insists on the surrender of the human heart to a "lonely" father-God who is needed by human beings but who also needs human beings. This theology of the heart, rooted in prophetic texts such as Jeremiah, indicates that the relationship between the divine and the human in *Clarel* is a love affair of the heart, not the mind. The etymology of the word "religion" is from the Latin *ligare*, meaning to bind or tie; thus, re-ligion is to re-bind the heart to God. Only through the heart—the seat of divine trust or Melville's divine incognito—can the paradox of protest theism, the difficulty of loving a hidden God, be resolved. Only by a theology of the heart can Melville's protest theism be finally understood. Protest theism explains how and why the unsatisfied human heart protests and loves: only by giving the heart in love to God can one's humanity be maintained. Because divine trust is hidden in the human heart and love is a human need, there can be a protest against human fate and a lament to a hidden God who is, nevertheless, loved in faith.

"RELIGION'S ANCIENT PORT": THE NEED FOR FAITH

The poem's strongest argument for faith is that there is no other realm in which to find solace. Listening to the "rival liturgies" sung in the Church of the Holy Sepulcher, Clarel imagines a liturgical condemnation of his own theological doubt:

> Thou who misgivest we enthrone
> A God untrue . . .
> . . . .
>   try Nature's reign
> Who deem'st the super-nature vain:

To Lot's Wave by black Kedron rove;
On, by Mount Seir, through Edom move;
There crouch thee with the jackal down—
Crave solace of the scorpion!
                    (1.6.21–22, 26–31)

Nature is "indifferent" and "awe nor reverence pretendest" (1.15.9–10). The Judean desert south of the Dead Sea is so inhospitable that not even a rich man could buy water there. The scorpion—an "unblest, small, evil thing" elsewhere in the poem (4.4.15)—offers terror rather than solace to Clarel's doubts and anxieties. When Nathan ponders nature's cruelty, where lambs are killed by lightning and mountain landslides bury his uncle alive, he cites "mother, Earth" as a source of terror: "Nature hath put such terror on / That from his mother man would run" (1.17.87, 85–86).

Faith is also unable to rely on any material proof, objective artifact, or biblical prooftext for its existence. Touring the crumbling archaeological ruins of Mount Zion, Clarel muses:

What object sensible to touch
Or quoted fact may faith rely on,
If faith confideth overmuch
That here's a monument in Zion:
Its substance ebbs—see, day and night
The sands subsiding from the height;
In time, absorbed, these grains may help
To form new sea-bed, slug and kelp.
                    (1.24.69–76)

The holiest spot for the Davidic lineage of kings in Judea crumbles and is washed away to form new seabeds. The highest spiritual spot for the Hebrews in all of Jerusalem becomes the lowest spot—below sea level. Those who go on a pilgrimage to Jerusalem to sustain their faith by viewing institutionally supported holy spots or archaeological digs and ruins are like those travelers in the Sinai desert, Bible in hand, eagerly tracing Moses' footsteps and searching for Mount Sinai. Biblical scholars admit that we have no assurance that the putative Mount Sinai is the actual mountain or whether Sinai (or Horeb) is a metaphor for holy geography or a name for a much larger land mass. Melville's point is that holy geography is no foundation or even support for faith.

Faith can rely, however, upon what the Dominican monk calls "strong compulsion of the need" (2.25.14). Such is the need that the monk sees reflected in three Protestants—Rolfe, Derwent, and Vine—singing the "Ave Maris Stella" by the Jordan—a Catholic rite. The rituals of Rome "not less of faith or need were born" (4.16.157). In other words, sectarian creed and ritual may divide people, but need unites them. Not all the characters in *Clarel* are fugitives from faith. The Dominican, the Syrian, and the Franciscan monk are all men of faith and are treated with respect by all except the irreverent Jew, Margoth. They represent what Vincent Kenny calls the "need that . . . all men have to root themselves in some belief."³ The reverent skeptic Rolfe is the poem's best spokesman for the need for faith:

> Though some be hurled
> From anchor, nor a haven find;
> Not less religion's ancient port,
> Till the crack of doom, shall be resort
> In stress of weather for mankind.
> Yea, long as children feel affright
> In darkness, men shall fear a God;
> And long as daisies yield delight
> Shall see His footprints in the sod.
> Is't ignorance? This ignorant state
> Science doth but elucidate—
> Deepen, enlarge. But though 'twere made
> Demonstrable that God is not—
> What then? it would not change this lot:
> The ghost would haunt, nor could be laid.
>
> (1.31.182–96)

Theism or nonsectarian faith is a port in the storm of human suffering, and as long as men fear God and delight in creation, God's presence will be felt. Science only discovers new fields of ignorance, more questions, and if it were possible to demonstrate the nonexistence of God, God's ghost would still haunt the streets.

The difficulty of a faith based on need is that we often cannot believe the dogmas of organized religion yet continue to need faith in something other than the human. The danger to a heroic doubter like Celio is that, after refuting all religious creeds and metaphysical schools, he will have no spiritual lifeboat to save him from sinking:

> When, counting Rome's tradition naught,
> The mind is coy to own the rule
> Of sect replacing, sect or school.
> At sea, in brig which swings no boat,
> To founder is to sink.
>
> (1.12.65–69)

The lifeboat of faith also keeps man afloat ethically—under control. Without the self-control represented by the Franciscan monk's "girdling cord," the senses will rebel and the human turn to brute (4.13.169). Without fear of God, we are subject to the "misrule of our selfish mind" (4.18.151). Fear of God is not a knee-knocking terror but an awe and amazement at something mysterious and beyond human intellect and control.

FAITH AND CIVILIZATION: THE RUIN OF AMERICA?

In the Civil War poem "The House-Top," Melville views the New York City draft riots of July 1863 as an example of the attenuation of faith—"priestly spells"—that no longer holds man's heart in awe; the result is that civilized human beings regress back to the indifferent brutishness of nature.

> All civil charms
> And priestly spells which late held hearts in awe—
> Fear-bound, subjected to a better sway
> Than sway of self; these like a dream dissolve,
> And man rebounds whole aeons back in nature.[4]

If faith dies, everything unethical is permitted.

In *Clarel*, when the pilgrims are by the Jordan River and look across at the wilderness of Moab, they see the river as a divine border separating them from the evil ground of barbarism:

> At this, some riders feel that awe
> Which comes of sense of absent law,
> And irreligious human kind,
> Relapsed, remanded, reassigned
> To chaos and brute passions blind.
>   (2.23.51–55)

The Dominican predicts a chain reaction among religions; if Rome falls, all religions might fall, and civilized man relapse into barbaric amorality:

> Rome stands; but who may tell the end?
> Relapse barbaric may impend,
> Dismission into ages blind—
> Moral dispersion of mankind.
>   (2.25.109–12)

The awful result of the abandonment of faith is not only the apocalyptic "doom reserved for earth" at the end of time (3.5.82) but also the more immediate exaggeration of man's arrogant power:

Lodged in power, enlarged in all,
Man achieves his last exemption—
Hopes no heaven, but fears no fall,
King in time, nor needs redemption.
(4.8.19–22)

The death of faith in a civilization has, to use a favorite Melvillean pun in *Clarel*, grave consequences. Once the fallibility of human beings goes unrecognized, man becomes a law unto himself—a "King in time." Faith has a civilizing mission in history, but once America's exaggerated belief in progress and mania for profit run out of control, there is trouble in American history. In lines we have noted before in a different context, Melville writes:

The impieties of 'Progress' speak.
What say *these*, in effect, to God?
How profits it? And who art Thou
That we should serve Thee? Of Thy ways
No knowledge we desire; *new* ways
We have found out, and better. Go—
Depart from us; we do erase
Thy sinecure: behold, the sun
Stands still no more in Ajalon:
Depart from us!—And if He do?
(And that He may, the Scripture says)
Is aught betwixt ye and the hells?
For He, nor in irreverent view,
'Tis He distills that savor true
Which keeps good essences from taint;
Where He is not, corruption dwells,
And man and chaos are without restraint.
(4.21.28–44)

Here Ungar explains that faith serves both the disciplinary needs of the cosmic and of the human. Once man refuses to "serve" God and rejects the possibility of miracles, such as the sun standing still over the valley of Ajalon during Joshua's holy war against the Amorites, God will abandon him. God will no longer preserve good; the result will be corruption in the human and chaos in the cosmos. Ungar predicts that the dangerous new American experiment of separating life and faith will fail. The abandonment of faith parallels the destruction of American democratic values: "What shall bind these seas / Of rival sharp communities / Unchristianized? . . ." (4.21.114–16). Without faith, a united America will turn into divisive rival communities as the Civil War proved—more *pluribus* than *unum*. In short, belief in God is necessary for human survival, for "Woe / To us; without a God, 'tis woe!" (4.20.132–33). If the idea of God is abandoned, everything is permitted, and, even worse, human beings become unrestrained gods, the Ahabian act of human self-deification that Melville feared.

THE REVERENTIAL IMPERATIVE

A denial of faith is a denial of God, and since God and man are both divine subjects in *Clarel*, the denial of the divine is a denial of the human. Like the discussion in *The Confidence-Man* between Goodman and Noble on the connection between infidelity (a lack of faith) and misanthropy (a lack of charity), Melville insists in his triad of theological virtues that faith is inextricably intertwined with reverence and charity.

> Bonds sympathetic bind these three—
> Faith, Reverence, and Charity.
> If Faith once fail, the faltering mood
> Affects—needs must—the sisterhood.
> 　　　　(1.25.92–95)

Despite the unknowability of God and the prevalence of skepticism, reverence is still Melville's concern in the poem. Reverence is an intellectual and spiritual need for the unknown, the concealed, the mysterious. One must simply recognize the imperative of reverence:

> Our New World's worldly wit so shrewd
> Lacks the Semitic *reverent* mood,
> Unworldly—hardly may confer
> Fitness for just interpreter
> Of Palestine. . . .
> 　　　　(1.1.92–96, emphasis mine)

Thus, in the very first canto, an unidentified American warns Clarel of the need for reverence. The New World's emphasis on self-reliance and this-worldly values are the wrong presuppositions for approaching Palestine as an interpreter. Here the suggestion is that, as in the theological interpretation of a text, the interpreter should not apply a method but adjust his thinking, even his belief, to the text called Palestine. When one interprets the word or place of God, one does not dominate; one serves the subject. The text appropriates the interpreter. An initial act of reverence, twice linked with the word "awe" (1.15.10; 4.2.198), is essential if one is to obtain understanding of a landscape, mind, text, or God. To someone secure in his knowledge, such as Margoth, the apostate Jewish geologist who mocks irreverently those who have different beliefs (see Margoth's jeer against Rome, 2.26.1–14), Palestine shall remain distressingly closed.

When postulating the endurance of Rome and its holidays, the Dominican monk recites a verse that teaches the way to wisdom—reverence:

> Arrested by a trembling shell,
> Wee tinkle of the small mass-bell,
>   A giant drops upon the knee.
> Thou art wise—effect as much;
> Let thy wisdom by a touch
>   Reverence like this decree.
>   (2.25.199–204)

Rolfe also chastises the New World for failure to instill in him the value of reverence: " 'Tis the New World that mannered me, / Yes, gave me this *vile liberty* / *To reverence naught*, not even herself" (2.26.151–53, emphasis mine). Here reverence is linked to human freedom. Rolfe tells Derwent that "men / Get tired at last of being free— / Whether in states—in states or creeds" (2.26.123–25). The twentieth-century reader may feel that Melville is condemning the human need for servitude, for the twentieth-century Western tradition is one of absolute freedom. But Rolfe is condemning too much freedom:

> For what's the sequel? Verily,
> Laws scribbled by law-breakers, creeds
> Scrawled by the freethinkers, and deeds
> Shameful and shameless. . . .
>   (2.26.126–29)[5]

Too much freethinking can cause the breakdown of laws, creeds, and good deeds. The realms of law, religion, and moral action all need a sense of obligation—a deliberate restraint of our natural instincts in order to obey a code of right and wrong. The ultimate ethical, religious hand-to-hand combat, Rolfe predicts, will be between the orthodoxy of Rome and the freethinking of atheism:

Rome and the Atheist have gained:
These two shall fight it out—these two;
Protestantism being retained
For base of operations sly
By Atheism.

(2.26.140–44)

The liberalism of Protestantism shall be used to the advantage of atheism; thus, the real fight shall be between the obligations of an orthodox creed and the freedom of no faith. Rather than an endorsement of Catholicism over Protestantism, Melville's point is that too much freedom can lead to shameless acts—the breakdown of ethical control. Too much "vile liberty" (2.26.152) leads to the failure to obey the spiritual and ethical imperative of reverence.

The narrator admirably illustrates the response of reverence to the mysteriousness of God's manifestations, whether supernatural or natural. While Derwent, Rolfe, and others watch the sunrise over the Valley of the Shepherds in Bethlehem, the narrator reminds us of the appearance of an angel of God to Mary and Joseph in Luke 2:10. He reverently compares the "splendor diaphanic" of the angel to the sight of a "phosphoric ocean" off the coast of Peru:

So (might one *reverently* dare
Terrene with heavenly to compare),
So, oft in mid-watch on that sea
Where the ridged Andes of Peru
Are far seen by the coasting crew—
Waves, sails and sailors in accord
Illumed are in a *mystery*,
Wonder and *glory* of the Lord,
Though *manifest* in aspect minor—
Phosphoric ocean in shekinah.

(4.9.37–46, emphasis mine)

The narrator's response to the mysterious manifestation of the Lord—the phosphorescent ocean seen as the Shekinah or the indwelling of God's Glory on earth often represented as radiance—is first to recognize the "mystery," then acknowledge the "Wonder and glory" of God.[6] The passage conveys a moment when one is stirred by mystery, wonder, and grandeur, when one goes beyond ordinary words and perceptions to make a brief discovery of God. Such moments evoke reverence.

CARITAS: "OF THE OLD CHRISTIAN
STYLE TOWARD MEN"

Clarel is thus an archival testimony to the existence of the greater meanings of Christianity, not only faith and reverence but also charity. The poem demonstrates a firm adherence to charity as an absolute criterion of human dignity. When Agath's shipmates must return to the sea, Agath is left "unto love / And charity" (3.12.163–64) with the monks at the Mar Saba monastery. Nehemiah also befriends a leper, just as the Catholic church cared for the lepers during the Middle Ages (1.26.72–76; see also "Huts"). Clarel even pays for Nehemiah's travel expenses on the pilgrimage in the highest possible way for one to give charity—anonymously: " 'Twas charity gave faith her due: / Without publicity or din" (2.1.219–20). The theological virtue of charity includes not only charity for mankind but also charity or love for animals. Seeing that the Banker's horse suffers under the heavy burden of the Banker's overweight body (the poem's biblical version of the fat, rich server of Mammon), Rolfe gives his steadier horse to the corpulent Banker, rather than see him and the horse suffer (2.12.21–24). The relationship between Djalea and his mare is even compared to the Song of Songs refrain of the lover to the beloved: "See man and mare, lover and loved" (4.1.171).

Derwent's charity takes the form of tolerance toward all views—"license to all" (3.21.96)—with a strong sense of Christian charity that can bear the verbal diatribes from Mortmain and others. Derwent tries to persuade Clarel that, if he wants to nurture his Christian faith, he must combine faith in Jesus—"Throw all this burden upon HIM" (3.21.157)—with the performance of good deeds:

> You'd do the world some good?
> Well, then: no good man will gainsay
> That good is good, done any way,
> In any name, by any brotherhood.
> (3.21.232–35)

Derwent's nonsectarian charity is no mere liberal enthusiasm given by a supposedly shallow character, but a part of the larger issue of theodicy. If those who ascribe goodness to a monotheistic God are left in a hopeless quandary by the problem of evil and undeserved suffering, then those who believe in a malevolent God and universe are also left in a hopeless quandary by the problem of good. The mystery of charity not motivated by selfish interests should be as amazing as the mystery of an innate disposition toward evil.

The result of the weakening of faith will be threefold according to Ungar:

the end of charity, the accompanying shame of poverty, and the inability to recognize evil—"All recognition they forego / Of Evil . . ." (4.20.100 101). With the dissolution of faith comes the dissolution of "bonds of duty" (4.20.66) and the end "of the old Christian style toward men" (4.20.83). The harsh treatment of workers in England's mines and mills—"grimy in Mammon's English pen"—is in sharp contrast to the paupers that Jesus "helped and comforted" (4.20.87, 90):

> Thou, Poverty, erst free from shame,
> Even sacred through the Savior's claim,
> Professed by saints, by sages prized—
> A pariah now, and bastardized!
> (4.20.91–94)

Without some faith in God, charity seems impossible.

THE NEED FOR FAITH AND THE TOLERANCE FOR RELIGIOUS HYPOCRISY

In Melville's utilitarian approach to theism through human need, false faith or even hypocrisy does not threaten the existence or worth of an innate spiritual disposition in mankind. Melville recognizes that religious behavior can be the most deceptive human behavior. Certain credal beliefs are idolatrously regarded as absolute and inspire fanaticism. A community of faith will commit itself to a dogma that promises certainty. A community of faith will submit itself to the absolute authority of an idea, especially if covered with a patina of divine sanction. Often such ideas become substitutes for God. Infallibility, such as the Deist's trust in the infallibility of reason or the early Protestant's trust in the infallibility of the individual mind to understand scripture (*sola scriptura*), can produce theological corruption:

> By what art
> Of conjuration might the heart
> Of heavenly love, so sweet, so good,
> Corrupt into the creeds malign,
> Begetting strife's pernicious brood,
> Which claimed for patron thee divine?
> (1.13.86–91)

The revelation of Jesus and his teachings have been distorted to the cruelest corruption. The intersympathy of creeds described by Clarel in his portrayal of the universal spiritual urge to travel on pilgrimages of faith even unto death

(see the canto "Clarel") is debased to rival interpretations and jealous feuds
over holy ground:

> The wrangles here which oft befall:
> [in the Church of the Holy Sepulcher]
> Contentions for each holy place,
> And jealousies how far from grace:
> O, bickering family bereft,
> Was feud the heritage He left?
> (1.6.37–41)

Theological corruption and the idolatry of creed can even lead to bigotry
when the Mar Saba friars refuse to bury Mortmain within the monastery walls
because he was a disbeliever. "Bigotry did steer" Mortmain's "poor bier," but
"heaven that disclaims, and him [Mortmain] beweeps / In annual showers;
and the tried spirit sleeps" (3.32.68, 67, 75–76).

Even so-called theological error is accepted tolerantly in *Clarel*. When the
Moslem shepherds turn their back on Bethlehem to pray to Allah, Derwent
insists that, nevertheless, "Christ listens" and does not "stay / Upon a syllable
in creed" (4.10.69, 70–71). Clarel implies that the Jewish rejection of the
light of Christ is also theologically in error. When viewing the intense suppli-
cation of the Jews, their heads leaning against the Wailing Wall, he says,

> Yon Jew has faith; can faith be vain?
> But *is* it faith? ay, faith's the word—
> What else? Faith then can thus beguile
> Her faithfulest. Hard, that is hard!
> (1.16.149–52)

The right or wrong of religious faith is a vexed affair. The narrator suggests
that Solomon's giant stones at the base of the Wailing Wall may have served
as the basis for the right religion—Judaism—but subserved the wrong—the
subsequent Roman, Turkish, and Moslem structures and faiths built on top
of the base: "Based these the Right? subserved the Wrong?" (1.16.12).

Melville's fear here is not that human beings are led into theological corruption and error. Rolfe readily admits that "perversion" naturally comes to all
faiths: "Pure things men need adulterate / And so adapt them to the kind"
(4.14.78, 81–82). Original teachings do become perverted. Rival interpretations do cause religious wars. Even monks display a lack of charity toward
unbelievers. Yet such hypocrisy and error do not call into question the value
of the original disposition to believe in God. Melville's fear is that human
beings will have no God to serve. Thus his assumption throughout *Clarel* is

that any transcendent or immanent God—Allah, Christ, Yahweh—is better than no God.

Melville's remarkable spiritual honesty in *Clarel* includes the honesty not only of one who lacks a normative faith and is wrestling with doubt but also of one who admits the widespread evidence of religious hypocrisy. Such hypocrisy does not prove, however, that experiential faith is bogus. Certainly many assent to the so-called correct credal beliefs but do not act a Christian life. And whether the Christian, Jewish, or Islamic faith is the right or wrong one matters not—faith is needed. Thus Melville is concerned more with relevance than with validity, with the application of faith as a human need, rather than with religious claims as divine truth. Yet, like most other Victorians, Melville does not represent a secular morality, could not separate God from ethics, and would not entertain the twentieth-century notion that an atheist could be as moral as a Christian. Charity, reverence, faith, and an ethic of self-control—all are traditional, if not orthodox, Christian virtues sympathetically represented in the poem by a so-called Christian rebel, Herman Melville.[7]

Melville even accommodates certain religious frauds to the human need for faith. The canto "The Easter Fire" is a long disquisition on the issue of orthodoxy versus reform inspired by the violence witnessed in the Church of the Holy Sepulcher during St. Basil's Easter. In spreading the fires that are supposedly ignited by an angel or by prayer to all Greek monasteries, pilgrims are trampled to death or beaten by Moslem guards trying to maintain order. The true danger of such zeal is not that these Easter flames are "fraudful fires"—theological error—but that the Moslem's own faith is weakened when he sees the violence of the "Christian fakirs" by the tomb of the Prince of Peace (3.16.52, 72). Melville's pun includes the meanings of both a "fakir," an alms-seeker, a poor religious person, a mendicant; and a "faker," an illusionist, a magician, even a hypocrite. Even if the Greek Orthodox Church is "orthodoxy petrified" (3.16.95), its rites still can elicit good:

> it may so befall
> That, as yon docile lamps receive
> The fraudful flame, yet honest burn,
> So, no collusive guile may cleave
> Unto these simple friars, who turn
> And take whate'er the forms dispense,
> Nor question, *Wherefore?* ask not, *Whence?*
> (3.16.113–19)

The truthfulness of a rite or belief in religious life is dependent not upon its form but on its application. *Homo religiosus* takes "whate'er the forms dispense." In other words, there are instances in which belief is not true—not corresponding with any fact—but may still inspire one with honest values and even help one to strive for a more worthy life. Furthermore, in a time of doubt, it is dangerous to drop any credal assertion or religious rite because with each reform comes a corresponding loss in hope and support for mankind. As Melville's contemporary Matthew Arnold wrote one year before the publication of *Clarel* in *God and the Bible,* "soon enough will the illusions which charmed and aided man's inexperience be gone; what have you to give him in the place of them?"[8] Religion may be a crutch, but if it helps one to walk, *Clarel* recommends crutches.

> Greek churchmen would let drop this thing
> Of fraud, e'en let it cease. But no:
> 'Tis ancient, 'tis entangled so
> With vital things of needful sway,
> Scarce dare they deviate that way.
> (3.16.133–37)

The advice is to *"Never retract"* (3.16.144) because as "some doctrines fall away from creeds," so do "hopes, which scarce again, / In those same forms, shall solace men" (3.16.152, 153–54). Orthodoxy may be rigid, but if reformers "lengthen out the cable's tether" (3.16.161), the believers may never return to faith. If the word "religion" means to tie one to God (*ligare*), it is best that man know the length of his tether.

Theological hypocrisy is really not an issue in *Clarel* because if faith crumbles, hypocrisy also will no longer survive: "Hypocrisy, / The false thing, wanes just in degree / That Faith, the true thing, wanes: each pales" (4.20.77–79). In fact, in what are perhaps the most extreme lines of religious temporizing in the poem, Derwent suggests that in a time without faith it is best to feign a faith:

> the priest in view
> Bowed—hailed Apollo, as before,
> Ere change set in; what else to do?
> Or whither turn, or what adore?
> What but to temporize for him,
> Stranded upon an interim
> Between the ebb and flood? . . .
> (3.21.210–16)

Such noble religious fraudulence, "to temporize," is a utilitarian need, for man must serve, "adore," something. In the canto "Song and Recitative,"

Derwent recites a poem during the drinking party in the monastery: "Who is the god of all these flowers?— / . . . who knows? / None the less I take repose— / Believe, and worship here with wine" (3.13.75–78). One believes even if one does not and cannot know God. Even a fictitious faith is better than no faith at all, especially during an age that is stranded between the cyclical flow of faith and doubt.

THE CYCLICAL TIMES OF DOUBT AND FAITH

That Melville, according to William Shurr, sees "history as repetitive and cyclic"[9] implies a historical continuity to faith. Since "Time, God, are inexhaustible" (1.31.265), faith may return. Time implies the possibility of hope. If time is inexhaustible, there is no teleological end of history for Melville. Thus the full range of belief is possible. The nineteenth-century crisis in belief is not permanent; faith will come again and go again. As Clarel wrestles with the universal presence of doubt, he poses one of the central questions put forth by the entire poem: Will faith come again?

> 　　　　　　With what sweep
> Doubt plunges, and from maw to maw;
> Traditions none the nations keep—
> Old ties dissolve in one wide thaw;
> The Frank, the Turk, and e'en the Jew
> Share it; perchance the Brahmin too.
> *Returns each thing that may withdraw?*
> The schools of blue-fish years desert
> Our sounds and shores—but they revert;
> The ship returns on her long tack:
> The bones of Theseus are brought back:
> A comet shall resume its path
> Though three millenniums go. But faith?
> 　　　　　(3.14.100–112, emphasis mine)

The bluefish, the ship, Theseus's bones, and the comet—all imply the possibility of a return of faith, a turning to God of "each thing that may withdraw." Even man's withdrawal from God or God's withdrawal from man in the form of concealment may end.

Melville does not begin in *Clarel* with an a priori statement of faith such as God will return or men will be faithful to God. He infers such statements from the cyclical nature of history. Such truths about faith and doubt will come through history and time, not despite history and time. Cyclical history bears witness to the possible knowledge of God. For example, after Caesar

professed his atheism before the Roman Senate, no one would imagine that
Christ would soon come:

> Tully scarce dreamed they [the gods] could be won
> Back into credence; less that earth
> Ever could know yet mightier birth
> Of deity. He died. Christ came.
> And, in due hour, that impious Rome,
> Emerging from vast wreck and shame,
> Held the fore front of Christendom.
> The inference? the lesson?—come:
> Let fools count on faith's closing knell—
> Time, God, are inexhaustible.
>
> (1.31.256–65)

Since faith may return, Melville suggests, there is a theological relevance to
history. Historical events—the rise and fall of empires—are not just confusion and contingency. Recurring factors are discernible: the ebb and flow of
faith and doubt. Time is not only "inexhaustible" but also "ambiguous," and
"periods unforecast" may come (4.16.187, 188). "Circumstance" and "Time"
"are charged with store of latencies" (4.21.76, 77). Furthermore, cyclical
faith is part of the Melvillean recognition of comparative religions and their
effect on the psychology of faith (see 3.6.81–88). Since it is futile to debate
the truth of one religion or one holy book against another, and since creeds
and religions change or die and return, one's present belief should not be read
as more true than earlier so-called primitive or false faiths. The birth and
death of different faiths indicate the importance of tolerance and theological
openness when responding to anyone's affirmation of faith. As Derwent says,
"Have Faith, which, even from the myth / Draws something to be useful
with: / In any form some truths will hold" (3.21.184–86).

The changes and chances of time and the need for a utilitarian ("useful")
faith suggest that faith may appear in the most secular of forms:

> Suppose an instituted creed
> (Or truth or fable) should indeed
> To ashes fall; the spirit exhales,
> But reinfunds in active forms:
> Verse, popular verse, it charms or warms—
> Bellies Philosophy's flattened sails—
> Tinctures the very book, perchance,
> Which claims arrest of its advance.
>
> (3.21.190–97)

The referent for the pronoun "its" in the last quoted line is the spirit of faith, and the passage implies that everything has the potential to bear witness to faith in God—poetry, philosophy, and even those secular works that deny faith's advance. Faith is interwoven with doubt, but it would be a mistake to ignore the possibility of faith in any idea or movement. Doubt may drive belief to a new, tested, resilient faith, but, if pushed too far, doubt may foster dogmatic atheism. Doubt can also, however, reverse itself—what Melville calls a "recoil." Earnest searchers are "strong natures" who "have a strong recoil" (4.5.58), and men like Nathan who are immersed in skepticism may not only return but, even more radically, recoil to a new vehement faith:

> how earnestness,
> Which disbelief for first-fruits bore,
> Now, in recoil, by natural stress
> Constrained to faith—to faith in more
> Than prior disbelief had spurned;
> As if, when he toward credence turned,
> Distance therefrom but gave career
> For impetus that shot him sheer
> Beyond. . . .
>
> (1.17.232–40)

The cyclical nature of faith implies a two-way theological road from faith to doubt and from doubt to faith. There is neither steady positive progression nor steady negative regression in the history of doubt and faith. Rolfe, Ungar, Mortmain, Celio—too many characters in the poem express a disbelief in continuous human improvement. Melville, contrary to so many of his age, had no belief in nor commitment to steady human progress. Good is not gaining ground on evil. Generations do not progress through history into a state of more faith. Generations emerge over and over again from doubt into faith and from faith into doubt, repeating the same mistakes, responding to God in similar ways.

THE AESTHETIC IMPERATIVE

The problem in tracing faith through cyclic periods of its presence or absence is that faith does not provide rational answers to the question of the existence of a hidden and silent God. Instead, *Clarel* represents a faith that arouses an ethical-poetic approach to the world. Without faith, ethical control is lost. Without faith, reverence is lost, and the religious veneration of mystery is replaced by the rationalist's explanation of mystery. Even more troubling to Melville, however, is that an attenuation of faith may mean an attenuation of its handmaiden: imagination. As the power of human imagination linked with faith diminishes, there may occur a loss of aesthetic appreciation or even a drying up of the sources of poetic art.

One of the sources of poetry is religious legends. Derwent suggests that although Rome's legends have been ignored since Luther's Reformation, once faith returns ("days divine"), they shall serve as material for the poets:

> Her legends—some are sweet as May;
> Ungarnered wealth no doubt is there
> (Too long ignored by Luther's pride),
> But which perchance in days divine
> (Era, whereof I read the sign)
> When much that sours the sects is gone,
> Like Dorian myths the bards shall own—
> Yes, prove the poet's second mine.
>   (2.26.86–93)

When Christianity was "green" in its youth, before the divisiveness of sects arose, Christianity was able to "summons poets to the truth" (2.21.112, 114). Legends such as the one about Arculf and Adamnan cultivate an attitude of veneration and hope that modern science can never replace:

> Those legends which, be it confessed,
> Did nearer bring to them the sky—
> Did nearer woo it to their hope
> Of all that seers and saints avow—
> Than Galileo's telescope
> Can bid it unto prosing Science now.
>   (1.35.110–15)

In the canto "The Sepulchre," Melville differentiates between fancy and imagination. Fancy is a "light achiever" and is linked with those who "wouldst mock" God and faith, those who know "everything above, below" but not the wisdom of the "deep human heart" (1.3.181, 159, 155, 156). Imagination, however, is "earnest ever" (1.3.182) and allows one not only to conjure up a word-picture of an event but also to relive it empathically. The imagination "re-lives the crucifixion day" and shares with the "three pale Marys" the shock and disappointment at Jesus' empty tomb by empathizing with a faith tinged with obstinacy that can still "invoke him who returns no call" (1.3.184, 186, 193). Only through the imagination can one understand the faith, the "fears," and the "terror linked with love" that Jesus' followers experienced before witnesses of the resurrection testified that they had seen Jesus again (1.3.194, 195).

Faith is also an aesthetic phenomenon because of its ability to transfigure the profane into the sacred. Salvaterra, in the canto "Soldier and Monk," "transfigured Ungar's sword" (4.15.12), and Vine compares Salvaterra's ability to elevate objects into the realm of the sacred (even swords) to a Franciscan who, in Mexico, elevated a flower to the "emblems of Christ's last agony" (4.15.26) and named it the passion flower:

> What beauty in that sad conceit!
> Such charm, the title still we meet.
> Our guide, methinks, where'er he turns
> For him this passion-flower burns;
> And all the world is elegy.
> A green knoll is to you and me
> But pastoral, and little more:
> To him 'tis even Calvary.
>
> (4.15.30–37)

Salvaterra can transfigure a green hill into Calvary via his faith and his imagination. Unlike the rationalist's demand for ocular proof—I'll believe it when I see it—faith's response is, I'll see it when I believe it. Faith can change perception so that a sword is a cross; a hill, the scene of the Passion.

Faith not only has its practical results—fulfilling a spiritual need, supporting ethical conduct, keeping reverence and charity alive—but it also implies a relationship with God. In the struggle to express this relationship between the human and the divine, biblical authors relied upon the figurative language of flesh and blood—anthropomorphism. To take such figurative language literally is to misunderstand biblical language completely. To take such metaphorical language as only a poetic device is also to misunderstand the complex theological relationship represented by biblical metaphors.

WITH THE FATHER ALONE

The biblical metaphor Melville chose to describe the relationship between the human and the divine is that of the child and the father. Throughout the Hebrew Bible, God is the father (even "a father of the fatherless," Psalms 68:5), and Israel is a child. Even if one believes that Christ mediates between the human and the divine, a Christian still approaches God as father via the name of Christ: "Whatsoever ye shall ask the Father in my name, he will give it to you" (John 16:23). In the Bible, the metaphor of a child can evoke the return to God after moral backsliding: "Return, ye backsliding children, and I will heal your backslidings" (Jeremiah 3:22). Yahweh carries Israel out of Egypt and bears Israel through exile in the wilderness, as a father finds an abandoned child: "He [God] found him [Israel] in a desert land, and in the waste howling wilderness; he led him about, he instructed him, he kept him as the apple of his eye" (Deuteronomy 32:10). In *Clarel*, Israel's beginning as a nation, its spiritual rebirth, is evoked in terms of the child-father metaphor: "When Israel was a child, then I loved him, and called my son out of Egypt" (Hosea 11:1; and in *Clarel* 1.31.222–23). Christians are called "children of God by faith in Christ Jesus" (Galatians 3:26), and the metaphorical model for receiving the kingdom of God is a child: "Except ye be converted, and become as little children, ye shall not enter into the kingdom of heaven" (Matthew 18:3). In Romans and Galatians, the child-father metaphor expresses a complex spiritual relationship: "but ye have received the Spirit of adoption, whereby we cry, Abba, Father. The Spirit itself beareth witness with our Spirit, that we are the children of God. And if children, then heirs; heirs of God, and joint heirs with Christ" (Romans 8:15–17). Paul claims that Christians can go from slaves, to sons, to children, to heirs of God who will inherit God's future world. As sons of God, adopted heirs, the Spirit of God's Son cries Abba through them. The key biblical metaphor of child-father-Abba is exploited by Melville to express a wide range of spiritual meanings: wayward children, abandoned children (orphans), adopted children, and even a father's inheritance to children.

The child-father relationship is usually one of trust, a kind of trust that can be viewed as unreasonable but humanly understandable. The son who is last to see that his father is guilty of a crime or sin is considered to have overlooked evidence but to be pardonable. This argument is used by secularists who judge that the trust that believers place in a father-God is unreasonable, a trust that takes the good will of the father for granted despite the counterevidence of a hidden silent God who does not answer the questions raised by a son's death and undeserved suffering. Such a trusting faith may be dismissed as childlike, but both the Hebrew and the Christian Bibles do not use the criterion of maturity that such a dismissal ("child-like") implies. Melville adopts the biblical child-father metaphor to insist that children of faith should trust their father despite the counterevidence. Trust in the father becomes a moral resolution formed in the light of an ideal—the ideal relationship between child and father—and faith becomes "child-like" (1.3.118, 1.13.25, 1.35.17), an innocent trust that faith requires (rather than the pejorative "childish"):

> Unvexed by Europe's grieving doubt
> Which asks *And can the Father be?*
> Those children of the climes devout,

On festival in fane installed;
Happily ignorant, make glee
Like orphans in the play-ground walled.
(1.3.135–40)

The community of faith—"children of the clime devout"—like orphans search for the father God. The passage implies that the faithful are "ignorant" of the skepticism outside the "play-ground walled," the skepticism that doubts the existence of God: *"And can the Father be?"* Even if the father has abandoned the children—"Where is the foundling's father hidden?" (*Moby-Dick*)—the faithful still address God with the familiarity of children addressing their father. It is essential to note that Clarel, like Ishmael in *Moby-Dick*, is another Melvillean orphan in search of a father and a mother: "Clarel, bereft while still but young" (1.39.17). Even the devil, during the Syrian monk's temptation, acknowledges the familial relationship between the human and the divine: "Is yon the Father's home? / And thou His child cast out to night?" (2.18.97–98). When the Dominican monk asserts that it is impossible to know God from nature, he also insists that " 'Tis Abba Father that we seek, / Not the Artificer" (2.25.158–59). The Dominican suggests here that mankind wants God as father, which implies a collapse of the distance between the human and the divine. Mankind does not want a God who is an artificer, for an artisan creates something different from himself and often distant. The Dominican wants adoption—a reconciliation between child-orphan and father.

Of the many metaphors to describe God in the Bible, Jesus chooses Abba to address God (Mark 14:36; one of the few Aramaisms preserved in the *koina* Greek New Testament)—not Lord, Master, Lord of Hosts, Groom, or Shepherd, but Father. In addition to the traditional orthodox Christian interpretation that the child is of the substance of the father, as Jesus is the son or begotten of the father, Jesus' cry to Abba—Father—implies a desire for closeness and oneness despite any divine self-concealment or abandonment. The child-father metaphor explains why prudent, self-controlled men of war such as Djalea still remain "half a child" (4.29.27). The epithet "child" does not refer to an immature infatuation versus the "passion deep of man mature" (4.29.26) but to the relationship a man has to a God, despite divine hiddenness and silence, approached as a child approaches his father. Even the crusader King Louis IX is still "a child / In simple faith" who has "trust" (2.13.7–8, 11) in God just like the "child-like thousands" who sing the Easter liturgy, the "hallelujah after pain" (4.33.20, 21).

If the expression of the human condition before God is that of a child before a father, the relationship can be broken or reversed—that of an orphan before a hidden or absent father. In fact, a father who has had the child-father relationship broken or ignored is a lonely father. During the Mar Saba masque, the monk playing the wandering Jew says that he is "more lonely than an only god" (3.19.77). A flaw exists at the very heart of the child-father relationship: God, like humans, is self-exiled and lonely. A God who can feel loneliness is a personal God, a "Thou" instead of an "It" in Martin Buber's terms. Such a lonely God is not merely a linguistic convention but a divine Thou who responds as a lonely father. Divine loneliness implies that the divine has need of the human. In other words, the notion of the human created in the image of God gives us permission to reverse the process. In *Clarel*, by looking at the human, we learn what God is like. Just as Celio, Mortmain, and Clarel fail to commune with each other, just as Derwent, Nehemiah, and Vine all experience a need for spiritual and emotional sympathy, God also suffers loneliness and needs communion. Even the patriarch Abraham, who originally received God's covenant promise of presence, experiences God as alone: "Even he which first, with mind austere, / Arrived in solitary tone / To think of God as One—alone" (2.20.4–6). The word "alone" may refer to both Abraham and God, but its closeness to the word "God" suggests that here again God is a lonely God, just as "isolation lones" Jesus' "state" (1.13.78). The phrase "God as One—alone" is one of several revelatory windows through which we can get a glimpse of Melville's knowledge of the Hebrew Bible and rabbinic responsa.

Although Melville's theology library is lost to us, *Clarel* demonstrates that Melville had some knowledge of rabbinic commentaries. The oneness of God is the most basic assertion in the Hebrew Bible and the primary and principle theme of the Book of the Covenant, Deuteronomy. Melville here alludes to the verse called the *Shema,* which implies not just outer obedience to legal rules but inner acceptance of God in love: "Hear [*shema* in Hebrew], O Israel: The Lord our God is one Lord" (Deuteronomy 6:4). This basic Hebrew assertion of the oneness and uniqueness of God is repeated eight times in Deuteronomy. But two of the most famous medieval rabbinic commentators, Rashbam and Ibn Ezra, translated the Shema as "Hear, O Israel, The Lord is our God, the Lord *alone.*" The juxtaposition of "One—alone" in *Clarel* suggests that Melville was not only familiar with the Shema, a biblical commonplace, but with the rabbinic controversy over the reading and translation of the Hebrew word *ehod*: "one" or "alone."

Melville's notion of the one lonely God is not a God of abstraction, like Thomas Hardy's First Cause or Prime Mover. He may dwell in loneliness, but He is sought in intimacy. A lonely God needs intimacy, and *Clarel* suggests that a restoration of the relationship between the human and the divine, as a child to the father, can be achieved if one gives one's heart in love to God. Just as "a god-like mind" cannot live "without a God," the hidden human heart can be given in love and trust to a hidden God.[10] How this is so may be suggested by an examination of Melville's language and theology of the heart and by a final look at the Epilogue of the poem.

A THEOLOGY OF THE HEART

Melville had a biblical love for the word "heart" in *Clarel*. The recurrence of this master word suggests the increasing importance of a heart motif that goes beyond the common notion of the heart as the seat of human emotions and affectivity. Melville adopts the biblical notion of the heart as the seat of divine immanence and trust, recurrently using the biblical metaphor of proving or testing the human heart and then turning the human heart to God. Of the almost eight hundred references to the heart in the Hebrew Bible, most occur in the prophetic text Jeremiah. In Jeremiah, we are called upon to "wash thine heart from wickedness" (4:14), to remove the "foreskins of your heart" (4:4), to return to God with the "whole heart" (3:10), and to search for God "with all your heart" (29:13). The new covenant which the Lord will make with the house of Israel will be written "in their hearts" (31:31–34). Just as Melville turned to the poetic energy of Jeremiah for the lament form and for the polarity of mood and emotion in *Clarel*'s structure, so he grapples with the problem of God by using the biblical symbol of the Jeremianic heart.

Like Ezekiel's and Jeremiah's uncircumcised heart that must be circumcised to God (to remove the metaphorical foreskin of unfeeling fat around the heart and thereby be sensitized to God), the Melvillean "unsatisfied" heart (3.30.149) insists that the only way to establish a relationship with a hidden, silent God, the only way to satisfy the heart, is to give the heart on fire and in love to God. As Clarel says, "And make my heart to burn with love" (1.7.51). Clarel's wish is no mere romantic metaphor but is an allusion to another important biblical co-text for understanding *Clarel*: the deeply ironic road-to-Emmaus passage in Luke 24:13–35. Here, two of the disciples are walking from Jerusalem to Emmaus, and Jesus, as divine incognito, joins them. Their eyes are "held" ("holden" in the King James translation), or prevented from recognizing Jesus, and they begin to speak about what has happened recently in Jerusalem—the Passion. The irony is that the disciples tell Jesus the things that have just happened to him. Jesus answers like a truly ironic and hidden God: "What things?" (Luke 24:19). On the road to Emmaus, Jesus gives perhaps the most famous scripture lesson in history: "And beginning at Moses and all the prophets, he [Jesus] expounded unto them in all the scriptures the things concerning himself" (Luke 24:27). When the disciples' eyes are opened and they recognize Jesus, he vanishes, again like an ironic hidden God. Then the disciples say to each other: "Did not our heart burn within us, while he talked to us by the way, and while he opened to us the scriptures?" (Luke 24:32). The image of the disciples' and Clarel's heart on fire can have two contrary meanings. First, one could claim that heart-on-fire implies the sheer pleasure of learning scripture, especially with a master teacher, Jesus. Clarel yearns for such a sage-scholar: "Some stranger of a lore replete, / Who . . . Would question me, expound and prove" (1.7.47–50). Yet the images of heart-on-fire and Jesus' vanishing from the scene also imply an incomplete exegesis, a partial revelation of divine knowledge and purpose that does not completely satisfy. Of course, in Luke 24, Jesus appears again and gives a second, more complete instruction, but Melville does not refer to this second post-Resurrection appearance. The walk-to-Emmaus co-text in the seventh canto of the very first book of Clarel is the perfect paradigm to understand Clarel, a lapsed divinity student, and his desire to find and to love God revealed through scripture. Yet, at the same time, the Luke co-text enables us to understand the inherent difficulty of loving an ironic, hidden-yet-present God who works through mysterious events such as Jesus' death and is partially revealed through biblical words that are difficult to interpret and are incomplete. The disciples' failure to recognize the hidden Jesus is parallel to Clarel's failure to find the hidden God who is capable of ironically playing with human perception and understanding. The disciples' blindness is cured by the second appearance of the risen Christ, and they return to Jerusalem "with great joy" (Luke 24:52). But Clarel's eyes in Melville's poem are still "held" from seeing clearly.

The heart burning with fire is also a central image in Jeremiah, one of the biblical co-texts essential to understanding Clarel's Epilogue: "Then I said, I will not make mention of him, nor speak any more in his name. But his word was in mine heart as a burning fire shut up in my bones, and I was weary with forbearing, and I could not stay" (Jeremiah 20:9). Jeremiah is in the grip of an emotion so deep and compelling that it must find expression: "My heart maketh a noise within me; I cannot hold my peace. . . ." (4:19). These two heart passages are often interpreted as Jeremiah's futile attempt to turn his back on his prophetic mission or as a sign of his wild swings in mood in the five poems called Jeremiah's confessions or complaints. But the passages are central to understanding what Melville does in the Epilogue: within the human heart is something that we cannot hold in, something that must rise up: God's word in Jeremiah, divine trust in Clarel. The hunt for the hidden God in Clarel, the desire to know and to interpret the words of Jesus in Luke, and the inability to hold in the word of God in Jeremiah—all are problems in hermeneutics. In a sense, both Bible readers and Clarel readers are on the way to Emmaus. We have evidence for God; at times we think we understand God; at times we are skeptical; at times our eyes are "held" or kept from seeing the hidden God; and sometimes our hearts are on fire, and we cannot hold in our sense of the reality of God despite the evidence of protest and suffering.

Melville wrote the following inscription in his copy of the New Testament: "Who well considers the Christian religion, would think that God meant to keep it in the dark from our understandings, and make it turn upon the motions of our hearts."[11] *Clarel* also insists that we go beyond thought, beyond will, beyond emotion to think and to feel faith in the heart. In a 1 June 1851 letter to Nathaniel Hawthorne, Melville gives an early hint of what becomes in *Clarel*, twenty-five years later, a theology of the heart: "I stand for the heart. To the dogs with the head! I had rather be a fool with a heart, than Jupiter Olympus with his head. The reason the mass of men fear God, and at bottom dislike Him, is because they rather distrust His heart, and fancy Him all brain like a watch."[12] In *Clarel*, faith has not only a utilitarian dimension—faith out of need, faith as ethical control—but also an ontological dimension. Faith is God approached and perceived by the heart, not the mind.

The word "heart" in *Clarel* is a synecdochic manifestation of the divinity within the human—a part of the whole and the whole in the part, a symbol. The heart not only pumps blood to the brain and is given symbolic primacy over the intellect and will. The heart is also symbolic of how far the human has receded from God or how far the human has returned to God. The heart is a hyphen between the human and the divine. The heart as synecdoche also enunciates the whole person, as when Nehemiah calls Clarel and others by the synecdochic epithet "heart" (1.9.9). Or when Derwent compares a man to a book and claims that "through Nature each heart looks / Up to a God . . ." (2.32.79–80). Rather than characters, *Clarel* contains hearts that run the entire range of rejection, doubt, denial, and faith. Judas, who rejected Jesus, has "a fiend-heart in the human one" (1.30.49); Clarel sees himself as a "heart profane" because of his doubt (1.6.18). Ruth and Agar have cold hearts that indicate not only their unhappiness in Palestine but also their inability to approach God: "It was with hearts but chill and loath; / Never was heaven served by that / Cold form . . ." (1.27.97–99). Those within a community of faith who have a close personal relationship with God have very different hearts: Helena's "warm emotional heart" (1.31.115), the faithful's "settled hearts" (3.5.127), John the Baptist's "pure" heart (2.11.90), Salvaterra's "pure heart" (4.13.96), and faith's "loyal heart" (4.10.85).

Clarel's heart-hunger for God remains unsatisfied because he cannot give his heart to God. Clarel's heart is a lover hungering for love, seeking, waiting in anticipation for spiritual, physical, and emotional communion, guidance, and security in life, repose for the soul or self and, most important, knowledge of God. The difficulty, however, is that there is a continuum between knowing and loving. For Clarel, one can love only what one knows; what is unknown, remote, hidden, and silent is difficult to cherish. Clarel cannot give his heart to an unknown God. Clarel's unsatisfied heart is desperate to burn with love. Possessing Ruth as his love object does not satisfy his deeper love for God: "Possessing Ruth, nor less his heart / Aye hungering still, in deeper part / Unsatisfied . . ." (3.30.147–49). Clarel's "passionate mood," as "long as hungering unfed," will reject "all else" (2.27.108, 109, 110) and cannot be fed by any heterosexual or homosexual love (see 2.27.123–28). Clarel knows that the "*other* love" he seeks is the love that God-intoxicated saints such as "St. Francis and St. John have felt": "That *other* love!—Oh heavy load— / Is naught trustworthy but God?" (3.31.50, 53–54). Eros must yield to agape. Even the devil warns the Syrian monk that "heart-peace" is impossible for man as long as "each pure nature pines in dearth" (2.18.129, 130). When Clarel tries to read the Bible to make his heart burn with love—a unity made up of the "Fathers" or Hebrew Bible and the "Evangelists" or Christian Bible—he cannot:

> He sought the inn, and tried to read
> The Fathers with a *filial* mind.
> In vain; *heart* wandered or *repined*.
> The Evangelists may serve his need:
> Deep as he felt the beauty sway,
> Estrangement there he could but heed,
> Both time and tone so far away
> From him the modern. . . .
> (1.41.78–85, emphasis mine)

Clarel tries to read Hebrew Scripture with a "filial mind," a mind that approaches the father-God as a child does. He cannot. His heart repines, not only in the sense of complaining or discontent but also in the archaic sense of a lover's painful longing. Finally, his heart is estranged, distanced from God. Since Clarel is unable to trust God as a child trusts a father, Clarel's heart wanders from God. Eventually, Clarel is in danger of losing his heart— "dissolving heart" (4.2.186)—and becomes a "heart bereft" (4.33.56)— bereft of Ruth and of God.

Clarel's spiritual struggle is the same as the psalmist's: although his mind is embittered, his heart also grieves inwardly (Psalms 73:21–22). Clarel suffers from "the complex passion" (1.5.217), for he cannot love an unknown, hidden God; he cannot place any degree of trust in a divine presence in absence who surpasses all human knowledge: "How think to sound God's deeper heart!" (2.32.111). Clarel cannot grasp the great paradox of protest theism, setting one's hope and trust in a hidden God: "And I will wait upon the Lord, that hideth his face from the house of Jacob, and I will look for him" (in the sense of hope and trust; Isaiah 8:17).

In the canto "In Confidence," Derwent tries to change Clarel's heart, but he makes the mistake of accommodating faith to reason or subordinating the heart to the head. Derwent wants to say to Clarel, "Throw all this burden upon HIM" but does not, and Clarel's "freighted heart" sinks "lower and lower" (3.21.157, 322, 321). Yet Derwent admits that "there's here and there a heart / Which shares at whiles strange throbs alone," and that he understands Clarel's frustration with a hidden God: "we dote / To dream heaven drops a casting vote, / In these perplexities takes part!" (3.21.164–65, 167–69). After Clarel cries to God in his confusion, Derwent preaches nonsectarian good deeds and charity and also appeals for the heart: "do you know / That what most satisfies the head / Least solaces the heart?" (3.21.241–43). The canto ends with Clarel's envying Nehemiah's response to faith that is the abdication of the head—reason—for the heart: "that folly of the cross / Contemned by reason, yet how dear to you?" (3.21.325–26).

Since the exact nature of God will always be the great unknown, Melville does not posit an "ideal balance of head and heart" but favors the heart over the head.[13] In terms of the distance between the human and the divine, the head as the seat of reason, will, and freethinking estranges the human from the divine, but the heart binds man to God. Even though Celio's skepticism insists that Christ is responsible for the dove and the shark—good and evil—he still recognizes that some people are enthralled to Christ because "the head rejects; so much the more / The heart embraces" (1.13.68–69). To retain the primacy of the heart is difficult for people because the heart often yields to the head: "Does intellect assert a claim / Against the heart, her yielding kin?" (1.36.9–10). The "misrule of our selfish mind," along with the "ills by fate assigned," is the source of much self-inflicted human suffering (4.18.151, 150), and "what most satisfies the head / Least solaces the heart" (3.21.242–43). When Rolfe describes the loving "reverence" that pilgrims give to Shakespeare's house in Stratford, Derwent insists that those who truly understand Shakespeare would not "idolize" his home as a "shrine" (4.7.64). Rolfe's rebuttal demonstrates that Derwent has missed the point and does not understand the "vital affections" of the pilgrim heart:

> Nay, 'tis the heart here, not the head.
> You note some pilgrims hither bring
> The rich or humble offering:
> If that's irrational—what then?
> In kindred way your Lutheran
> Will rival it; yes, in sad hour
> The Lutheran widow lays her flower
> Before the picture of the dead:
> Vital affections do not draw
> Precepts from Reason's arid law.
>   (4.7.66–75)

Here Rolfe connects the heart with reverence and sets the irrational but vital heart against the rational but arid "Reason." Rolfe insists that we must turn not to reason to understand the personal value placed on shrines or graves but to the deeper and more personal affections of the heart. The deepest affection of the heart is not against reason but a completion of reason. For the use of reason that denies the meanings of the heart cuts itself off from meaning. Derwent even associates the head with the pride and vanity of complex theological "controversies": "Behead me—rid me of pride's part / And let me live but by the heart!" (3.6.65, 68–69).

Mortmain questions Derwent's desire to live only by the heart, by asking the central prophetic question of Jeremiah and Ezekiel: "Hast proved thy heart? first prove it. Stay: / The Bible, tell me, is it true, / And thence deriv'st thy flattering view?" (3.6.70–72). Mortmain challenges Derwent to prove the truth of his heart and then suggests that the testing of the heart rather than the head is a biblical notion. To "prove" the heart in *Clarel* is to demonstrate the crux of protest theism: that one can give one's heart to a hidden God despite the question, in human terms, of whether a hidden God deserves such a gift. In fact, giving one's heart is a powerful reminder for God to keep His promises to man because the greater the gift, the greater the responsibility one has to the giver. At the very beginning of the pilgrimage, the narrator also implies that Clarel will face such a testing of the heart: "In heart what hap may Clarel prove?" (1.44.49).

The fact that Derwent and Clarel are unable to prove their heart-affair with God does not negate the ceaseless striving for God that is in the human heart. The narrator asks the most central question of the poem in terms of Clarel's failure to achieve a theology of the heart: "So willful! but 'tis loss and smart, / Clarel, in thy dissolving heart. / Will't form anew?" (4.2.185–87). Here, the narrator corrects Clarel's willful and uncharitable reading of the mercenary Ungar, who claims that the human voice is comparable to a gun. The narrator hopes that during the pilgrimage, Clarel will form a new heart. The biblical prophets knew from the testing, proving, and forming anew of the human heart that the intricate relationship between one's outward behavior and inner motivation—between deed, word, and thought—is notoriously difficult to read and fathom. Yet only if the heart is read can it be known whether one trusts God, whether, in prophetic terms, one is obedient to God and a true prophet. Jeremiah knew that the human heart is deceitful and opposes man and God: "The heart is deceitful above all things, and desperately wicked: who can know it? I the Lord search the heart . . ." (Jeremiah 17:9–10). Only God can test or prove the integrity of a human heart—this is Mortmain's point. Derwent may be lying to others or to himself.

Clarel, like the Hebrew prophetic texts, is really an ordeal of the testing of the human heart, not for God to repay human goodness with rewards, but to understand whether within the human heart there is a genuine turning toward God. The problem is that humans alone cannot test the mettle, so to speak, of the human heart. The narrator's desire for Clarel's heart to form anew is also inspired by the prophetic texts Ezekiel and Jeremiah: "And I will give them an heart to know me, that I am the Lord: and they shall be my people, and I will be their God: for they shall return unto me with their whole heart." (Jeremiah 24:7). In Jeremiah, Yahweh gives his people a new heart to recognize that He is their God and they are His people—the covenant formula that defines the relationship between Yahweh and Israel, a relationship of a possessive lover-God to the lost heart of the beloved-Israel. Ezekiel tells of a similar God-given gift of a new heart: "I will give them one heart and I will put a new spirit within you; and I will take the stony heart out of their flesh, and will give them an heart of flesh" (Ezekiel 11:19). Here, the strong hardness of human nature which closes men against God and their fellow men would be broken and made into a human heart of flesh. Yet, in Ezekiel, the new heart does not seem to be a unilateral gift of divine grace. Ezekiel understood the more difficult forming anew of the human heart: "Cast away from you all your transgressions, whereby ye have transgressed; and make you a new heart and a new spirit . . ." (Ezekiel 18:31). In *Clarel*, the human heart must also be given without the divine gift of a new heart and is thus much more difficult to achieve. As in Ezekiel, Clarel must make his own new heart.

The dilemma in *Clarel* is not merely that Melville would not trust the human mind as the organ of truth, as many Unitarians and even Transcendentalists did, but that a biblical difference exists between a receptive heart and an unreceptive heart, between a heart of flesh and a heart of stone. Although Nathan becomes overzealous for his newfound Judaism, it is still his initial "receptive heart" that enables him to apprehend his wife's faith (1.17.225). Ungar, however, raises counterevidence for the callousness of human beings who are often unreceptive, in this case to Christ's parables:

> There is a callousness in clay.
> Christ's pastoral parables divine,
>
> . . . .
> how many feel?
> Feel! rather put it—comprehend?
> Not unto all does nature lend
> The gift; at hight such love's appeal
> Is hard to know, as in her deep
> Is hate; a prior love must steep
> The spirit; head nor heart have marge
> Commensurate in man at large.
> (4.18.121–22, 124–31)

Many do not understand Jesus' parables. Ungar seems to deny the head-heart dilemma by insisting that neither symbolic dimension of humanity can feel and comprehend the love of Jesus. Ungar's notion of a "prior love" that "must steep / The spirit" is not a thunderbolt of grace from without but a prior love and trust from within. One must bring a measure of openness and trust to Jesus' words. As Jesus said in the parable of the measure, "with what measure ye mete, it shall be measured to you: and unto you that hear shall more be given. For he that hath, to him shall be given: and he that hath not, from him shall be taken even that which he hath" (Mark 4:24–25). The difficulty, however, in interpreting the words of Jesus is that interpretation is not an easy task. There will always be readers and listeners who have eyes that do not see and ears that do not hear (Mark 8:18). Although "hearts change not in the change of gods" (4.18.141; cf. 2.26.159) implies that "man's hard heart" (4.18.163) stays the same, those few who do go to Jesus with trust and openness own him in the heart, not the head: "More minds with shrewd Voltaire have part / Than now own Jesus in the heart" (4.18.144–45). Melville's Civil War poem "The Conflict of Convictions," which qualifies the notion of human progress, also stresses the changelessness of the human heart: "Age after age shall be / As age after age has been / From man's changeless heart their way they win." Unreceptive hearts are changeless; receptive hearts, though, can change.

For Ungar and Rolfe, just as for the biblical authors, hard-heartedness or callousness is the root of all sin. In fact, Ungar compares the weakening of faith and the various sects to a "hard heart aged grown" (4.20.71). The receptive heart enables one to turn to God; an unreceptive heart keeps one in a state of ignorance and even malice. The stiff-necked unwillingness, however, to give the heart to an ironic, hidden, silent God suggests the difficulty of drawing close to such a lonely God. Unreceptive hearts suggest the difficulty of knowing the human and the divine heart: "But if in vain / One tries to comprehend a man, / How think to sound God's deeper heart!" (2.32.109–11).

THE HEART OF THE MYSTERY

Melville's emphasis on theism as a support for ethical self-control is directly related to his recognition of the human capacity for malice without end. Although spirits are personified in the poem, what drives the course of human events in *Clarel* is not a titanic struggle between God and Satan but unreceptive, callous human nature. Melville has no need for gargoyles; the demon is within. The field of battle is the human heart, and the contending armies do not hail from foreign lands. With his deep respect for the fallibility or fallenness of humanity, Melville would have appreciated the sign above the life-size mirror in the gorilla house of New York's Bronx Zoo. After viewing some of the world's most dangerous and intimidating animals, human beings stand in front of the mirror, look, and read these stinging words: "You are looking at the most dangerous animal in the world!" This similar recognition of the "callousness in clay" causes Mortmain to view death as a sanction against human wickedness and Ungar to claim that the "deterring dart" of Mosaic Law should be "graved on man's hard heart," for only "penalty makes sinners start" (4.18.121, 159, 163, 164).

Just as "the heart / Of heavenly love," the teachings of Jesus, can be corrupted into "the creeds malign" (1.13.87–88, 89), the human heart can also be filled with evil and the spirit of malice. As we have noted before in the canto "Prelusive," Melville's narrator sees Piranezi's etchings of the Roman prisons as a symbol of the mystery of iniquity within the heart:[14]

> The thing implied is one with man,
> His penetralia of retreat—
> The heart, with labyrinths replete:
> In freaks of intimation see
> Paul's "mystery of iniquity:"
> Involved indeed, a blur of dream;
> As, awed by scruple and restricted
> In first design, or interdicted
> By fate and warnings as might seem;
> The inventor miraged all the maze,
> Obscured it with prudential haze;
> Nor less, if subject unto question,
> The egg left, egg of the suggestion.
> (2.35.20–32)

The mystery of iniquity as represented in *Clarel* is much more than an Emersonian absence of good. Evil is active in *Clarel*. Several characters— Mortmain, Rolfe, Ungar—testify to the "malevolence / In man toward man" (4.13.226–27). Mortmain recognizes the presence of goodness and wisdom but, according to his embittered point of view, claims: "The good have but a patch at best, / The wise their corner; for the rest— / Malice divides with ignorance" (2.4.90–92). The lines in "Prelusive," however, indicate not only that artists deliberately obscure meaning but also that God ("the inventor") hides the evil but still leaves the egg of its suggestion. The context darkens here. How can man give his heart to God if that heart conceals evil? As Mortmain reasserts, "some hearts die in thrall" of "wickedness" (2.36.23, 26). If what Melville insists upon in *Clarel* is man's creation in the image of God, can there be divine immanence in an evil person? And if "the inventor miraged all the maze" (2.35.29), if all of nature is in fact concealed, how can we recognize good or evil within the human or the divine heart? The essence of iniquity is a mystery.

The answer to the dilemma is Melville's notion of human polarity. We are dust and ashes and a little above the angels. The human is caught between heaven and hell: "hearts which dwell / Helots of habit old as earth / Suspended 'twixt the heaven and hell" (3.31.61–63). In the Epilogue, man is "ape and angel, strife and old debate— / The harps of heaven and dreary gongs of hell" (4.35.12–13). Here Melville refers not only to evolution versus creationism but also to the duality of human nature and of the human heart. One can be in thrall of wickedness and/or of goodness: "Evil and good they braided play / Into one chord" (4.4.27–28). Human malevolence is qualified by human benevolence—charity, tolerance. Within the context of human polarity, the "Prelusive" canto does not deny that human beings are endowed with a created spirit. That spirit—the heart—can be either in a lost relation to God—evil—or in a renewed relation to God—good. One has the freedom to choose good or evil, to choose for or against God.

Because the inventor deliberately hides the meaning of the heart, the egg of a suggestion may be the mystery of evil or may be trust in the divine:

> Consult the heart!
> Spouse to the brain—can coax or thwart:
> Does *she* renounce the trust divine?
> Hide it she may, but scarce resign;
> Like to a casket buried deep
> Which, in a fine and fibrous throng,
> The rootlets of the forest keep—
> 'Tis tangled in her meshes strong.
>   (4.18.77–84)

The implication here is that the heart is the seat of a radical trust in God. Divine trust may be hidden but not absent. Just as the Creator plays hide-and-seek with his creation, man also hides from God his trust and love. Just as the Creator-Inventor conceals evil in the heart, the created can also "hide" divine trust in the human heart. The degree of sensitivity to God is determined by the degree of sensitivity to the hidden divinity within the heart. Within the human heart is the seed of eternity, which is the source of the desire for the presence of God and for the understanding of His ways. Those who irreverently mock the Church of the Holy Sepulcher are those who are "versed / In everything above, below— / In all but thy deep human heart" (1.3.154–56). Without well-versed knowledge of the heart, without the proving or testing of the heart, the heart cannot be given in trust to God.

In Melville's biblical imagination, the human heart, like every other dimension of human experience, can be claimed by good or counterclaimed by evil. If mankind had no inclination toward the divine, if the divine found no immanent hospitality within the heart, then evil would run out of control, and only an overwhelmingly unambiguous divine self-disclosure could reveal the divine to the human. Such a revelation would be coercion, not choice. To be cognitively free toward the divine, human beings possess an innate tendency to trust God. Evil competes with such immanence, however, and the human is obviously able to repress the divinity within without doing manifest violence to his nature. The choice against the evil side of the dual human nature is helped by the ethical control offered by faith. Although Clarel claims that the hint of evil hidden in the weak human lips of the portrait of Beatrice Cenci cannot be restrained—"Desire is none, nor any reign" (3.7.24)—faith does offer the hope of some reigned control throughout the rest of the poem. Some people need God's "Thou shalt not" upon them.

Of course, that protest theism as a faith includes the courage to protest against God and to retain faith as ethical control and as a surrender of the heart to God, to love God as a child loves and trusts a father, does not prove the existence of a loving God. God is a hidden, ambiguous, multi-faced being—an image of His creation, man. The surrender of the human heart to God, however, has a significance and purpose internal to itself—not dependent on any verifiable revelation or definition of God. The unsatisfied heart is a call for a response to a lonely God. Rather than a heart-to-heart connection with God as the fruits of faith, the unsatisfied heart is now the essence of faith. God hides from man, in a sense, so that He might know the choice of the human heart—to turn to or away from God.

EPILOGUE AND ENTELECHY

The Epilogue of *Clarel* is a combination of the turn to and away from God, a combination of love and protest, a faith tinged with obstinacy: protest theism. Although faith bleeds "from her wounded trust," the trust often broken between child and father, Melville stubbornly insists on *"the spirit above the dust!"* (4.35.9, 11). Although the polarity of human nature—"ape and angel," "star and clod"—along with the debate between science and faith may never be resolved as long as God is hidden, Melville still metaphorically suggests a response to God. Although the theodicy question of why is there undeserved suffering and death—"Wherefore ripen us to pain?" (4.35.21)— remains unanswered, Melville suggests that we give the heart to God:

> Then *keep thy heart*, though yet but ill-resigned—
> Clarel, thy heart, the *issues* there but mind;
> That like the crocus budding through the snow—

That like a swimmer rising from the deep—
That like a *burning secret* which doth go
Even from the bosom that would hoard and keep;
Emerge thou mayst from the last whelming sea,
And prove that death but routs life into victory.

(4.35.27–34, emphasis mine)

"Keep thy heart" is a sign to remember the divinity within the heart, not a sign of selfish hoarding. One could read this last stanza as metaphorically similar to "Ishmael's deliverance from the wreck of the *Pequod*," as Merlin Bowen suggested.[15] But *Clarel's* Epilogue is much more than the coffin suddenly turned into a life buoy, more than Ahab's "theoretic bright side," after the much darker "side of death" (*Moby-Dick*). The last stanza of the Epilogue is an intertextual biblical theology of the heart. The "burning secret" from the "bosom" is very similar to Jeremiah's inability to hold in his impulse toward God: "But his word was in mine heart as a burning fire shut up in my bones . . ." (Jeremiah 20:9). The divine trust shut up within the human heart is what some people hide, but the Epilogue counsels that, "like a burning secret which doth go / Even from the bosom that would hoard and keep," the love that Clarel first yearned for—"and make my heart to burn with love" (1.7.51)—may unfold from within at the last. The burning secret of *Clarel* is divine immanence, the seed of eternity within the human heart, and the choice of unfolding the heart in love to God. The budding crocus, the swimmer, and the secret from the heart are not so much hints at resurrection and immortality as they are an unfolding from within of the divinity of man that "prove[s] that death but routs life into victory."[16]

The Epilogue is not the narrator's advice to bypass the entire dialogic process of twenty thousand lines of theological debate, but it is an invitation to reread the poem within the biblical context of a theology of the heart that is the second half of protest theism. The heart has been discussed throughout the pilgrimage, and the Epilogue is not a sudden, unprepared-for panacea for Clarel's doubt. The great enemy of faith in *Clarel* is not Godlessness—"if God but be—but be!" (2.15.73). The enemy is heartlessness. The ignoring of the human heart and the callousness toward the human and the divine cause the collapse of charity, tolerance, and ethical control.

Even rebellion against God is at least passionate in *Clarel*, as the human is allowed to lament, protest, and object to God. But, after protest, one pledges the human heart to come near to God. What is essential to notice in the Epilogue is the dialogical fusing of prooftexts from both the Hebrew and the Christian Bibles. First is the unique verbatim quotation "Keep thy heart" that occurs only once in the Bible: "Keep thy heart with all diligence; for out of it are the issues of life" (Proverbs 4:23). The biblical idea and image of keeping the heart is also found in the famous phrase from Philippians 4:7: "And the peace of God, which passeth all understanding, shall keep your hearts and minds through Christ Jesus." The singular use of the word "heart," rather than the plural in Philippians, and the use of the word "issues" in the very next verse (4.35.27, 28) indicate that Melville had Proverbs 4:23 primarily in mind as his biblical co-text. But Philippians is also part of the semantic field of "keep thy heart," which now includes the connotation of the peace "which passeth all understanding." The key word "keep" has the metaphorical sense of watching and guarding the human heart, for the issues of the heart bring life, peace, victory: "prove[s] that death but routs life into victory." To "keep thy heart" also connotes the sense of learning from the heart—one of the goals of the entire pilgrimage—and the sense of guarding the divinity within the heart.

Clarel's Epilogue reinforces Melville's representation of a faith that is not a thunderbolt of grace from above but an upward movement of the human heart to God: "The spirit of man that goeth upward" (Ecclesiastes 3:21). Faith is not a revelation based on the sufficiency of divine grace—the spirit of God reaching down toward the human. Faith is the human spirit transcending itself to touch God out of need. A faith tinged with obstinacy "invokes him who returns no call" (1.3.193). The upward reach of the human heart to encounter the heart of the hidden God depends always on free choice—an a priori decision for or against God. Giving the heart to God, however, does not make of *Deus absconditus* a Deus ex machina. God does not suddenly emerge from hiddenness and silence. The human turns to God with the heart not to ensure an unambiguous revelation—no such revelation exists in Melville's theological worldview—but because the human has no choice if humanity is to be maintained. Melville also allows God to be God. God is free not to meet man on any human terms. The Clarelian pilgrim does, however, inquire after God. The only cure for the anxieties of questions and counterquestions is the heart—not the mind. Only through the heart can the paradox of a God hidden, but not absent, be resolved. If God is revealed in *Clarel*, He is revealed only to the heart, not to the eye. *Clarel*'s final testimony is not the radical ambivalence of agnosticism but the hope of an experiential faith called protest theism, which finds its mark in the human heart.

Conclusion

IN A FAMOUS NOTEBOOK ENTRY dated 20 November 1856, Nathaniel Hawthorne gave a revealing interpretation of Melville's spiritual struggles:

> he can neither believe, nor be comfortable in his unbelief: and he is too honest and courageous not to try to do one or the other. If he were a religious man, he would be one of the most truly religious and reverential; he has a very high and noble nature, and better worth immortality than most of us.[1]

Edwin M. Eigner has called this passage a description of the nineteenth-century condition of mind, and although he is discussing the structure of the romance, his gloss on Hawthorne's remarks illuminates Melville's theological reflection in *Clarel*:

> Thus for Hawthorne at least, it was dishonest and cowardly to remain willingly between doubt and conviction, and by extension, I would argue, dishonest and cowardly to write books merely descriptive of that condition. The brave man tries to fight his way through to a definite position, either to comfortable faith or, if necessary, to honest despair. Thus, while a sense of tormented doubt may have existed in Hawthorne and Melville, and while such a conflict is highly flattering to our own twentieth- century feeling for relativistic chaos, it is unlikely that open- ended ambiguity could have been the intended structure of their romances.[2]

Hawthorne predicted that Melville "will never rest until he gets hold of a definite belief."[3] I would qualify Eigner's remark by removing the "either/or" choice of faith or doubt, for Melville suggests a Pocahontas-wedding of such opposites into a "both/and" response to God. Yet, I agree with Eigner and Hawthorne that Melville does wrestle his way to a definite representation of belief in *Clarel:* protest theism. The governing claim of the poem is first to protest God and then to love God. In *Clarel*, human beings have an angry claim against God—the protest against death, divine concealment, and undeserved suffering. God has much to answer for, as it were, even though asking questions of God is not so much waiting for an answer as insisting that God keep his promises. To protest against God is also to accept the existence of God. Else why protest? The equal concern of the poem is theism—a giving of one's heart to God despite one's complaints, a heart-hunger for God as strong as any orthodox, traditional faith.

The steps toward a final stance of protest theism are humanly understandable if not strictly logical. *Clarel* demonstrates that human beings experience God as hidden and silent. The human has no unambiguous revelation, no ocular proof, no verifiable miracle to prove divine presence. The human response is to lament or to protest via questions the unknowability of God, to attack God's ways yet, at the same time, to maintain an implicit interest in addressing the divine. Reverent skeptics will also wrestle with the opposites of doubt and belief in the hope of acquiring a tested faith. Melville's protest theism is an interior faith, for it does not attach itself to any exterior, objective standard—no creed, no church. The impulse toward the divine is from the inside, from the heart. With the hope of immortality and the evidence of an inner divine voice, Melville recommends exteriorizing faith by turning to God out of need. Like a swimmer rising from the deep, one comes out from hiddenness to risk giving one's heart to a hidden God who controls a world containing more than a few corners of evil. Despite its longings for God, *Clarel* does not present a certain answer to the question of the nature of God. Melville shows a fierce opposition to the God of the rational philosophers, to a God that can be explicitly defined. In other words, Melville shows a direction in the search for God, a quest made up of questions, not a definition. The lack of certitude, however, is not a barrier to giving the heart to God. Melville's decision in favor of faith is both moral (charity, ethical control, tolerance) and ontological, for he presupposes the intuition of divine trust in the heart. The heart-hunger for faith breaks rebelliously with the traditional theological answers that offer stones for bread and rests in a biblical interpretation of protest theism that is a paradoxical combination of lament and love typical of the prophetic voice Jeremiah.

The emphasis on the heart, the presence of reverent narrative voices, the green hope of immortality, and the need for ethical control represent not tragic irresolution but metaphorical, narrative, and biblical evidence for faith. Yet Melville is a high-risk, high-profit teacher, for he often teaches by negative example. And thus the poem has a mixed, affective ending. Clarel's return to hiddenness suggests that suffering and loss do not always lead to learning and that many individuals cannot achieve a theology of hope or of the heart. Another reason for a mixed, affective ending to the poem is that the problem of evil which challenges any form of theism is given more narrative space than the problem of good. Yet Melville bypasses this imbalance between evil and good by refusing to decide whether creation is good with only accidental corners of evil or evil with incongruous corners of good. Melville claims a combination of good and evil, just as he claims the possibility of faith and doubt. Human beings, however, cannot weigh the probabilities of these interpretations. The human must simply give his heart to the divine, a spontaneous turn to God based on human need. The usefulness of faith interests Melville, not its claim to truth.

A theology of protest and love solves the problem of contradictory theological interpretations. There are aspects of human experience that invite a theistic belief, such as a sense of ethical obligation, a sense of divine immanence within the human heart, a hope for spiritual peace and immortality. Yet there are aspects of human experience that invite an atheistic lack of belief, such as divine hiddenness and silence, and the theodicy questions of undeserved suffering, doubt, and death. By focusing on biblical co-texts, narrative voices, and biblical ideas and metaphors more than on character, event, and setting, one can read from *Clarel* Melville's poetic evidence for faith.

One of the most baffling problems in Melville studies is the question of Herman Melville's final religious position. Through the novels rather than the later poetry, Melville scholars have attempted to identify Melville's religious commitment. Three widely accepted readings include William H. Gilman's sense of Melville as a "Christian rebel," Lawrance Thompson's notion of Melville's anti-Christian agnosticism and embittered pessimism, and T. Walter Herbert's claim that Melville struggled with and combined the opposing theologies of his father's liberal Unitarianism and his mother's conservative Calvinism. Recently a fourth gateway into understanding Melville's religious position has been opened by Walter D. Kring and Jonathan S. Carey, who discovered that Melville attended, and may even have been a communicant of, the All Soul's Unitarian Church in New York City, a congregation led at that time by the famous conservative Unitarian minister Henry Whitney Bellows.[4]

The theological reflection represented in *Clarel* that I call protest theism should take us beyond the desire to identify Melville with a specific creed or church, or even the combination of two theologies: Calvinism and Unitarianism. Like a liberal Unitarian, Melville was attracted in *Clarel* to ethics, not dogma; to Jesus, not Christ; to Spirit, not the incarnation. *Clarel* indicates that Melville, like the Unitarians, subordinated theology to ethics, demonstrated tolerance for other religions, and showed the dignity of human nature via man's altruistic impulses. Melville's emphasis on self-control and self-mastery is also an essential part of the self culture of the Transcendentalists and the Unitarians. Yet Melville seems closer to Calvinism in his attraction to the concept of Original Sin in *Clarel* and in his rejection of a faith based solely on reason or on empirical knowledge. And Melville's voices in *Clarel* certainly reject a Unitarian natural religion based on a beneficent deity and the belief in human perfectability. By focusing on the four great theological movements of American history and literature—Calvinism, Deism, Unitarianism, and Transcendentalism—we discover a Melville who identified with some of these doctrines but also distanced himself from them.

Clarel, however, seems to bypass the debate that has occupied so much of Melville studies. Faith in *Clarel* is a response not to dogma but to the burning questions about the nature of mortality, theodicy (good and evil), and divinity. Melville's theological reflection comes out of the tension between the traditional promises of faith, as in Calvinism and Unitarianism, and the experience of suffering. Only after Melville's estrangement from God and his wrestling with theodicy does he offer a protest theism based on hope, inner voices, human need, and the heart. In other words, the experience of suffering and death, the experience of estrangement from God provides both the occasion and the basis for Melvillean theological reflection in *Clarel*.

Melvillean protest theism is rooted in Melville's biblical imagination and in the intertextual relationship between *Clarel* and biblical texts, not in Unitarianism or Calvinism or Transcendentalism. The greatest credit to Melville's biblical habit of the heart, especially his Hebraic sensitivity to divine self-concealment, is that he presents the problem of divine hiddenness and silence as it presents itself in life. The question of the ultimate nature of God—of what is beyond human control—is left open, as it must be if one is serious in asking it. Any answer would be reductive and imply an all-encompassing human intellect—the very premise *Clarel* negates. Any answer would deny the power of protest theism—the personal, private confrontation between divine hiddenness and an unsatisfied heart. Melville also never mistakes the hidden God for an absent or dead God. Melville respects God enough to allow Him divine freedom and understands that God, although in hiding, reveals Himself in the ways and times (if at all) He chooses. Protest theism is not to be mistaken for theological certainty, for a formulation of creed or maxim. True to his earlier works such as *Mardi*, *Moby-Dick*, and *Pierre*, Melville returned to the Bible to insist that anything less than a deep-diving quest and question is untrue; any facile theological answer is pretentious.

Clarel's silence at the end of the quest, at the end of all his questions, is the most unsettling for a first-time reader. It is a silence that speaks of the futility of all that is human, of the death of all that he loves. What can Clarel, or anybody for that matter, say until God comes out of hiddenness and speaks?

And God never speaks in *Clarel*. But to the fourth- and fifth-time reader turned interpreter, the poem suggests a hopefulness in the face of hiddenness that is not merely a tired wisdom. In a spiritually honest combination of doubt and faith, of protest and love, *Clarel* offers a distinctly biblical perception of how to survive spiritually in a time when spiritual imagination wanes and the thirst for faith waxes. Perhaps a future time will come when all the questions, all the accounts, will be settled between the human and the divine. Agitated by thoughts of eternity, by hopes for immortality, by the human need for faith, by divine immanence and trust within the heart, Melville implicitly suggests that, like Jeremiah, we protest, and, like Isaiah, we wait, but we give our hearts in love. Melville's protest theism is ultimately the mark of all that is human. In writing *Clarel*, Melville did not create a dark, nihilistic poem, but he did, paradoxically, protest and love God unto death.

NOTES

INTRODUCTION

1. Bernard Rosenthal suggests that the poem's title refers to the "light of God" in "Herman Melville's Wandering Jews," in *Puritan Influences in American Literature*, ed. Emory Elliott (Urbana: University of Illinois Press, 1979), 182.

2. Vincent Kenny's *"Clarel,"* in *A Companion to Melville Studies*, ed. John Bryant (New York: Greenwood Press, 1986), 375–407.

3. Nathalia Wright, *Melville's Use of the Bible* (Durham, N.C.: Duke University Press, 1949); and Walter E. Bezanson, Introduction to *Clarel: A Poem and Pilgrimage in the Holy Land*, edited by Bezanson (New York: Hendricks House, 1960). Bezanson's classic introduction and notes have been reprinted as "Historical and Critical Note," in *Clarel: A Poem and Pilgrimage in the Holy Land*, ed. Harrison Hayford, Alma A. MacDougall, Hershel Parker, and G. Thomas Tanselle (Evanston and Chicago: North-western University Press and the Newberry Library, 1991), 505–639, 703–841.

4. Matthew Arnold, *God and the Bible: A Review of Objections to 'Literature and Dogma'* (New York: Macmillan, 1875).

5. Walker Cowen, *Melville's Marginalia* (New York: Garland, 1987), 2:633; cf. Bezanson, "Historical and Critical Note," 527.

6. For an example of the interchangeable use of the word "narrator" with "Melville," see Hershel Parker's "The Character of Vine in Melville's *Clarel,*" *Essays in Arts and Sciences*, 15 (June 1986): 94: "I will say 'narrator' or 'Melville' interchangeably, since I see no practical or theoretical value in talking about the narrator of this poem as a created character whose nature and voice differ from Melville's own."

7. Bezanson, *"Moby-Dick*: Work of Art," in *Moby-Dick: Centennial Essays*, ed. Tyrus Hillway and Luther S. Mansfield (Dallas: Southern Methodist University Press, 1953), 30–59. Bezanson reminds us again of the central narrative consciousness of Ishmael as narrator, the "discovered persona" of Herman Melville, a part of Melville but certainly not the whole Melville, in the more recent *"Moby-Dick*: Document, Drama, Dream," in *A Companion to Melville Studies*, ed. John Bryant (New York: Greenwood Press, 1986), 169–211.

8. See James Duban, "Chipping with a Chisel: The Ideology of Melville's Narrators," *Texas Studies in Literature and Language* 31 (1989): 341–85; and John Samson's *White Lies: Melville's Narratives of Facts* (Ithaca, N.Y.: Cornell University Press, 1989).

9. I still agree with Charles Feidelson, Jr.'s assertion that "Herman Melville (1819–91) remains largely unknown, so that all attempts to identify

the omnipresent voice of the novels with Melville as he lived and breathed have been self-defeating," in *Symbolism and American Literature* (Chicago: University of Chicago Press, 1953), 163.

10. According to Merton M. Sealts, Jr., "Next to the journal and the Bible, Stanley's *Sinai and Palestine* also contributed significantly to *Clarel. . . .*" *Melville's Reading* (Columbia, S.C.: University of South Carolina Press, 1988), 121. Sealts refers here to Melville's 1856–57 journal of his travels to the Levant; see Herman Melville, *Journals*, ed. Howard C. Horsford with Lynn Horth (Evanston and Chicago: Northwestern University Press and the Newberry Library, 1989). In addition to the three main sources mentioned above, Sealts notes that there were many theological works in Melville's library which may have influenced *Clarel*: "works that were scrapped after [Melville's] death as unsuitable for resale" (p. 122).

11. All quotations from the poem are cited parenthetically within the text by part, canto, and line numbers. Throughout, I use the new definitive Northwestern-Newberry edition: Herman Melville, *Clarel: A Poem and Pilgrimage in the Holy Land*, ed. Harrison Hayford, Alma A. MacDougall, Hershel Parker, and G. Thomas Tanselle (Evanston and Chicago: Northwestern University Press and the Newberry Library, 1991).

12. The pun here, "clew," refers to both clue or hint and clew, a nautical rope, tackle, or ring to tie down a sail. Thus, for some, the pilgrimage to find God has little evidence and little support or strength for the long voyage. Melville constantly strains for the topical or often archaic pun throughout the poem; here, he succeeds brilliantly.

13. Merrell R. Davis and William H. Gilman, eds., *The Letters of Herman Melville* (New Haven: Yale University Press, 1960), 275.

14. A slightly different version of Chapter 4 was published as "The Small Voice of Silence: Melville's Narrative Voices in *Clarel*," *Texas Studies in Literature and Language* 31 (1989): 451–73.

15. I refer to the moving scene in the film "Herman Melville: Damned in Paradise," in which Robert Penn Warren, sitting next to a cannon on a Civil War battleground, reads "Shiloh," deeply affected by the poem. Although I am not a great admirer of this film—my students call it talking heads—which includes a series of cameo readings and evaluations by Melville scholars, I cannot forget the Warren scene.

16. Book chapters that discuss *Clarel* (or even mention a few passages) include: "The Holy Sepulchre" in James Baird's *Ishmael* (Baltimore: Johns Hopkins Press, 1956), 404–28; "Poetry" in Edward H. Rosenberry's *Melville* (London: Routledge & Kegan Paul, 1979), 131–51; "The Art of Attaining Truth: *Battle-Pieces* through *Billy Budd*," in Martin Leonard Pops's *The Melville Archetype* (Kent, Ohio: Kent State University Press,

1970), 186–256; "Herman Melville's Wandering Jews" by Bernard Rosenthal, in *Puritan Influences in American Literature*, ed. Emory Elliott (Urbana: University of Illinois Press, 1979); *"Clarel"* by Vincent Kenny, in *A Companion to Melville Studies*, ed. John Bryant (New York: Greenwood Press, 1986), 375–407; "Wounds of Fratricidal Strife in Melville's Postwar Writings," in Carolyn L. Karcher's *Shadow over the Promised Land: Slavery, Race, and Violence in Melville's America* (Baton Rouge: Louisiana State University Press, 1980), 258–309; *"Clarel*: Cross Bearers All," in James E. Miller, Jr.'s *A Reader's Guide to Herman Melville* (New York: Octagon Books, 1973), 193–217; *"Clarel*: the Spirit above the Dust," in Ronald Mason's *The Spirit Above the Dust: A Study of Herman Melville* (London: John Lehmann, 1951), 224–45; "Under the Vault of Hollow Heaven," in Geoffrey Stone's *Melville* (New York: Sheed & Ward, 1949), 270–99; "'Life an Unfulfilled Romance': *Clarel*," in Edwin Haviland Miller's *Melville* (New York: George Braziller, 1975), 326–42; "The Endurance of Form: Melville's Poetry," in John Seelye's *Melville: The Ironic Diagram* (Evanston, Ill.: Northwestern University Press, 1970), 131–52; *"Clarel*," in Franklin Walker's *Irreverent Pilgrims: Melville, Browne, and Mark Twain in the Holy Land* (Seattle: University of Washington Press, 1974), 133–62; *"Clarel*," in William Ellery Sedgwick's *Herman Melville: The Tragedy of Mind* (Cambridge: Harvard University Press, 1944), 198–231; "'Just Reason, and Appeal for Grace,'" in Richard Chase's *Herman Melville: A Critical Study* (New York: Macmillan, 1949), 242–58; "Hellenic Cheer, Hebraic Grief," in Merlin Bowen's *The Long Encounter: Self and Experience in the Writings of Herman Melville* (Chicago: University of Chicago Press, 1960), 252–81; "The Long Search for Peace," in William Braswell's *Melville's Religious Thought: An Essay in Interpretation* (Durham, N.C.: Duke University Press, 1943), 107–27; "Divine Depravity," in Lawrance R. Thompson's *Melville's Quarrel with God* (Princeton: Princeton University Press, 1952), 335–38; "Alarums and Retreats," in Lewis Mumford's *Herman Melville* (New York: The Literary Guild of America, 1929), 292–326; "The Journey to Terra Damnata," in Dorothee Metlitsky Finkelstein's *Melville's Orienda* (New Haven: Yale University Press, 1961), 261–83; "The Long Quietus," in Raymond M. Weaver's *Herman Melville: Mariner and Mystic* (New York: George H. Doran, 1921), 349–85; *"Clarel* and *Billy Budd*: No Other Worlds but This," in Robert Grenberg's *Some Other World to Find: Quest and Negation in the Works of Herman Melville* (Urbana: University of Illinois Press, 1989), 190–213; "Long Decline," in Tyrus Hillway's *Herman Melville* (Boston: Twayne, 1979), 113–35; "The Customhouse," in Leon Howard's *Herman Melville: A Biography* (Berkeley: University of California Press, 1951), 283–319; "'The Cross Scarce Needs a Word': *The Confidence-Man* and *Clarel*," in

James Duban's *Melville's Major Fiction: Politics, Theology, and Imagination* (Dekalb: Northern Illinois University Press, 1983), 221–49.

17. Articles devoted to *Clarel* include: Robert Penn Warren's introduction to *Selected Poems of Herman Melville* (New York: Random House, 1967), 3–88; N. A. Ault, "The Sea Imagery in Melville's *Clarel*," *Research Studies of the State College of Washington* 27 (1959): 72–84; Nina Baym, "The Erotic Motif in Melville's *Clarel*," *Texas Studies in Literature and Language* 16 (Summer 1974): 315–28; Stanley Brodwin, "Herman Melville's *Clarel*: An Existentialist Gospel," *PMLA* 86 (May 1971): 375–87; Agnes Cannon, "Melville's Concepts of the Poet and Poetry," *Arizona Quarterly* 31 (Winter 1975): 315–39; Shirley Dettlaff, "Ionian Form and Esau's Waste: Melville's View of Art in *Clarel*," *American Literature* 54 (May 1982): 212–28; William B. Dillingham, "'Neither Believer nor Infidel': Themes of Melville's Poetry," *The Personalist* 46 (1965): 501–16; Joseph Flibbert, "The Dream and Religious Faith in Herman Melville's *Clarel*," *American Transcendental Quarterly* 50 (1981): 129–37; Richard H. Fogle, "Melville's *Clarel*: Doubt and Belief," *Tulane Studies in English* 10 (1960): 101–16; Basem L. Ra'ad, "The Death Plot in Melville's *Clarel*," *Emerson Society Quarterly* 27 (First Quarter 1981): 14–27; Bryan C. Short, "Form as Vision in Herman Melville's *Clarel*," *American Literature* 50 (January 1979): 553–69; William Wasilewski, "Melville's Poetic Strategy in *Clarel*: The Satellite Poems," *Essays in Arts and Sciences* 5 (July 1976): 149–59; Agnes Cannon, "On Translating *Clarel*," *Essays in Arts and Sciences* 5 (July 1976): 160–81; Wyn Kelley, "Haunted Stone: Nature and City in *Clarel*," *Essays in Arts and Sciences* 15 (June 1986): 15–31; Hershel Parker, "The Character of Vine in Melville's *Clarel*," *Essays in Arts and Sciences* 15 (June 1986): 91–113; Andrew Hook, "Melville's Poetry," in *Herman Melville: Reassessments,* ed. A. Robert Lee (London: Vision Press, 1984), 176–99; Helene Rozenberg-Sacks, "Allegory and Nominal Identity in Melville's Poem *Clarel*," *Literary Onomastics Studies* 1 (1974): 40–46; Douglas Robillard, "Melville's *Clarel* and the Parallel of Poetry and Painting," *North Dakota Quarterly* 51 (1983): 107–20; Warren Rosenberg, "'Deeper Than Sappho': Melville, Poetry, and the Erotic," *Modern Language Studies* 14 (1984): 70–78; James Duban and William J. Scheick, "The Dramatis Personae of Robert Browning and Herman Melville," *Criticism* 32 (Spring 1990): 221–40; James Duban, "From Bethlehem to Tahiti: Transcultural 'Hope' in *Clarel*," *Philological Quarterly* 70 (Fall 1991): 475–83.

18. The most recent dismissal of the Epilogue is by Robert Grenberg, who calls it "stunning in its misdirection," in *Some Other World to Find: Quest and Negation in the Works of Herman Melville* (Urbana: University of Illinois Press, 1989), 192. I think much more of the Epilogue than Grenberg does. See my Chapters 4 and 5.

CHAPTER 1: THE HIDDENNESS AND SILENCE OF GOD

1. Melville, "Timoleon," in *Collected Poems of Herman Melville*, ed. Howard P. Vincent (Chicago: Hendricks House, 1947), 215; Jay Leyda, *The Melville Log: A Documentary Life of Herman Melville* (New York: Harcourt, Brace, 1951), 1:508.

2. Henry W. Bellows, "The Suspense of Faith: An Address to the Alumni of the Divinity School of Harvard University" (New York: C. S. Francis, 1859), 18.

3. For Melville's supremely Protestant generation, the word "Bible" refers to both Old and New Testaments as one library. The terms "Hebrew Bible" and "Christian Bible" are used throughout this study to avoid the connotations of "Old" superseded by "New."

4. Merton M. Sealts, Jr., in *Melville's Reading*, documents that Melville underscored forty verses from Job, making it the most heavily underscored book in Melville's Bible. Ecclesiastes is second. Nathalia Wright, in *Melville's Use of the Bible*, first identified Hebrew Wisdom as a tradition implied throughout Melville's works (p. 77). She cites the unknowability of God as one of Wisdom's key metaphysical speculations (p. 106) and claims that Melville conveyed the idea of truth through the image of something hidden (p. 187). Wright is the starting point for this study. I, however, place the image of hiddenness in a much larger and more specific biblical and theological context.

5. All biblical quotations are drawn from the King James translation of the Bible—the version Melville read—and are cited in the text parenthetically. I cite chapter and verse in the hope that readers will read *Clarel* and the King James together, as co-texts. My references are selective, offering one prooftext from among hundreds that would have served equally well as analogies for Melville's theological reflection.

6. The Christian Bible also refers to divine hiddenness: "No man hath seen God at any time. . . ." (John 1:18). Since Melville's prime interest is in the human relationship with the hidden God, he speculates only indirectly in *Clarel* on the theological theories for divine self-concealment. One commonplace theory begins with the essential difference between God's identity (His essence) and God's manifestations (e.g., in nature). God's hiddenness or withdrawal from His creation occurred so that there would always be a distinction between identity and manifestation. This distinction is essential if human beings are to be cognitively free before God. God's concealment creates human freedom—the independent human free will. Of course, when human beings stop being humane and consistently choose evil, this theory becomes inconsistent with God's goodness. God's withdrawal to ensure free will also does little to answer the central problem in *Clarel* of an indifferent

nature. The key problem with the notion of a hidden God and the concomitant paradox of human freedom is theodicy: How can we accept any God (concealed or revealed) as good when we live in a world that contains so much undeserved human suffering and evil? One response to theodicy is to counter evil with the evidence of unselfish goodness in human beings. Why speak only of the problem of evil and not of the equally mysterious phenomenon of unselfish goodness, no matter how rare? One way of begging the question of theodicy is to deny the presence of any evil in the world, to deny suffering whether self-inflicted, caused by nature (e.g., viruses), or by human malice and ignorance—an answer that refuses to recognize human suffering. Such cosmic optimism is as insensitive in its way as the doctrine of total and unredeemed human depravity put forth by Calvinists. Another theological response is that there is some part of creation that the so-called omnipotent God cannot control—as if God created all of creation and, at the same time, a huge stone (evil) that He could not lift—a theory inconsistent with divine omnipotence. Yet another reading is that what human beings consider good is not what God considers good. Other responses include (1) the idea that the long-suffering God shows mercy in the face of human evil because God waits for the sinner's repentance; (2) the very Melvillean, as well as orthodox Christian and Jewish, belief that evil is a natural part of human nature that needs to be controlled; (3) the idea that undeserved human suffering is imposed on the righteous because they are strong enough to take it, and such pain will produce greater empathy for and brotherhood with fellow sufferers; (4) the famous orthodox response given by Job's so-called comforters that suffering is the proof and penalty of human sin and therefore appropriate punishment; and (5) the response that all the evil and suffering in this world will be righted in the next world, a response more readily accepted in Christian traditions than in Jewish traditions.

Perhaps the most subversive response to the problem of theodicy is that the Bible's anthropomorphic language may be all wrong: goodness may be no more a divine trait than politeness and hospitality are. That way lies madness— or dualism. Dualism is only acceptable to Christian theologies and is considered completely outside the pale of Jewish theologies. If we think God is good, why not imagine an evil adversary: Jehovah versus Satan, Ormuzd versus Ahriman? The end of dualism, however, may not necessarily be a victory for the good. This guide to the quagmire of theological explanations for the existence of evil, undeserved suffering, and the hidden God is included here to show that theology, as Melville sensed, cannot provide us with a solution to a God who perhaps can be described only circularly. As Djalea, the pilgrims' Druze guide, says, "No God there is but God" (3.15.117). I infer from Djalea's reply that we do not know the answer to the problem of evil and to God's purposes. In fact, the rabbis of the Talmud claimed that the existence of evil was the greatest mystery of the universe. To the rabbinic mind, all we can choose to do is hold on to a relationship with God in stubborn faith, a response that is represented in *Clarel* (see Chapter 5).

7. This study has also been inspired by a sentence that William Braswell wrote in *Melville's Religious Thought: An Essay in Interpretation* (Durham, N.C.: Duke University Press, 1943): "The question at the bottom of his [Melville's] reasoning concerned the nature of God" (p. 24). The nature of God is defined, though never determined, by the theological perspective of divine hiddenness. The notion of an "invisible God" has been mentioned by Richard H. Fogle, in "The Themes of Melville's Later Poetry," *Tulane Studies in English* 11 (1961), in poems such as "The Night March," "The Margrave's Birthnight," "Magian Wine," and "The Garden of Metrodorus." William H. Shurr, in *The Mystery of Iniquity: Melville as Poet, 1857–1891* (Lexington: University of Kentucky Press, 1972) describes part 7 of "Timoleon" as a "cry from the heart for the *deus absconditus* to show himself" (p. 155). In fact all of part 7 from "Timoleon" can serve as an excellent gloss on *Clarel*, but two stanzas in particular should be recalled:

> To second causes why appeal?
> Vain parleying here with fellow clods.
> To you, Arch Principals, I rear
> My quarrel, for this quarrel is with gods.
>
> . . . .
>
> Yea, *are* ye, gods? Then Ye, 'tis ye
> Should show what touch of tie ye may,
> Since ye, too, if not wrung are wronged
> By grievous misconceptions of your sway.
>   But deign, some little sign be given—
> Low thunder in your tranquil skies;
> Me reassure, nor let me be
> Like a lone dog that for a master cries.
>   (*Collected Poems*, 214–15)

The same combined sense of an arraignment of God and a deprivation without God runs throughout *Clarel*.

The hiddenness of God is also given special importance in the chapter from *Moby-Dick* entitled "The Tail." There the essence of whale is contextualized via the theme of the hiddenness of God in Exodus 33:17–23, where the ultimate mystery of God's nature remains hidden:

> Dissect him how I may, then, I but go skin deep; I know him not, and never will. But if I know not even the tail of this whale, how understand

his head? much more, how comprehend his face, when face he has none? Thou shalt see my back part, my tail, he seems to say, but my face shall not be seen. But I cannot completely make out his back part; and hint what he will about his face, I say again he has no face.

Both Ishmael and Moses are halted at this same metaphysical boundary. Moses asks God, "I beseech thee, show me thy glory." And God responds, "I will make all my goodness pass before thee, and I will proclaim the name of the Lord before thee; and will be gracious to whom I will be gracious, and will show mercy on whom I will show mercy. And he [God] said, Thou canst not see my face: for there shall no man see me, and live" (Exodus 33:18–20). Perhaps it is impossible to penetrate the full mystery of these lines, but they surely illustrate that with divine presence is always divine hiddenness. This was the paradoxical experience of the divine for Israel, for Ishmael, and for Melville in *Clarel*.

Rowland A. Sherrill, in *The Prophetic Melville: Experience, Transcendence, and Tragedy* (Athens: University of Georgia Press, 1979), discusses Melville's theological understanding in terms of Rudolf Otto's *The Idea of the Holy* and Jonathan Edwards's "hidden God." Although Sherrill does *not* discuss *Clarel*, I am still indebted to his reading of Melville's understanding of a hidden God who has not "stranded the universe" (p. 93). Sherrill fails to mention, however, that Edwards's source for divine hiddenness is Hebrew Scripture. *Moby-Dick* is a reverse image of *Clarel*: *Moby-Dick* is defiance of the hidden God; *Clarel*, ultimately, is reverence for the hidden God. Other than Sherrill on *Moby-Dick* and Fogle and Shurr on other poems by Melville, I have not found any examinations of the theological and biblical context and metaphor of divine hiddenness in *Clarel*.

8. Derwent is too readily dismissed by most critics for what Bezanson calls "his facile optimism" (in "Historical and Critical Note," 620). Bezanson places Derwent "low in the hierarchy of the poem" (p. 621) because of Clarel's and the monomaniacs' negative reaction to Derwent's theology of hope. If, however, one tracks the narrator's thematic concerns, some of Derwent's ideas coincide with the narrator's attempt elsewhere to say yea to the nay of the monomaniacs and Clarel. Derwent does not deny the presence of the serpent in the garden, but chooses to make life bearable by anticipating the fulfillment he hopes will be. If one can accept the narrator as central to the poem and the merging of the characters' voices with the narrator's voices (see Chapter 4), then Derwent comes out much higher in the poem's hierarchy. Melville also dialogically subverts the notion of an intellectually consistent and centered self. A character, such as Derwent, is capable of both deep-diving and superficial thought.

9. The relationship that Melville develops in *Clarel* between the hu-

man and the divine as one between child and father is discussed in Chapter 5 on faith.

10. Snow symbolizes atheism in *Moby-Dick:* "Or is it, that as in essence whiteness is not so much a color as the visible absence of color, and at the same time the concrete of all colors; is it for these reasons that there is such dumb blankness, full of meaning, in a wide landscape of snows—a colorless, all-color of atheism from which we shrink?" (p. 169—"The Whiteness of the Whale"). To be lost in a snowstorm in *Clarel* is to be cut off from the warmth of Christ.

11. The Elijah motif is discussed in Chapter 4, for it is the key to understanding one of the narrative voices in the poem, a voice patterned after that aerial voice of silence so dear to nineteenth-century Christians: the "still small voice" (1 Kings 19:12).

12. Stanley Brodwin, in "Herman Melville's *Clarel*: An Existentialist Gospel," *PMLA* 86 (May 1971): 379, glosses the Syrian monk's prayer quite differently, as an example of existential agony: "Either man must have absolute knowledge, or life loses its meaning and death becomes the only reality, yielding at least the grace of annihilation." Brodwin ignores the many intimations of immortality in the poem. Chapter 1 of this book demonstrates that Melville accepts the impossibility of absolute knowledge.

13. The received theological tradition teaches that Jesus' despair on the cross was an unusual situation in which Jesus was made to know the torment of hell and the absence of God to complete his earthly mission. Of course, there are times in the Christian Bible when God was not hidden to Jesus. Melville, however, does not mention these moments of presence nor the sense of Jesus' mission. Instead, Melville focuses on the suffering and death of Jesus, on the cruelty of the incarnation. His death is even more tragic because there is no communication with God when it is most needed; in death, God most consciously withdraws.

14. By "Melville," I refer to that consistent pattern of theological meanings, discussed in the Introduction, which one can identify as Melvillean. When a passage is elaborated in other parts of the poem, given a full development in serious, powerful poetry, and expressed by serious wisdom-characters or the narrator, we can be fairly sure that Melville is fully committed to the theme theologically, e.g., Jesus' sense of abandonment.

15. See Rosenthal, "Melville's Wandering Jews," 171.

16. See Chapter 5 on the loneliness of God.

17. Another example of the Melvillean "both/and" rather than the "either/or" of dualism is the combination of images and allusions from both the Hebrew and the Christian Bibles in his poem "The Great Pyramid" that suggests an idea of God derived from both Testaments: "turn the cheek," "Eld's [*el*] diadem," and "I AM."

18. The biblical motif of wrestling as a metaphor for the struggle with theological skepticism and for acquiring a tested faith is examined in Chapter 3.

19. The braided-cord passage qualifies Shurr's thesis that the universe in *Clarel* is predominately evil (*The Mystery of Iniquity*, 45–125).

20. The last verse of Job 28 gives us the definition of conventional Hebrew Wisdom teachings: "the fear of the Lord, that is wisdom; and to depart from evil is understanding." If one is willing to define "fear of the Lord" not as knee-knocking fear but as faith, reverence, and obedience, and if one is willing to define "to depart from evil" as moral self-control, then the Melvillean definition of faith delineated in Chapter 5 is quite close to the Wisdom teachings in Proverbs and Job 28.

21. Perhaps Melville's most overt statement of the hiddenness of the innermost human self is the description of a confessional box in his poem "In a Church of Padua":

Dread diving-bell! In thee inurned
What hollows the priest must sound,
Descending into consciences
Where more is hid than found.
(*Collected Poems*, 241)

22. See Thomas F. Heffernan, *Stove by a Whale: Owen Chase and the Essex* (Middletown, Conn.: Wesleyan University Press, 1981), 166–70.

23. Melville, *Journals*, 81.

24. Richard H. Fogle, "Melville's *Clarel*: Doubt and Belief," *Tulane Studies in English* 10 (1960); William B. Dillingham, "'Neither Believer nor Infidel': Themes of Melville's Poetry," *The Personalist* 46 (1965); and N. A. Ault, "The Sea Imagery in Melville's *Clarel*," *Research Studies of the State College of Washington* 27 (1959)—all mention the theme of loneliness or estrangement, although not in the context of a hidden God. Fogle claims that "the characters do not genuinely interact with each other" (p. 106). Dillingham states that "Melville built much of his work on the theme of man's loneliness. In his view man was an island and could never know God or another human being even though warm, superficial relationships were possible" (p. 509). Ault says that "one of the poem's major themes is the loneliness of modern man. Robbed by modern science and religious sectarianism of the simple verities of the past, the pilgrims (like man) are a lonely group as isolated from each other as from any ultimate understanding of the meaning of life" (p. 77).

25. See Bezanson, "Historical and Critical Note," 564.

26. See Nina Baym's "The Erotic Motif in Melville's *Clarel*," *Texas Studies in Literature and Language* 16 (Summer 1974): 315–28.

27. In his "Discussions" in the Northwestern-Newberry edition of *Clarel*, 756–57, Bezanson points out the biblical allusion to Psalm 102.

28. Bryan C. Short, "Form as Vision in Herman Melville's *Clarel*," *American Literature* 50 (January 1979): 568.

29. Another interesting sleep-trance occurs in Melville's poem "America," where the allegorical woman—America—first reveals terror and then calm in her contorted sleep (*Collected Poems*, 106–7).

30. C. Vann Woodward, *The Burden of Southern History* (Baton Rouge: Louisiana State University Press, 1960), 116.

31. A reciprocal, imitating relationship between the divine and the human is suggested in Melville's sketch "The Marquis de Grandvin": "Yes, and as the prophets of old announcing the mind of their deity, in some instances dramatically put on his personality, even so will I assume that of de Grandvin . . . I will imitate the inimitable," *Great Short Works of Herman Melville*, ed. Warner Berthoff (New York: Harper & Row, 1969), 401. Further evidence that Melville pondered the image and idea of reciprocal divinity can be found in a quotation written on the inside back cover of his copy of the New Testament:

> If we can conceive it possible, that the creator of the world himself assumed the form of his creature, and lived in that manner for a time upon earth, this creature must seem to us of infinite perfection, because susceptible of such a combination with his maker. Hence in our idea of God man there can be no inconsistency with our idea of God: and if we often feel a certain disagreement with Him & remoteness from Him, it is but the more on that account our duty, not like advocates of the wicked Spirit, to keep our eyes constantly on the nakedness and wickedness of our nature: but rather to seek out every property & beauty, by which our pretension to a similarity with the Divinity may be made good.

This quotation is taken from a letter dated 1671 from St. Evermond to the Mareschal de Crequi, in Cowen, *Melville's Marginalia*, 1:351. William Braswell, *Melville's Religious Thought*; F. O. Matthiessen, *American Renaissance: Art and Expression in the Age of Emerson and Whitman* (New York: Oxford University Press, 1941); and Leonard Martin Pops, *The Melville Archetype* (Kent, Ohio: Kent State University Press, 1970), write of the divinity rooted in human nature. Pops sees Melville's search for the God within each person in the Jungian terms of individuation and the subconscious (pp. 1–26). Braswell writes that Melville believed all men have in them the "spark of divinity" (p. 140). Matthiessen claims that the great change in nineteenth-century theological thought was "from God-man [birth of Christ] to Man-God" or "the potential divinity in every man" (p. 446). Matthiessen's point, however, is that this sense of God within man can become, in its extreme form, a kind of human self-deification such as Ahab's. Melville's emphasis in *Clarel* is on reverence, not defiance. The divinity in man is a theme throughout the works of the early nineteenth century. One need only recall Emerson's famous dictum that "the highest revelation is that God is in every man" ("Self-Reliance") or Whitman's famous cry in "Passage to India": "Trinitas divine shall be gloriously accomplish'd and compacted by the true son of God, the poet. . . ."

    32. Bezanson claims that the attributes of Rama as described in this canto must refer to either Vine or Rolfe ("Discussions," 750).

    33. A Melvillean theology of the heart is discussed in Chapter 5.

CHAPTER 2: MELVILLE'S LAMENT

    1. Several critics have noted the presence of questions in *Clarel*, although without discussing them in the biblical context of lament and theodicy. I am indebted to the work of John Seelye, Vincent Kenny, and William Wasilewski. John Seelye, although not referring directly to *Clarel*, writes that "Truth, for Melville, is a question, not an answer, and by abandoning the answers imposed on existence by his questers, he only the more emphasized the final question. The emergence of Melville's final style, which is not the baroque rodomontade of *Moby-Dick* or the mannered irony of *The Confidence-Man* but is rather a hesitant, inquiring, parenthetical, and qualified syntax—a circling interrogation mark without a period, perfectly suits the revised proportions of his diagram. It suggests that if Melville has at last come to some terms with Mystery, he celebrated that final acquiescence by withdrawing behind mysteries of his own," *Melville: The Ironic Diagram* (Evanston, Ill.: Northwestern University Press, 1970), 10. Vincent Kenny identifies the tone of *Clarel* as Hebraic: "The tone is thus one of Hebraic lamentation. Without direct borrowing of lines or incidents, the sorrows of Job and Jeremiah are paralleled in Clarel's sad journey. The tragic human condition, in which reclamation can come only from a source outside oneself, echoes the sad cries of Ecclesiastes," *Herman Melville's Clarel: A Spiritual Autobiography* (Hamden, Conn.: Shoe String Press, 1973), 98. My only corrections to Kenny's significant insight are that *Clarel* does directly borrow from the Hebrew laments, Job, and Ecclesiastes and that, as I show in Chapter 5, it does speak of a source of the divine inside oneself. William Wasilewski writes that "this crisis of faith finds articulation in questions whose very tone punctuates them with despair," "Melville's Poetic Strategy in *Clarel*: The Satellite Poems," *Essays in Arts and Sciences* 5 (July 1976): 153.

2. In a poem that demonstrates that one can no longer address God directly and expect an answer, one could explain the presence of questions in *Clarel* as the natural rhetorical mode for a poem about theological doubt. Such a reading would suggest that Melville was unable to resign himself to the will of God; he had to question and rebel against the decrees of divine will, which earlier ages, more secure in their faith, accepted with greater submissiveness. This reading makes Melville at one with many of his Victorian contemporaries. Melville was, however, very much more spiritually complex than Tennyson or Arnold. Clarelian questions show a much wider range of reflection on theological problems. Melville's questions go beyond the subjects usually associated with the interrogative mode; they go beyond theological doubt. A more secure reading is to view *Clarel* as a lament and as a theodicy, as a poem that displays a similarity of genre, language, and thought to the biblical voices of lament and theodicy in books such as Jeremiah, Job, Psalms, Lamentations, and Ecclesiastes.

3. This question is answered in Chapter 5 on protest theism.

4. One can say, as is found in Proverbs 20:9, Job 4:6–7, and elsewhere, that no one is innocent, no one is wholly righteous before God and the Law. Melville is certainly drawn to the notion of the innate human evil that causes transgressions and guilt, but there are an equal number of questions in *Clarel* concerning the death of the innocent (Ruth and Agar) and the death of the righteous (Nehemiah). Although Melville is willing enough to proclaim human guilt, he is, via the lament, unwilling to proclaim God's innocence in the presence of human suffering and death.

5. The promise of life or death is given in Deuteronomy 30:15–20, and the Abrahamic covenant or promise of divine presence, progeny, and promised land is referred to throughout the Pentateuch, especially in Genesis, chapters 12, 15, and 17.

6. Shurr first pointed out the theodicy nature of this "audacious question" in the Epilogue, although he claims that "wherefore ripen us to pain?" is addressed to a "malevolent deity," *The Mystery of Iniquity*, 122.

7. Bezanson mistakes the source of the bride and groom allusion in his "Discussions," 723. He claims the source is Revelation, but the author of Revelation is quoting Jeremiah, as the Christian Bible authors so often do. The strongest evidence for claiming Jeremiah as the source Melville had in mind is that Melville calls the author of this line "the greater prophet" (1.7.19), an epithet used to describe any of the three major prophets in the Hebrew Bible: Isaiah, Jeremiah, and Ezekiel.

8. Jeremiah's voices are heard elsewhere in *Clarel*. Rachel weeping for her children is mentioned in 4.29.113 (see Jeremiah 31:15). References to the bitter draft "wormwood" as in 1.32.25 come from Jeremiah as do the references throughout *Clarel* to the balm of Gilead. Derwent refers to Ungar's

"Jeremiad spells" (4.23.23), and the Prodigal claims that beautiful Hebrew women, "witches," ignore the lament and sorrow of Jeremiah: "Of Jeremiah what reck they?" (4.26.226). One should also note the use in *Clarel* of the word "woe," a distinctly biblical word marking pain and disappointment (e.g., 1.33.68; 1.42.51; 3.19.119; 4.20.132–33).

9. Bezanson, in "Discussions," 809, first pointed out that this canto is based on Jeremiah. My reading of this canto includes more biblical resonances than Jeremiah alone.

10. See Chapter 3 on contraries.

11. Disillusionment is frequently mentioned in many Melville studies but not adequately developed in readings of *Clarel*. Two helpful critics have been Lawrance Thompson and Milton R. Stern, although neither author discusses disillusionment in *Clarel*. Stern sees Melville's words as demonstrating his sense of the end of idealism in Western civilization in *The Fine-Hammered Steel of Herman Melville* (Urbana: University of Illinois Press, 1957), 1–28. Thompson discusses disillusionment as Melville's "habit of mind," as a perception of two values—a true value and a false value—and the illusion experienced when one turns away from the once true value in *Melville's Quarrel with God* (Princeton: Princeton University Press, 1952), 148–49.

12. *Clarel* qualifies other ideal visions. Joseph G. Knapp points out that the American Dream of westward expansion is undercut by pilgrims who go east to seek wisdom. See his *Tortured Synthesis: The Meaning of Melville's Clarel* (New York: Philosophical Library, 1971), 3.

13. Bezanson, "Discussions," 784.

14. See Shurr, *The Mystery of Iniquity*, 259. Elsewhere, Shurr writes that Melville "viewed the New Testament with a mixture of nostalgia and regret that such a beautiful story could not actually be true" (p. 189).

15. According to Stanley Brodwin in "Herman Melville's *Clarel*, 375–87, the poem's quest for faith "arises out of the central phenomenon of annihilation" (p. 380). Basem L. Ra'ad offers an optimistic reading of death as a "constructive kind of bereavement," where Clarel learns "how to accept the finality of death without bringing perpetual agony upon himself" in Ra'ad's "The Death Plot in Melville's *Clarel*," *ESQ* 27 (First Quarter 1981): 25. Another overly optimistic reading that tries to explain away death is Joseph Knapp's opinion that "death is an eclipse that is real to the viewer, but is, in terms of ultimate certitude, only a transitory condition," *Tortured Synthesis*, 38. To discuss death only as a passing or even instructive state, however, is to ignore the painful questioning of death in the poem. Annihilation was one of Melville's complaints—a frightening one for him. The key question in the poem is how to have any faith in the face of death that cannot be explained away.

16. In Melville's Civil War poem "The Conflict of Convictions," in *Collected Poems*, 7.

17. Melville, *Journals*, 62.

18. The possibility of immortality will be addressed in Chapter 4. The eternal life promised by Christian faith is accessible only through death. We must first die. Melville is aware that faith and resurrection do not change the human condition of suffering and death.

19. Shurr writes that "the force of Melville's words here seems to be that the Encantadas (and the Holy Land) are not at all godforsaken, but the nature of that presiding god must be recognized for what it is in Melville's developing symbol," *The Mystery of Iniquity*, 65. The nature of that God, for Shurr, is evil. But evil is only one face of Melville's God; another is hidden and possibly good.

20. Kenny, in *Herman Melville's Clarel*, 109, writes that "the cross symbolizes pain and sorrow. It must be carried or endured, not as a redemptive act guaranteeing immortality but simply because there is little else in life except suffering." The other half of *Clarel's* theological story asserts that there is more to life than suffering. See my Chapters 4 and 5.

21. For readings of Clarel's endurance and tragic awareness, see Knapp, *Tortured Synthesis*, 103–15; Kenny, *Herman Melville's Clarel*, 148–51; and Merlin Bowen, *The Long Encounter: Self and Experience in the Writings of Herman Melville* (Chicago: University of Chicago Press, 1960), 279.

22. Robert Penn Warren, Introduction, *Selected Poems of Herman Melville*, edited by Warren (New York: Random House, 1967), 88.

CHAPTER 3: GOD-WRESTLING

1. Melville, *Collected Poems*, 231.

2. Shurr characterizes "Art" as "the terrifying contest with ultimates," *Mysteries of Iniquity*, 243.

3. Several passages in *Clarel* suggest Jacob's voice, including references to his dream at Bethel: "Bethel high / Saw Jacob, under starry sky, / On stones his head lay . . ." (2.10.5–7). Three other Bethel references that help describe the stairs leading up to the Mar Saba palm—symbol of heaven, peace, and immortality to some—are in 3.30.135, 3.32.23, and 3.32.53. A reference to the proto-Exodus of Jacob's funeral train leaving Egypt is in 4.26.76–78.

4. Wrestling is more than an aspect of self and faith in *Clarel*; it is a cosmic metaphor. An example of such cosmic strife is the canto entitled "In the Mountain" (3.1), where there are four extended metaphors of conflict: the "Armageddon" of good and evil (3.1.41–43) that supports Shurr's thesis in *The Mystery of Iniquity*, 58, of a personified Melvillean universe; the "two human skeletons inlaced / In grapple as alive they fell"; the "crime and earthquake, throes and war" of Siddim; and Mortmain's view of the warrior

God—"the striding God of Habakkuk" (3.1.82–83, 116, 144–69). Structurally, *Clarel* also juxtaposes opposites, as one canto is followed by its antithesis (discussed later in this chapter).

5. The reconciling of oppositions is also an aesthetic hallmark of the romantic tradition in nineteenth-century American and European literature. Certainly Melville was influenced by the romanticism of Coleridge, Emerson, the Schlegel brothers, and others, but the oppositional nature of biblical texts is also a primary point of contact for Melville's aesthetics. For an overview of the scholarship on Melville's debt to romanticism and organicism, see Shirley M. Dettlaff, "Melville's Aesthetics," in *A Companion To Melville Studies*, ed. John Bryant (Westport, Conn.: Greenwood Press, 1986), 625–65.

6. Cowen, *Melville's Marginalia*, 1:315–16.

7. Brodwin, "Herman Melville's *Clarel*," 379.

8. Bowen, in *The Long Encounter*, 256, writes that "closer study confirms Clarel's first impression of Vine: he is indeed a union of opposites. In him, heart and head exist in delicate balance."

9. Bowen makes a similar observation: "But what seems in Rolfe a lack of all fixed conviction appears more clearly later as a settled opposition to all attempts to freeze experience into rigid artificial forms," *The Long Encounter*, 260.

10. See Thompson, *Melville's Quarrel with God*; T. Walter Herbert, Jr., *Moby-Dick and Calvinism: A World Dismantled* (New Brunswick, N.J.: Rutgers University Press, 1977); and Seelye, *The Ironic Diagram*, 133, 144.

11. Fogle, "Melville's *Clarel*," 101–16.

12. Melville, *Moby-Dick*, "The Fountain." The Pocahontas-wedding habit of mind is very much a part of *Moby-Dick*: "The more so, I say, because truly to enjoy bodily warmth, some small part of you must be cold, for there is no quality in this world that is not what it is merely by contrast. Nothing exists in itself," "Nightgown."

13. Nathaniel Hawthorne, *The English Notebooks*, ed. Randall Stewart (New York: Oxford University Press, 1941), 432.

14. Brodwin writes that "unlike Kierkegaard, Melville does not see doubt as a necessary, though paradoxical, element in the very nature of faith, a faith that must dynamically transcend the doubt of which it is ontologically a part. Neither Clarel, Vine, Derwent, nor Rolfe have the 'faith to doubt,' though the Monk, in his statement 'He *is*, though doubt attend,' edges toward that view," "Herman Melville's *Clarel*," 379. Brodwin does not consider the differences between common and heroic doubt nor the balance of contraries.

15. Kenny, *Herman Melville's Clarel*, 212.

16. The canto "The Easter Fire" may seem to modify the notion of the wedding of opposites in thought and self, but it only again demonstrates the range in Melville's thinking. Rolfe, here, seems to criticize Derwent's habit of

mind: "Things all diverse he would unite: / His idol's an hermaphrodite" (3.16.173–74)—the way of thinking Melville seems to have admired. Rolfe then qualifies his critique in three different ways and, finally, practices the same uniting of things diverse he accuses Derwent of. First, Rolfe admits that Derwent does not err but only "overstates" what his "heart avers" (3.16.186–87). Second, Rolfe contrasts Derwent with the dissembling plastic "pulpiteers," who do not follow "the Truth not for a day" (3.16.189–90; see "the truth of the Lord endureth forever," Psalms 117:2), but try to harmonize extremes in a superficial manner rather than wrestling heroically. Rolfe does not criticize Derwent but the sciolists who, like circus men, ride with one foot on each horse and rein together wildly different ideas: "Moses and Comte, Renan and Paul" (3.16.199). Such superficial comparative thinking, with its huge leaps across time, only adds to intellectual pretentiousness. Third, Rolfe admits that certain "astute ones" do unite opposites in their battle between faith and science by placing "The King a corpse in armor led / On a live Horse . . ." (3.16.208–9). In what is perhaps an allusion to *El Cid*, Rolfe claims that the opposition of a God who is considered dead by some but still revered by a tenacious ("live") religious faith that refuses to accept the death of God may be the only tenable response. After Rolfe's long dialog, Clarel catches him red-handed in building his own hermaphrodite idol, for Rolfe earlier espoused the appeal of Catholicism and faith and now reverses himself in implying that all creeds are folded in doubt. Thus Clarel accuses Rolfe of a noncommittal "manysidedness"—a positive trait of all those who demonstrate openness and tolerance and can balance opposites such as "earnestness and levity" (3.16.263, 261).

17. Bezanson, "Historical and Critical Note," 623.

18. Seelye makes a similar observation about the juxtaposition of opposites in other works by Melville. We reach very different conclusions, however, about Clarelian faith. Seelye also does not place the Melvillean literary form of opposition within a biblical intertextual analytic. He writes that Melville was "an artist who regarded his art as a system of tensions produced by diagrammatic contrasts, a symposium of opposed viewpoints," *The Ironic Diagram*, 137. T. Walter Herbert, Jr., "Calvinist Earthquake: *Moby-Dick* and Religous Tradition," in *New Essays on Moby-Dick*, ed. Richard H. Brodhead (Cambridge: Cambridge University Press, 1986), 138, also makes a similar observation about content and form: "His [Melville's] art invokes opposed perspectives simultaneously, establishes vehement thematic premises and then reverses them, fuses horror with mildness and self-destruction with apotheosis." And Douglas Robillard, in his introduction to *Poems of Herman Melville* (New Haven: College and University Press, 1976), 12, 22, writes that there is in Melville's poetry the "powerful meeting of opposites" and "paradox." See, for example, the sea that is inhuman but heals and purifies in *John Marr*

and the "warmth and chill of wedded life and death" in Melville's poem "Pontoosuce."

19. The voices of the Psalms are heard in several cantos. Nehemiah sings a chant that is a conflation of Job 29:3 and Psalms 23:4:

> Though through the valley of the shade
>   I pass, no evil do I fear;
> His candle shineth on my head:
>   Lo, he is with me, even here
>   (2.28.44–47)

The verse is a reinterpretation of line 4 of the classic psalm of psalms, Psalm 23: "Yea, though I walk through the valley of the shadow of death, I will fear no evil: for thou art with me; thy rod and thy staff they comfort me." Job 29:3 reads: "When his candle shined upon my head, and when by his light I walked through darkness." Both verses convey the sense of God's guidance and protective presence in and through times of trouble. When the narrator tells of the violence committed during the fraudulent lighting of the candles during St. Basil's Easter in the Church of the Holy Sepulcher, he refers to "ferocious psalms" that reflect the violent zeal of the priests and communicants. There are several psalms that convey fierceness or ferociousness: "Happy shall he be, that taketh and dasheth thy little ones against the stones," a reference to Babylonian babies and the retributive justice that the Babylonians bring upon themselves for their unkind treatment of the Jews in exile (Psalms 137:9). The "Penitential Psalms" that Galileo was forced to recite are referred to in *Clarel* (3.5.69) as is Psalm 102 in which the psalmist compares himself to a lone sparrow ("The Sparrow," 1.38.9–27).

CHAPTER 4: THE SMALL VOICE OF SILENCE

1. For examples of the anti-faith argument, see Dettlaff, "Ionian Form and Esau's Waste: Melville's View of Art in *Clarel*," *American Literature* 54 (May 1982): 223; Kenny, *Herman Melville's Clarel*, 144; and Bezanson, Introduction to *Clarel*, cix.

2. The referential power of an Elijah motif is evident throughout the poem. There are two specific references to the small voice of silence. When Mortmain returns from his lonely sojourn in the desert to rejoin the pilgrimage, he is compared to Elijah, who hid from Jezebel by the brook called "Cherith" and later heard God's still small voice or what Melville calls a "voice aerial" (2.34.20–22). Derwent uses God's voice of silence as a contrast to the garrulity of his friend Don Hannibal: "Not thou com'st in the still small

voice" (4.20.1). The Elijah motif also helps portray the character Mortmain. He is twice directly compared to Elijah with the epithets "the Gileadite" (3.32.15—Elijah was from Gilead) and "the Tishbite" (3.11.228). Mortmain, as a prophet of doom estranged from his culture, has much in common with Elijah and other biblical prophets. He is passionate in his search for God, and he condemns human wickedness. The entire Elijah-Elisha narrative sequence played an important part in Melville's imagination: Elijah's "chariot" is mentioned in 2.16.32; in 4.1.156–59, the hills south of Jerusalem are "leprous" as Naaman, the Syrian leper cured in the Jordan by Elisha; and Nehemiah, like Elijah, is fed by a bird, Ruth (1.22.61). And, of course, Elijah is a central prophetic character in *Moby-Dick*. It should be noted that one essential difference between the Elijah passage and Melville's intertextual use of it in *Clarel* is that, on Mount Horeb, God teaches Elijah by silence and then by word, while in *Clarel*, God never reveals himself in direct speech.

3. Most *Clarel* critics discuss the human divine relationships in the poem but insist that the poem's final theological resting place is agnostic or endlessly vacillating between faith and doubt. Hope, if mentioned, is dismissed. For example, see Fogle, "Melville's *Clarel*," and Kenny, *"Clarel."* Melville does offer, however, a way to faith based on divine immanence and a theology of hope.

4. Several critics assume that the narrator is Melville himself (e.g., Shurr, *The Mystery of Iniquity*, 102; Hershel Parker, "The Character of Vine in Melville's *Clarel*," *Essays in Arts and Sciences* 15 [June 1986]: 94). Melville is behind every word of *Clarel*, but to say that the narrator is Melville does not take us very far into the poem. The questions of perspective (who sees, who speaks), the dialogicity of the narrative voices, and the nature of the narrative consciousness are more important for signaling Melville's intentions to the reader.

5. Before listening to Melville's narrative voices in the context of the Elijah motif, we must remember that *Clarel* is a retrospective narration, an after-the-fact retelling of the suffering, reflection, and confusion of the narrator and his fellow pilgrims. The narrator reveals his retrospective technique by telling us before the pilgrims even reach Mar Saba that the abbot of the monastery has told him of the biannual flooding of the wadis (3.1.97). The narrator also reveals to us in a flashforward that Clarel will learn of Nehemiah's charity to the lepers after his actual encounter with Nehemiah and Toulib the leper (1.26.72–76).

6. This narrative mode of retelling a story told by one character who heard it from another is cited by Shurr as a distancing technique: "The narrative technique here is complex: × reports to y who reports to z, about M. Mortmain is remote and distant, isolated in his present monomania; and

the narrative technique helps emphasize the distance," *The Mystery of Iniquity*, 88. The reader may be far from a character, but the narrator who so consciously reveals his technique also brings us closer to him.

7. Bezanson, "Historical and Critical Note," 572.

8. Kenny, *Herman Melville's Clarel*, 130, 127.

9. I have used the term "voice" rather than mood or function to indicate the obsessively dialogical nature of the poem, and because all four voices in the poem are more than literary functions. They demonstrate an attitude that the narrator shows toward his material in varying gradations of distance or closeness. The word "voice" also suggests the narrator's language choice that again demonstrates an attitude toward his material such as reverence or skepticism. Although the voice we hear is written, we also hear its shifting timbre. In fact, I am suggesting that Melville deliberately does not give key lexical or graphic signposts, even to the point that we are not sure of the speaker's identity and the addressee, in order for us to listen to the narrator's different voices. Melville consciously strives to make the reader aware of the tale's teller.

10. Bezanson, "Historical and Critical Note," 566.

11. The literary source for Melville's enigmatic Syrian monk in *Clarel* is Henry Whitney Bellows's travelogue *The Old World in Its New Face*, vol. 2. Bellows, Melville's famous Unitarian minister, traveled to the Levant in 1867–68. At Jericho, Bellows recorded the appearance of an Abyssinian anchorite descending Mount Quarantania. For demonstrable evidence indicating that Melville's Syrian monk is derived from Bellows's anchorite in many of his aspects (appearance and language), see my article, "A New Source for Melville's *Clarel* and 'Fruit of Travel Long Ago': H. W. Bellows's *The Old World in Its New Face* (1867–1868)," in *The Melville Society Extracts* (September 1992).

12. The narrator of *White-Jacket* also emphasizes the importance of the color green in ecological renewal: "but rather would I be urned in the trunk of some green tree, and even in death have the vital sap circulating around me, giving of my dead body to the living foliage that shaded my peaceful tomb" (chapter 74).

13. Bowen, *The Long Encounter*, 260.

14. Bowen, *The Long Encounter*, 271. Bowen is one of the few critics to see a significant spiritual change in Mortmain: "Mortmain, his pride of knowledge put aside, has passed, as Rolfe has not, through the gateway of despair and come out into a freedom where, though all is lost, nothing is regretted, and where, having wholly given over this world, his hands are free to reach out, at least toward another" (p. 274).

15. Kenny, *Herman Melville's Clarel*, 65.

16. Seelye, *The Ironic Diagram*, 144.

17. Bowen, *The Long Encounter*, 279.

18. Kenny, *Herman Melville's Clarel*, 218.

19. Rosenthal, "Melville's Wandering Jews," 188, 189. Although he discusses hope in a completely different context and his essay is in a collection that might easily be overlooked by the *Clarel* reader, Rosenthal is the only critic who gives hope its due in *Clarel*, and who recognizes the importance of the character Derwent to the theme of hope.

20. The word "illusion" in *Clarel* is often used within the context of a subjective vision or dream and is not necessarily a word denoting a sarcastic dismissal. "Illusion" is often juxtaposed with "calm" (1.7.60, 62) or with the conflation of "dream," "legend and event" (1.10.67–68). Vine, when reciting the lyrics of a Florentine artist, claims that the amaranths—a floral symbol of immortality—are an "illusion" (3.14.40). The Armenian funeral procession is also called an "illusion," yet one that is very real to Clarel (4.16.103). The word is also used to describe visions: Clarel's vision of the dead (4.32.85) and the Syrian monk's debate with Satan (2.18.43). Many critics have also noticed the use of what Shurr calls "the doubt-filled subjunctive," the hypothetical "if" and the words "may" and "mayst" in the Epilogue, *The Mystery of Iniquity*, 204. This "pondering repose of IF" (*Moby-Dick*, "The Gilder") does not detract from divine immanence and the victory of life over death suggested in the Epilogue. Hypothetical dialog occurs throughout the poem as evidence of the non-omniscient narrator and as a thematic warning against spiritual pride and pretentious, theological certitudes.

21. The starting point for every *Clarel* student is Walter E. Bezanson's introduction to the Hendricks House edition of *Clarel*. Bezanson's view of the faith-doubt question in the poem basically follows Hawthorne's famous evaluation of Melville: "He can neither believe, nor be comfortable in his unbelief; and he is too honest and courageous not to try to do one or the other," *The English Notebooks*, 432–33, 437. Bezanson calls this condition of mind a "double vision" ("Historical and Critical Note," 512) and claims, counter to my reading, that in the Epilogue the "agnostic pro and con" is the poem's summary rather than "the concluding images of possible rebirth" (571). Although he does recognize the St. Saba palm as "a central symbol of the hope of immortality, or grace, or at least peace" (561), most of his comments focus on the "con." For instance, he claims that the "central theme of the poem" is "the deadness of faith" (545) and that the only insight of the poem is the tragic view of the need to endure the opposites of doubt and belief. Bezanson consistently uses the word "dilemma" to describe the poem's theological ideas and adopts Melville's phrase "complex passion" to describe the "total historical, theological and psychological dilemma which permeates the poem" (564). By privileging only one half of the evidence in the poem, Bezanson apprehends only one half of Melville's final theological stance. Just

as God has many faces that are usually expressed in pairs—mercy versus judgment, love versus anger, presence versus hiddenness—*Clarel* also explores both doubt and faith, despair and hope. Furthermore, what Bezanson and other *Clarel* scholars do not see is that with each step that God takes in retreat from the external world of the poem—no revelation, no miracles—divine inwardness advances another step. In other words, there is an inverse relation in *Clarel* between the hiddenness of God—*Deus absconditus*—and God's presence within. In a sense, Bezanson sees this inwardness on the part of characters and the narrator but places it in a movement "away from theology towards . . . speculative psychology" (572). Bezanson therefore sees "moments of sudden, unconscious, self-revelation" and the emphasis in the poem (575) on human hiddenness but sees such inwardness as a part of depth psychology. In *Clarel,* however, psychology is the handmaiden of theology, and every human character, in some sense, is a mirror image of the divine being's hiddenness or presence.

CHAPTER 5: THE UNSATISFIED HEART

1. Melville, *Letters*, 125.
2. Melville, *Letters*, 125.
3. Kenny, *Herman Melville's Clarel*, 138.
4. Melville, *Collected Poems*, 7.
5. The canto continues, "Men get sick / Under that curse of Frederick / The cynical: For punishment / This rebel province I present / To the philosophers" (2.26.129–33). In his "Discussions," 781, Bezanson correctly identifies Frederick "the cynical" with Frederick the Great of Prussia (1712–86) but writes that the "particular 'curse' (lines 131–32) has not been located." The historical context for this allusion is Voltaire's idea of the founding of a highly civilized society of philosophes on Frederick II's lands in Cleves. The idea, of course, was merely a jest, but Melville seems to suggest that the curse is too much freedom. Frederick's response to Voltaire's experiment of self-government based on reason and dedicated to individual freedom was both sardonic and cynical.
6. See Bezanson, "Discussions," 826. For a far more detailed explanation of the sources of Shekinah, see Gershom G. Scholem's *Major Trends in Jewish Mysticism*, rev. ed. (New York: Schocken Books, 1950), 230.
7. William H. Gilman, *Melville's Early Life and Redburn* (New York: New York University Press, 1951), 242.
8. Arnold, *God and the Bible*, 378.
9. Shurr, *The Mystery of Iniquity*, 82.
10. Leyda, *Melville Log*, 2:508.
11. William Braswell first located Melville's heart inscription in "Saint

Evremont's letter of 1671 to the Mareschal de Crequi," *Melville's Religious Thought*, 23, 132. But it was James Duban who found the source of Melville's inscription: in the 1710 English translation of Pierre Bayle's *Dictionary* that Melville owned. See James Duban, "The Translation of Pierre Bayle's *An Historical and Critical Dictionary* Owned by Melville," *The Papers of the Bibliographical Society of America*, 71 (3rd Quarter, 1977): 347–51.

    12. Melville, *Letters*, 129.

    13. Agnes Cannon, "Melville's Concepts of the Poet and Poetry," *Arizona Quarterly* 31 (Winter 1975): 317. Knapp was the first to mention the "dual confusion" of the head versus the heart dilemma but did not suggest that the heart takes primacy in *Clarel, Tortured Synthesis*, 7. Although James A. Baird, in *Ishmael* (Baltimore: Johns Hopkins University Press, 1956), 355, never explicated the ending of *Clarel*, he described Melville's art eclectically in terms of primitivism: "the poem ends with Clarel's rejection of reason and his acceptance of only the 'primitive' heart." Joseph Flibbert, in "The Dream and Religious Faith in Herman Melville's *Clarel*," *American Transcendental Quarterly* 50 (1981): 132, noted that "in matters of faith, reason and the senses are subordinate to the imagination and the heart." Although Flibbert does not discuss the heart, he does conclude that dream visions help Clarel develop acceptance and endurance via the imagination.

    14. See Shurr, *The Mystery of Iniquity*, 114–15.

    15. Bowen, *The Long Encounter*, 280.

    16. Shurr's intriguing application of the two meanings of the word "prove"—to establish the truth of something or to test the nature of something—seems on target, *The Mystery of Iniquity*, 123. To "prove" the heart does suggest a testing of the ability to give the heart to God. In terms of the meaning of truth, I do not think Melville would use the word to indicate any degree of falsehood.

CONCLUSION

    1. Hawthorne, *The English Notebooks*, 432–33.

    2. Edwin M. Eigner, *The Metaphysical Novel in England and America* (Berkeley: University of California Press, 1978), 174–75.

    3. Hawthorne, *The English Notebooks*, 433.

    4. See Gilman, *Melville's Early Life*; Thompson, *Melville's Quarrel with God*; Herbert, *Moby-Dick and Calvinism;* and Donald Yannella and Hershel Parker, eds., *The Endless Winding Way in Melville: New Charts by Kring and Carey* (Glassboro, N.J.: Melville Society, 1981).

WORKS CITED

Arnold, Matthew. *God and the Bible: A Review of Objections to 'Literature and Dogma.'* New York: Macmillan, 1875.

Ault, N. A. "The Sea Imagery in Melville's *Clarel.*" *Research Studies of the State College of Washington* 27 (1959): 72–84.

Baird, James A. *Ishmael.* Baltimore: Johns Hopkins University Press, 1956.

Baym, Nina. "The Erotic Motif in Melville's *Clarel.*" *Texas Studies in Literature and Language* 16 (Summer 1974): 315–28.

Bellows, Henry W. "The Suspense of Faith: An Address to the Alumni of the Divinity School of Harvard University." New York: C. S. Francis, 1859.

Bezanson, Walter E. Introduction. *Clarel: A Poem and Pilgrimage in the Holy Land.* By Herman Melville. Edited by Bezanson. New York: Hendricks House, 1960.

———. "*Moby-Dick*: Document, Drama, Dream." *A Companion to Melville Studies.* Ed. John Bryant. New York: Greenwood Press, 1986, 169–211.

———. "*Moby-Dick*: Work of Art." *Moby-Dick: Centennial Essays.* Ed. Tyrus Hillway and Luther S. Mansfield. Dallas: Southern Methodist University Press, 1953.

Bowen, Merlin. *The Long Encounter: Self and Experience in the Writings of Herman Melville.* Chicago: University of Chicago Press, 1960.

Braswell, William. *Melville's Religious Thought: An Essay in Interpretation.* Durham, N.C.: Duke University Press, 1943.

Brodwin, Stanley. "Herman Melville's *Clarel*: An Existentialist Gospel." *PMLA* 86 (May 1971): 375–87.

Cannon, Agnes. "Melville's Concepts of the Poet and Poetry." *Arizona Quarterly* 31 (Winter 1975): 315–39.

Cowen, Walker. *Melville's Marginalia.* 2 Vols. New York: Garland, 1987. (Reprint of Cowen's 1965 Harvard Ph.D. thesis.)

Davis, Merrell R., and William H. Gilman, eds. *The Letters of Herman Melville.* New Haven: Yale University Press, 1960.

Dettlaff, Shirley. "Ionian Form and Esau's Waste: Melville's View of Art in *Clarel.*" *American Literature* 54 (May 1982): 212–28.

———. "Melville's Aesthetics." *A Companion to Melville Studies.* Ed. John Bryant. Westport, Conn.: Greenwood Press, 1986, 625–65.

Dillingham, William B. "'Neither Believer nor Infidel': Themes of Melville's Poetry." *The Personalist* 46 (1965): 501–16.

Duban, James. "Chipping with a Chisel: The Ideology of Melville's Narrators." *Texas Studies in Literature and Language* 31 (1989): 341–85.

———. "The Translation of Pierre Bayle's *An Historical and Critical*

Dictionary Owned by Melville." *The Papers of the Bibliographical Society of America* 71 (3rd Quarter, 1977): 347–51.

Eigner, Edwin M. *The Metaphysical Novel in England and America.* Berkeley: University of California Press, 1978.

Feidelson, Charles, Jr. *Symbolism and American Literature.* Chicago: University of Chicago Press, 1953.

Flibbert, Joseph. "The Dream and Religious Faith in Herman Melville's *Clarel.*" *American Transcendental Quarterly* 50 (1981): 129–37.

Fogle, Richard H. "Melville's *Clarel*: Doubt and Belief." *Tulane Studies in English* 10 (1960): 101–16.

———. "The Themes of Melville's Later Poetry." *Tulane Studies in English* 11 (1961): 65–86.

Gilman, William H. *Melville's Early Life and Redburn.* New York: New York University Press, 1951.

Goldman, Stan. "The Small Voice of Silence: Melville's Narrative Voices in *Clarel.*" *Texas Studies in Literature and Language* 31 (1989): 451–73.

Grenberg, Robert. *Some Other World to Find: Quest and Negation in the Works of Herman Melville.* Urbana: University of Illinois Press, 1989.

Hawthorne, Nathaniel. *The English Notebooks.* Ed. Randall Stewart. New York: Oxford University Press, 1941.

Heffernan, Thomas F. *Stove by a Whale: Owen Chase and the Essex.* Middletown, Conn.: Wesleyan University Press, 1981.

Herbert, T. Walter, Jr. "Calvinist Earthquake: *Moby-Dick* and Religious Tradition." *New Essays on Moby-Dick.* Ed. Richard H. Brodhead. Cambridge: Cambridge University Press, 1986.

———. *Moby-Dick and Calvinism: A World Dismantled.* New Brunswick, N.J.: Rutgers University Press, 1977.

Kenny, Vincent. "*Clarel.*" *A Companion to Melville Studies.* Ed. John Bryant. Westport, Conn.: Greenwood Press, 1986.

———. *Herman Melville's Clarel: A Spiritual Autobiography.* Hamden, Conn.: Shoe String Press, 1973.

Knapp, Joseph G. *Tortured Synthesis: The Meaning of Melville's Clarel.* New York: Philosophical Library, 1971.

Leyda, Jay. *The Melville Log: A Documentary Life of Herman Melville.* 2 vols. New York: Harcourt, Brace, 1951.

Matthiessen, F. O. *American Renaissance: Art and Expression in the Age of Emerson and Whitman.* New York: Oxford University Press, 1941.

Melville, Herman. *Clarel: A Poem and Pilgrimage in the Holy Land.* Ed. Walter E. Bezanson. New York: Hendricks House, 1960.

———. *Clarel: A Poem and Pilgrimage in the Holy Land.* Ed. Harrison Hayford, Alma MacDougall, Hershel Parker, and G. Thomas Tanselle. Vol.

12 of *The Writings of Herman Melville*. Evanston and Chicago: Northwestern University Press and the Newberry Library, 1991.

———. *Collected Poems of Herman Melville*. Ed. Howard P. Vincent. Chicago: Hendricks House, 1947.

———. *Great Short Works of Herman Melville*. Ed. Warner Berthoff. New York: Harper & Row, 1969.

———. *Journals*. Ed. Howard C. Horsford with Lynn Horth. Vol. 15 of *The Writings of Herman Melville*. Evanston and Chicago: Northwestern University Press and the Newberry Library, 1989.

———. *Moby-Dick*. Ed. Harrison Hayford and Hershel Parker. New York: W. W. Norton, 1967.

———. *White-Jacket*. Ed. Harrison Hayford, Hershel Parker, and G. Thomas Tanselle. Vol. 5 of *The Writings of Herman Melville*. Evanston and Chicago: Northwestern University Press and the Newberry Library, 1970.

Parker, Hershel. "The Character of Vine in Melville's *Clarel*." *Essays in Arts and Sciences* 15 (June 1986): 91–113.

Pops, Martin Leonard. *The Melville Archetype*. Kent, Ohio: Kent State University Press, 1970.

Ra'ad, Basem L. "The Death Plot in Melville's *Clarel*." *ESQ* 27 (1st Quarter 1981): 14–27.

Robillard, Douglas. Introduction. *Poems of Herman Melville*. New Haven: College and University Press Publishers, 1976.

Rosenthal, Bernard. "Herman Melville's Wandering Jews." *Puritan Influences in American Literature*. Ed. Emory Elliott. Urbana: University of Illinois Press, 1979.

Samson, John. *White Lies: Melville's Narratives of Facts*. Ithaca, N.Y.: Cornell University Press, 1989.

Sealts, Merton M. *Melville's Reading*. Revised and Enlarged Edition. Columbia, S.C.: University of South Carolina Press, 1988.

Sedgwick, W. E. *Herman Melville: The Tragedy of Mind*. Cambridge: Harvard University Press, 1944.

Seelye, John. *Melville: The Ironic Diagram*. Evanston, Ill.: Northwestern University Press, 1970.

Sherrill, Rowland A. *The Prophetic Melville: Experience, Transcendence, and Tragedy*. Athens: University of Georgia Press, 1979.

Short, Bryan C. "Form as Vision in Herman Melville's *Clarel*." *American Literature* 50 (January 1979): 553–69.

Shurr, William. *The Mystery of Iniquity: Melville as Poet, 1857–1891*. Lexington: University of Kentucky Press, 1972.

Stern, Milton R. *The Fine-Hammered Steel of Herman Melville*. Urbana: University of Illinois Press, 1957.

Thompson, Lawrance. *Melville's Quarrel with God*. Princeton: Princeton University Press, 1952.

Warren, Robert Penn. Introduction. *Selected Poems of Herman Melville*. Edited by Warren. New York: Random House, 1967.

Wasilewski, William. "Melville's Poetic Strategy in *Clarel*: The Satellite Poems." *Essays in Arts and Sciences* 5 (July 1976): 149–59.

Woodward, C. Vann. *The Burden of Southern History*. Baton Rouge: Louisiana State University Press, 1960.

Wright, Nathalia. *Melville's Use of the Bible*. Durham, N.C.: Duke University Press, 1949.

Yannella, Donald, and Parker, Hershel, eds. *The Endless Winding Way in Melville: New Charts by Kring and Carey*. Glassboro, N.J.: Melville Society, 1981

INDEX

Ahab, 137
Arnold, Matthew, 5, 10, 77, 99, 144

Bahktin, 6
Baird, James A., 193n.13
Bellows, Henry Whitney: "The Suspense of Faith," 13; Melville's minister, 168
Bezanson, Walter E., 5, 6, 10, 93, 108, 113, 171n.3, 183n.7, 192n.5; his reading of *Clarel*, 191–92n.21
Bible (Hebrew): divine hiddenness in, 13–14, 177–78n.7; "either/or" contraries in, 76; father-child metaphor in, 149–51; heart motif in, 153, 159; lover-beloved metaphor in, 33–34; the many faces of God in, 24–25; theodicy in, 48–50, 183n.4, 183n.5
Bowen, Merlin, 8, 9, 121, 124, 126, 164, 186nn.8,9, 190n.14
Braswell, William, 177n.7, 181n.31
Brodwin, Stanley, 77, 179n.12, 184n.15, 186n.14
Browning, 86

Cannon, Agnes, 157, 193n.13
Carey, Jonathan S., 168
Clarel: and aesthetic comparisons with other American poems, 10; the American cantos in, 17, 40; animals in, 140; the anti-faith critical reading of, 103–4, 188n.1, 189n.3; the anti-hope critical reading of, 125; anti-semitism (absence of) in, 108; archaelogy (biblical) in, 133; authority (scriptural) in, 120; Bibles (the battle of the) in, 25–26; bibliography of, 172–74nn.16–17; "both/and" versus "either/or" thinking in, 99–100; characters (interchangeable) in, 111; characters (subsumed by narrator) in, 112, 115, 129; characters (unconvincing authority of) in, 110–11, 113; charity in, 140–41; child-father metaphor in, 149–151; character (main) in, 11, 80; contraries (wedding of) in, 77–78; death in, 59–63, 118–19, 121–22; Derwent (character of) in, 16, 178n.8; dialog (hypothetical) in, 109–10; dialogical nature of, 6, 15, 17, 117; divine distance (paradox of) in, 12–13; divine hiddenness and silence in, 8, 13–14, 18–23; divine immanence in the human in, 6, 41–44, 116, 123, 164–65; divine trust in, 154, 162; divinity (reciprocal) in, 40–42, 181n.31; dolphins and rainbow images in, 126–27; doubt (common versus heroic) in, 81–86; doubt and faith in, 86–91, 101, 145–147; dramatic *agon* (gnostic quest), *Clarel* as, 14–17; dramatis personae in, 15–17 (see also *Clarel*: character); dream visions (sleep) in, 115–16, 122; dualities (human) in, 78–81, 162; Easter, 120, 127; ecology in, 120; "Eld" (pun) in,